CW01066933

TOO GOOD TO BE TRUE

TOO GOOD
TO BE TRUE

*How to Survive in the
Casino Economy*

Rowan Bosworth-Davies

THE BODLEY HEAD
LONDON

The author and publishers gratefully
acknowledge the Society of Authors for their
kind permission to reproduce the poem by
John Masefield, as the literary representative
of the estate of John Masefield.

British Cataloguing in Publication Data:
Bosworth-Davies, Rowan
Too good to be true: how to survive in the casino economy
1. Securities fraud—Great Britain
1. Title
362.1'68   HV6699.G7
ISBN 0 370 31048 9
© Rowan Bosworth-Davies 1987
Printed in Great Britain for
The Bodley Head
32 Bedford Square
London
WC1B 3EL
by
Redwood Burn Limited, Trowbridge, Wiltshire
First published 1987

'There's a sucker born every minute.'
Phineus T. Barnum

Contents

Acknowledgements

Many people had a hand in assisting me in the preparation of this book and if I have failed to include their names here, I can only beg their forgiveness and say that failure to include them was not due to any fault other than my own.

I owe a considerable debt of gratitude to the following, who are named in order of my memory. Oonagh MacDonald MP, and her personal staff, who provided me with so much background material. Sir Peter Tapsell MP, Dennis Skinner MP, who first introduced me to the concept of the Casino Economy, Tim Yeo MP, Brian Gould MP, Tim Smith MP, and Professor 'Jim' Gower. All these busy people willingly gave up their time to assist me and agreed to be interviewed. From America, I must acknowledge the help and assistance given to me by officers of the Securities and Exchange Commission and the Commodity Futures Trading Commission. These good people were somewhat bemused by the appearance of a 'Scotland Yard Cop' in their offices, but they gave unstintingly of their time. In particular, I should like to acknowledge the help of Gary Lynch, Head of Enforcement of the SEC and of Dennis Klejna, Head of Enforcement of the CFTC. In addition, their staff members have given me immeasurable help and it is a pleasure to acknowledge the help of Rick Norell, Stuart Allen and Robert MacNamara II. In addition, Stuard Young Jr. made my researches so much easier than they might have been.

Returning home, I must mention the part played in my 'education' by two dear friends, Barbara Conway, now with the Securities and Investments Board and Lorana Sullivan, of the *Observer*.

Others whom I did not know so well, but who gave me permission to use their published work were Dr Michael Levi of Cardiff University, and Stephen Fay. I must include the other influences which assisted me in this book, the music of Mark Knopfler, the constant encouragement of my agent, Maggie Hanbury, without whose work none of this would have been accomplished, and the invaluable help of my publisher and editors, Chris Holifield, Sara Kerruish and Susanna Nicklin. To my friends and ex-colleagues at 'C6' I say 'Keep the faith' and last, but by no means least, to Hans, wherever he might be, I say, 'There's still a warrant for your arrest issued at Bow Street Magistrates Court.'

Preface

This has been a very personal book, most of which was written before the Financial Services Act came into force. In addition, a considerable amount of what I have said was written before the Securities and Investments Board had published the rules and regulations upon which basis they have applied to become the designated agency. If what I have said has become superseded by the passage of time, or, indeed, any mistakes of fact have been occasioned because of last-minute changes in legislative intention, I can only ask the reader to pardon my failing.

This book has been a personal statement for me and I am conscious that many people will find material in it with which they might take offence. I can only say now that my intention has never been to offend the honest or genuine practitioner in the City and if anything I have written might appear to include the honest man, I ask to be given the benefit of the doubt. To that group of dishonest men who have attempted to besmirch the good name of the City of London, I say, 'Do not think that this proviso applies to you.'

The most important influence upon my research and upon my subsequent work has been my friendship with Lorana Sullivan, an investigative financial journalist with the *Observer* newspaper. When she became aware that it was my intention to write this book, she made available to me all the papers and documents which she had collected during the course of her professional activities in dealing with alleged financial frauds. Even at a time when she and her employers were under the greatest pressure, faced with a very expensive libel action and under considerable suspicion from a number of official agencies, her help and support has never wavered. She made her information available to me subject to the only condition that I make the most use of it in my researches. I owe her a debt of gratitude I shall always find hard to repay.

The most important person to whom I should address my thanks is my wife, Carolyn, whose support and encouragement during the hard times has been invaluable and without whom I doubt if one word would have been written.

Introduction

If you owe the bank £1000, they can make your life a misery. If you owe them £10 million, then you own the bank. If you invest £500 for a client, he will be constantly on the phone to you. If you invest £100,000 for him, he'll never bother you. The greater the amount of money you can steal from a client, the less chance you have of being nicked.

This philosophy was first explained to me by a very successful fraudsman whose affairs I had been investigating during my posting to the Fraud Squad. He was charming, unscrupulous and totally unprincipled and had made and lost several fortunes by setting up fictitious commodity investment companies which he used to divest foreign investors of their money.

I shall call him Hans, although this is not his real name. He will appear again in this book and to date he has never been convicted of any offence relating to his fraudulent activities in the United Kingdom. He had been less than careful in one of his scams and had been threatened by a group of German con-men, then operating in London. Believing his life to be in danger and being well aware that the Director of Public Prosecutions would not sanction his prosecution, he had come to the Fraud Squad, to ask for protection.

In return for immunity from any further prosecutions, he was prepared, he said, to describe the activities of a generation of fraudsters who were operating from London and who were rapidly destroying the good name of the City of London as a place in which to conduct speculative investment for profit.

Hans made one fundamental mistake. He knew that he would not be prosecuted for the offences which our department had already investigated. The DPP had declined to conduct any criminal proceedings against him. He could not believe however that the Director's office would be prepared to be so lenient again when they learned the truth of his other activities and he was firmly of the opinion that prosecution would follow as surely as night follows day.

I was prepared to keep him in this blissful state of ignorance while he told his story and accordingly he would come to my office on a weekly basis and fill in more gaps in our knowledge.

So unfolded one of the strangest stories I had ever heard. In its telling I was to discover the philosophy of the fraudsman whose victim, the private investor, is the most vulnerable in an economy which sets great store by a policy of investment for the future, whether it be for income or for growth, and which makes facilities available for the entrepreneur to promote investment schemes.

Poor Hans: if only he had known that the DPP couldn't have cared less about his activities.

In common with most professional con-men who spend their entire working lives pretending to be something other than they are, he had believed that he could talk his way out of trouble, in the shape of the Law, when it arrived. He was shrewd enough however to realise that he would eventually offend one of his fellow adventurers, who would be more likely to settle the matter in a way which would be highly prejudicial to his continued well-being. Believing that his only bargaining card was an offer of complete immunity in return for a total exposé of his criminal accomplices, he told his amazing story.

He might just as well have saved his breath but I didn't have the heart to tell him.

Much later, when he discovered that his confessions had been totally ignored he rang me. He found it incredible that the 'Prosecutor', as he called him would simply discard his evidence. 'You guys must be mad,' he said; 'They're stealing the world from under your noses and you do nothing about it. You deserve everything that's coming to you.'

I never told him as much, but privately, I agreed with him.

Hans' philosophy was a simple one. People who have money to invest are all looking for the greatest return for the minimum outlay. Essentially, he believed, this was equivalent to greed and as far as he was concerned, greedy people were legitimate targets. He would offer them an investment in a scheme which offered fantastic returns and he would then proceed to steal their money.

'People who believe the sort of stuff I tell 'em, must be stupid and they deserve to get ripped off,' he would say.

At first, I thought that this was just one man's cynical interpretation and one which would not enjoy wide support. As I proceeded to investigate other investment-related frauds, I found that this attitude was widespread among investment advisors and promoters and far from being unusual. The investor was considered to be fair game for any ruse or device which parted him from his money. The true expert, I discovered, was the man who could steal a client blind, and then go back and get him to invest even more money, in the hope of recovering his initial investment. Needless to say, this money soon disappeared as well.

I began to reconsider the cases in which I had been involved, to see if I could discern a pattern which might identify the sort of person who was most likely to become the victim of the fraudster. A number of different tests were applied and in each case, no unifying thread could be observed. A number of elements were common in most cases but there was little that could be said to be a persistently common factor.

Greed was a fairly regular feature in most investment-related scams. I thought that I had discovered a unifying common link in the greed element, until I came to investigate the affairs of David Langford, a Licensed Dealer whose activities will be discussed at far greater length later. Nevertheless, greed, on the part of the investor did play a significant part in bringing the investor and the fraudsman together. I was to discover that one of the most appealing influences in the decision to invest money in a speculative scheme was where the investor believed that the particular investment was dishonest or illegal.

If you doubt the truth of this, next time you see an unlicensed street trader working a crowd, watch the behaviour of the purchasers who are induced to believe that what they are buying has not been honestly acquired by the salesman. It is the 'something for nothing' syndrome which is present, I suppose, in all of us to a greater or lesser degree. The street trader isn't really selling stolen goods, he's got too much sense, but the buyer allows himself to be induced into believing that there is something 'not quite right' about the goods. For some strange reason, he believes, because the goods look like the real thing, but are considerably cheaper, that he is getting better value and parts with his money quite happily.

I saw an illustration of this most clearly in a case where the investors genuinely believed that their investments were being made in a scheme which was completely illegal in America. The scheme promised fantastic rewards, trading on inside information concerning the potential performance of certain shares which was allegedly being supplied by a Stock Market trader in the United States. Discovery of this practice would, the investors were told, result in the entire funds under management being frozen and sequestered by the American authorities, with a consequent loss of the entire investment. Nevertheless, investors flocked to put their money in. One loser, a successful businessman, invested his entire life's savings and mortgaged his house to put in a figure in excess of £250,000. Wasn't it Schiller who said: 'Against stupidity the gods themselves struggle in vain.'?

Needless to say, he lost the lot. When I interviewed him, his anger was directed not at the fact that he had been deceived into parting with his money but that the promoter of the fraud, a friend of a friend, hadn't told him to get his investment out before it crashed.

This example proved the truth of yet another of Hans' philosophies. 'Always steal from your friends first. They're far easier to convince and much less likely to report you.'

The only factor they had in common was that of ignorance of the investment method proposed to the client. I found it more and more incredible that supposedly educated, intelligent adults would part with considerable sums of money, to persons they had never previously met, sometimes as a result of nothing more than an unsolicited telephone call. When interviewed subsequently, they would be unable to describe in practical detail the techniques which were supposedly to be adopted to provide them with the enormous promised returns.

When pressed for details, the hapless loser would in many cases prove to know absolutely nothing about the promoter, the investment or its methods of working. He or she would shyly produce a tattered bundle of papers which might purport to be contract notes or account statements but when questioned as to their knowledge of the contents, there would follow a period of embarrassing silence before the scarcely audible admission that they could not understand the figures or the accounting, had been too embarrassed to query the contents and had simply hoped that everything would be all right.

In many cases, I came away with the real belief that many investors were half aware, almost from inception, that they were being conned and appeared to be unable to prevent it happening to them. Latterly, I came to the belief that the fraudster does not have to go looking for his victims. In most cases, they will come to him.

Sometimes, the embarrassment gave way to anger. Not, as you might suppose aimed at the con-man, but at the Fraud Squad. I lost count of the times that losers were prepared to vent their spleen on me and my colleagues. In one particular case, the loser, who had been deceived into parting with the sum of £2000, which he could ill afford to lose, accused me of having been responsible for losing his money on the basis that he had been assured by the promoters of the investment that nothing was wrong with the company but it had been forced to cease trading because the investigations of the police had made it impossible for the fund to trade with an unblemished reputation. Even when he was shown evidence that the company had spent all his money on having a good time and that it had not been invested in any of the ways he had been promised, he still was not convinced, preferring to believe the word of a man he had met but once in his life and to whom he had handed a cheque for £2000, rather than the evidence of his own eyes.

At first, I found a loser's anger aimed at me instead of the fraudster hard to understand. Was it because we had finally confirmed what they had long suspected but were too frightened to admit to themselves, which was that they had been conned?

Slowly, it became clearer that one of the big weapons in the fraudsman's armoury is the fear of ridicule on the part of the loser. This fear is so real that some victims will stand the financial loss sooner than admit that they have been fooled. This factor is not restricted to private investors but is very common among large business corporations. If questioned closely, the directors of these companies will say that they prefer to keep the knowledge of these losses to themselves to minimise the bad publicity for the company. There may be something in this argument but I am convinced that the fear of personal ridicule plays a larger part in the decision.

Why should this be? The whole point of the fraudsman's skill, surely, is to instil in the mind of his victim the honestly held belief that all is as it should be and that his investment is in the safest hands available. Far from being ridiculed, the fraudsman's victim is deserving of sympathy because he has been deceived into believing that one state of affairs exists when the converse is true.

The second weapon in the armoury of investment fraud is the close resemblance that the fraudulent business has to a genuine investment company. One important element in the definition of an investment is time. The time aspect is present in every investment contract, whether it be a matter of days, months or years. How can you tell, when you have agreed to tie up your capital for a minimum period of twelve months, if your friendly account executive is busy siphoning off your money to some off-shore bank and preparing for his getaway? You can't and that's an end to it. It is a very brave, or conversely, foolhardy detective who goes charging in with a search warrant alleging fraudulent practice in an investment company, without having very strong evidence. The usual end-result is a series of writs, returnable in the High Court, alleging serious libels and grave financial loss and demanding injunctions and punitive damages. I know what it's like, because it happened to me. The High Court can be a lonely place when you are defending one of these actions, no matter how honest or genuine your motives may have been.

The difference between the honest and the dishonest company can sometimes only be discovered when the time comes to pay out the proposed profits or dividends, by which time it may be too late, if the money has long since gone and the promoters have fled the country. Any subsequent investigation, while it may eventually ascertain the truth of the situation, is most unlikely to recover the money invested. Yet this is the only thing the unfortunate investor wants to recover.

The loser may be unwilling for his gullibility to be aired in public but while he thinks that there is a chance that he may recover some, if not all of his original investment, he will co-operate with police enquiries. If he is told that the chances of recovery are minimal, then his willingness to assist, in many cases, evaporates rapidly.

Even assuming it is possible to get total co-operation from the losers, what problems then present themselves? In many cases, the promoters have fled the country. The initial invested capital is in some off-shore bank, deposited under the name of a company registered in yet another off-shore haven. Rarely will these organisations permit unfettered access to their records and, in some cases, their legal jurisdictions have laws expressly forbidding disclosure of beneficial interests.

Extradition from foreign states is fraught with difficulties and can take many months, if not years, to achieve. As time goes by, witnesses become harder to trace, memories fade, documents get misplaced and the potential for a judicious outcome slips farther and farther away.

During my time at the Metropolitan and City Police Company Fraud Department, I saw the first glimmerings of what I later came to call the vicious circle of fraud. I first coined the phrase in a report which I prepared for the Commodity Futures Trading Commission, in Washington, dealing with the activities of a group of commodity traders and convicted criminals who had applied for membership of the New Orleans Commodity Exchange. It was one of Hans' little scams and he nearly got away with it. Had he succeeded, we should have been entirely at the mercy of his friends who would have been enabled to 'close the vicious circle of fraud', and we should have been unable to prove that what they were doing was dishonest. The Americans got the message and revoked all the membership applications, but it was a close-run thing.

Much later, I travelled to America, where I studied with the Securities and Exchange Commission and the Commodity Futures Trading Commission and I visited the major Exchanges in Chicago, Philadelphia and New York. This visit taught me that if we in the United Kingdom were ever going properly to confront the growing menace of investment fraud, then we should have to alter our views radically with regard to the degree of seriousness which we ought to invest in the professional investigation of these and similar allegations.

My belief in the urgency of such a revision of attitudes was given an added impetus by the Financial Revolution currently taking place in the City of London, the so-called 'Big Bang'.

The City of London is an institution in itself. When money men around the world talk of 'The City', it is the City of London to which they refer. The City has slowly developed from ancient origins, through a number of revolutions, both historically inevitable and man-inspired, to emerge in its present form. The City is in a constant state of change and, at the moment, it stands at yet another cross-roads in its historical development.

Big changes have come in the way the United Kingdom conducts its financial business and the City of London has been forced to change with the times. These changes have altered the traditional face of established financial dealings and they will be reflected in the High Street Banks, Building Societies, and Insurance Companies as well as in the ways in which the public are invited to enter into schemes for the management of their savings or investments, whether they be for pensions, housing, education, or simply as a means of 'putting something aside for a rainy day'.

Our perceptions of the role of the investment broker will change dramatically. Where before, you might have been inclined to visit a Building Society if you wanted a mortgage, an Insurance company if you wanted a pension, a bank if you wanted to arrange a loan or a stock broker if you wanted to buy some shares, these organisations and individuals now compete for each other's and, perhaps more importantly, the customer's business with varying degrees of success and efficiency.

New and hitherto untried methods of investment will be available for the private investor. New schemes will be promoted, offering varying rates of return. New definitions of 'investor' will be dreamt up by those responsible for marketing the new opportunities. Of one thing you can be absolutely certain. Somewhere in this brand new, bright tomorrow lurks the con-man, the fraudster, the promoter of the fantastic opportunity which cannot fail. He is as inseparable from the investment arena as is the limpet from the end of the pier.

The new regulatory proposals contained in the Investor Protection Legislation are intended to weaken the hold of the limpet and make life considerably more difficult for him. The well publicised recent activities of a number of stock cheats, investment fraudsmen and financial incompetents prove, if proof were needed, the urgency with which such investor protection methods should be introduced. Take Justin Frewen for instance. This high-living, old Etonian commodity broker-cum-swindler was sentenced to two years' imprisonment after the collapse of his company, Imperial Commodities. At his trial, the jury were told of the opulent life style which he maintained while he proceeded to lose £500,000 of his clients' money. He was described by the judge as a 'liar' and an 'arrogant young man'. Frewen might have been temporarily removed from circulation but there are plenty more like him, only too happy to step into the gap caused by his absence.

Norrey Brooke, otherwise known as Guy FitzSimmons Brooke or any of the many aliases used by him during his colourful past, springs immediately to mind. He was sentenced to six months' imprisonment, suspended for two years in 1985 for parting investors from $400,000 in his bogus investment scam trading under the name of Global Capital Growth.

What about Keith Hunt, the overweight, Warwickshire-based commodities fraudsman who disappeared leaving £13 million adrift? Rumoured to be at present propping up a fly-over on the M25, the police file on him is still open.

When the idea for this book was first proposed, my publishers asked me whom I most wanted to address. I had given the matter some considerable thought and I told them that while I hoped that it would be of interest to all readers, I wanted to appeal particularly to the man or woman who was thinking of entering into a new form of investment opportunity, perhaps for the first time in their lives.

I was thinking particularly of the person who may have recently have come into possession of a substantial sum of money. We live in a country with, at the time of writing, approximately 3 million people unemployed. Daily we read of more and more redundancies in the traditional areas of industrial manufacturing. To some, redundancy need not mean a bleak future of enforced unemployment, but may indicate simply an opportunity to take early retirement. That man or woman may have received a redundancy payment, or severance allowance. They may be in receipt of sums of money arising out of the commutation of pension schemes, or alternatively, have decided to remove their pension contributions to seek alternative forms of pension planning. Whichever is the case, there are probably many more people alive today in possession of fairly sizeable sums of disposable cash than ever before.

At the same time, the Conservative Government is committed to extending the concept of a property-owning democracy, what Mrs Thatcher has called 'Popular Capitalism'. This is not just restricted to the encouragement for people to buy their own homes but has extended to the purchase of shares and securities. For many people, purchasing shares in British Telecom represented the first time they had ever bought or considered buying an 'investment' in the form of a share in their life.

In fairness, it must be said that many of them had little understanding of the ramifications involved in such a purchase, indeed, it was only necessary to follow some of the agonising correspondence which appeared in the financial publications following on from the sale of BT to realise that many hundreds, perhaps thousands of people, spurred on by the seductive advertising, had entered into a transaction, the natural outcome of which was to have dramatic consequences on their lives.

What a lot of first-time purchasers did not perhaps realise was that in buying shares in a public company, their names, as shareholders, became registered with the Share Registrar of British Telecom. This register of shareholders is a public document, and one which is scrutinised by marketing organisations preparing new lists of potential recipients of unsolicited mail offering everything from new share issues in similar established companies, to the more esoteric offerings in time-share opportunities, container leasing or pooled commodity funds.

As an aside, many of these people found themselves the unfortunate recipients of unsolicited calls from unscrupulous market makers and licensed dealers who offered to buy their BT shares at a premium and then followed up this first, profitable transaction, with other, less profitable offers, which quickly extinguished any profits that had been made and exposed these persons to additional expense and subsequent loss which they had neither foreseen nor sought. It struck me then that the British Telecom affair was symptomatic of a dichotomy facing the Government. On the one hand, committed to a policy of de-nationali-sation, to be achieved by promoting a greater degree of individual share ownership by the privatisation of hitherto nationalised industries, the Government intends to extend the share-owning franchise to more people than ever before. This policy would undoubtedly have a two-fold benefit, for by encouraging more people to invest in shares and securities, the Tory vision is spread farther afield and the money released in the purchase of this new range of securities enables the Government to make more money available for realising further tax concessions. On the other hand, the Government are introducing more people than ever before to an investment strategy which a great many of them do not understand and about which there has been little attempt to stimulate any degree of public education. The dangers inherent in this policy are that the unscrupulous operators in the financial sector, sensing a range of rich pickings at the expense of this new but relatively unsophisticated investment market will move in on a tide of speculative euphoria and enrich themselves at the expense of the investors.

Much comparison will be made with the American experience of market regulation. I make no apology for this, believing that our American cousins have a lot they could teach us about financial regulation, were we but willing to learn. It is not possible to say that all their methods would necessarily work well in the United Kingdom but we ignore their experience at our peril. I am firmly of the belief that there is a body of opinion in the City and the Financial Establishment which will resist change at any turn. There is a powerful lobby actively engaged in an attempt to weaken and dilute the effective strength of proposed legislation for financial regulation. I do not believe that all these people are necessarily engaged in the practice of fraud or fraud-related activities. They represent simply an entrenched attitude of mind which is the product of years of City practice and tradition and which they do not want to see changed.

At the same time, there has been a vociferous body of opinion which has championed opposition towards any move to enable the proposed regulatory organisations to resemble their counterparts in the United

States. What these conservative elements appear to fail to realise is that the fraudsman will happily catch a free ride on their coat tails, taking full advantage of the heady days of deregulated free-for-all, while appearing to speak with the voice of traditional City values.

It is only a question of time before we have to face up to the reality that the City of London is but one component part in an international financial community, committed to trading around the clock on a twenty-four-hour basis. Business which might hitherto have been conducted in London will, just as easily, be conducted in New York or Tokyo. The successful market in the future will be that in which the investor perceives he is getting the best deal. The traditionalists in the Square Mile who resist the new climate of regulatory change are simply fooling themselves if they believe that they can continue in their time-honoured way without loss to themselves. They are certainly not fooling anyone else.

The debate on the changes in the City has, hitherto, concentrated on the practitioners and business participants. The one group which appears to have been ignored is that group which will become the captive market of the future, the private investor. I hope that this book will be of value to the man and woman who, confronted with the mass of investment advice and promises of profit which will flow from the promoters of the Casino Economy, will be able to look at what is on offer, benefit from other people's mistakes and be able to identify more easily the possible hallmarks of the con-man. An old friend of mine, Barbara Conway, was the guiding light behind the 'Scrutineer' column in the *Daily Telegraph*, before moving to take up a post with the Securities and Investments Board. She has written many cautionary articles, warning the public of the dangers posed by the City cheats and fraudsters. I would like to associate myself with the following quotation which I have culled from one of her pieces. She said:

'I do not believe that people should be coddled to protect them from their own folly. But I do believe, particularly when major changes are taking place in the financial markets and when the public is urged to paddle in often unfamiliar investment waters, that the paddlers are entitled to expect all reasonable measures to be taken to keep those waters shark free.'

In one way, it is easier to describe this book by telling you what it isn't. If you are merely looking for investment advice, then this book will be a waste of your time and money. I am no investment expert and what I know about the relative benefits to be obtained from the many different, competing investment opportunities on offer, could be written on the back of a postage stamp. This is not a textbook on the workings of the City. I have ignored vast areas of historical description and laudatory background. If you want to discover the difference between the Baltic Exchange and the London International Financial Futures Market then I have no doubt you can find such a book on another shelf. What this book is not intended to be is a technical, abstract treatise on financial theory and it will not make you rich, although I hope that it might prevent you from becoming potentially poorer. There are men in the City of London whose business affairs have been identified by the hallmarks of sound practice, fair dealing and honest conduct. It is these men whose traditions are tarnished by the activities of the other group whose methods are identified by sharp practice, deceit and dishonesty and it is about these men that I seek to write.

CHAPTER ONE
The Vicious Circle

Next time you go into your local newsagent, go to that section of the shelves which holds the magazines and periodicals which deal with business, money and financial investment and just count up how many there are. It will surprise you. Look at the price of some of these publications, which may surprise you even more, and then choose the glossiest, most sophisticated one you can find and open it.

Now, start counting. Count how many advertisements you can find in the first ten pages which offer you an investment service. Now, count the ones which say they will be a personal opportunity for you to benefit fully from the professional expertise of the fund managers, brokers or investment advisers, and will enable you to participate in an exciting new world of investment opportunities.

Having conducted this small personal survey, multiply the number you have found by the number of magazines on the shelves and then, having discovered the amazingly large number of remarkably similar services on offer, ask yourself this question: 'If the facilities these companies have to offer are so efficient, why do they need to spend so much money advertising their services?'

Having so recklessly exposed you to temptation and possible danger, I urge you to put the magazine back on the shelf and find somewhere to wash your hands. As a final precaution, repeat the following phrase three times, or as many times as it takes to put the contents of the magazine out of your mind. 'Reading investment magazines can seriously damage your wealth.' It is the wealth warning which ought to be printed compulsorily on the front cover of every such periodical in the same way that the Government warns smokers of the danger to their health on the side of every cigarette packet.

All joking apart, it is an instructive exercise to review the vast number of investment services which are currently available. Yet what is it that these advertisers have to offer? And why is their market growing so rapidly? As a starting point, therefore, let us look at what makes up an investment.

I have no doubt that my definition is one to which any number of highly qualified economists could find cause to take exception. So be it. My aim is to create a workable definition which will be capable of simple explanation but which will, at the same time, contain all the necessary components for accuracy.

An investment is a commitment of funds, present or future, by an individual, private group, public body or State, for a (usually) defined period of time, for the expected purpose of deriving a future return in the form of the original sum plus an additional sum of money, income or money's worth, the additional amount of the realisable return being proportional to the degree of risk of total loss of the original invested capital, such risk being known to the investor at the time of making the commitment.

The investor can immediately be seen to be different from the speculator, who while possessing many of the characteristics of this definition, is really more akin to the gambler. His financial commitment rarely includes the defined aspect of the time element and his risk/gain ratio is far less quantifiable. The investor expects to realise a return on his money. The speculator merely hopes to make a profit. The act of investing, because of the time and risk element involved, indicates an act of commitment by the investor and is an indicator of the degree of confidence he holds in the society in which he lives.

The risk/gain ratio is the factor by which the investor decides whether he is prepared to commit his own capital in an enterprise, which has the potential to provide a return but contains an element of risk of loss of the initial investment. The natural, or market risks are inherent in every investment decision and determine the degree of return which the investor expects to realise. The decision whether or not to invest can only be made by the individual investor, having taken into consideration the relevant risk factors concerned. This should, however, be the only variable element he needs to consider. The amount of money to be invested and the amount of time which the investor decides is a sufficient commitment, are merely matters of degree which can be determined upon once the decision to undertake this particular risk has been reached.

If we accept that it is in the long-term interests of civilised societies to encourage the concept of private and social investment, then it follows that it is in the interests of those societies to provide the means to enable the investor to invest fairly. Once the investor finds that he is being expected to assume risks other than those which naturally occur in the normal course of investment events, then he will lose confidence in the system in which he is expected to risk his capital and will seek markets where the extraneous risks are better controlled.

It is not part of my aim to launch into a detailed analysis of the economic theory of investment but it is a quantifiable measure of the health of a nation and a reflection of its political stability that people are prepared to undertake investment in its fabric, its industries or its financial services. That investment can be in the form of committing money to provide oneself with a pension for one's old age or to provide an income, which can be called personal investment or to build a factory or fund a business which can be called social investment. The volume of investment in any society is determined by the entrepreneur whose decisions are governed solely by the risk/gain ratio. The greater the degree of income achieved from investment, the greater will be the amount of investment undertaken. A second factor in the determination of the volume of investment is the rate of interest currently available. If a man can earn a greater rate of return by committing his capital in personal investment areas, he will be less disposed to make social investments, as he must calculate among the costs involved in his social investment the loss he has sustained by not investing in high interest-bearing areas of private investment. Social investment has a direct influence upon employment and consumption, personal investment leads to a greater individual ownership of property which, in theory, aids social stability.

It is the disparity in the potential return available between social and personal investment which can lead to an overconcentration of investment in one sector of the economy to the detriment of the other, and lead to the accusation being made that the City exists to serve the interests of those who profit most from the manipulation of money (the casino economy) at the expense of those who create wealth through manufacturing industry. Inevitably, this has a tendency to be identified in political terms. Dennis Skinner, MP, no friend of the Conservative Government, put it this way:

'By and large, the Tory party represent the interests of the City, what I call more generally the Casino Economy . . . I suppose this Tory Government has characterised more than any other the fact that they wanted to support the Casino Economy as against what I call the

Industrial Economy. By the Casino Economy I mean the City, the Stock Exchange, Lloyds, banking, insurance, as opposed to those people who provide goods and public services. The Casino Economy has benefited by this Government's actions to a greater degree than many others, and when you have interest rates in double figures, then the opportunity to make money has been much easier, you can hardly fail to make money in the Casino Economy, when interest rates are in double figures.'

Lest the temptation should exist to dismiss Dennis Skinner's arguments out of hand, simply because he is one of the most well-known critics of the Conservative Government, I sought other views. In a leading article in *The Sunday Times*, Roy Hattersley, the Labour Shadow Chancellor, made the following observations:

'Self-interest and emotion combine in encouraging Conservatives to do what is best for the City. As a result, the Chancellor's economic policy increasingly reflects City prejudices, to the detriment of manufacturing industry . . . The privatisation of public assets has put several fortunes into City pockets, not all of them the products of reputable Merchant Banking practices. The City grows fat on the current wave of mergers and take-overs which flourish within our sloppy monopoly policy—most of them unrelated to competitive efficiency or the economies of scale . . . Yet commitment to the City's interests prevents the Government doing what is best for industry as a whole. Britain, almost alone among the industrial states of Europe, lacks institutions that work closely with industry to offer substantial amounts of medium and long-term credit, often at preferential interest rates, to special category customers.'

Bryan Gould, MP, a Labour Front Bench spokesman, put it another way. He said:

'I think that one of the peculiar features, perhaps the one character-istic feature of British economic policy-making over a very, very long time, is that where more successful countries than we have run their economies in the interests of people who make things in factories and sell them in international markets, in other words, trading economies like the Germans and the Japanese, we have, for well over 100 years, and this is perhaps the last hang-over of an Imperial economy, we have run the economy in the interests of people who hold assets, who deal in money, and, as a consequence, we're very sensitive to the particular interests of the City, and we'll jettison manufacturing industry, no problem at all. The present Government happily threw away a fifth of all British manufacturing industry in the space of eighteen months at the beginning of the 1980s, but let something go wrong in the City, JMB or whatever, and every resource is summoned to prop it up. If the price we have to pay for having a successful City is that they totally dominate economic policy making, to the disadvantage of all of the rest of us, so that we are a weaker economy than we need be, then we've got to look carefully at the balance of advantage.'

Whichever area of investment a person chooses, however, it is accepted that it is in the interest of the State to encourage such practices. It is one of the functions of capitalist economies to provide technical means whereby the disparity between personal and social investment can be levelled and these efforts can be made by the taxation of certain profitable earnings or the providing of tax incentives for certain kinds of investment practice.

Generally speaking, acts or behaviour which benefit the State are deserving of State encouragement or assistance and the protection of investors is an acceptable aspect of social control within capitalist societies. That protection is not aimed at stifling entrepreneurial activity, which would be a regressive step, but at providing the necessary environment in which the investor may commit his capital, in the sure knowledge that he is aware of all the relevant risks involved in the proposition and thus is able to make the necessary decision.

One aspect of our historical tradition of investor protection has been to emphasize the degree of personal responsibility which is placed upon the individual investor for the making of his decisions. Prior to the introduction of the concept of the limited company, was opposed to a partnership, or sole trader, the concept of investment was limited to the overall ownership of assets by individuals. The prevailing laws dealt, in the main, with the inalienable rights of property ownership and were strictly interpreted and enforced.

The development of the limited liability company introduced another dimension into our understanding of the responsibilities regarding legal ownership and created a concept of investment in property without immediate physical possession or, necessarily, ownership. An additional concept has been added by the introduction of forms of indirect investment where an investor has committed funds to a unit trust or managed fund, which is itself merely part of an even bigger investment in a series of disparate investment opportunities.

Whatever the nature of the investment medium offered, the fundamental requirements are that either the investor must rely on his own judgement or he must be given a degree of protection, and, to assist this, two identifiable traditions have developed.

In the case of the man with the experience of investing his money in entrepreneurial schemes, the concept of 'disclosure' was developed, which required all the pertinent facts surrounding the proposed investment in question to be disclosed, prior to subscription, ie telling the putative investor the full facts concerning the enterprise and then leaving him to make his mind up as to whether the proposal was the sort of investment in which he wanted to get involved. The Davey Committee which reported on the requirements of certain aspects of Company Law in 1895 stated:

'It may be a counsel of perfection and impossible of attainment to say that a prospectus shall disclose everything which could reasonably influence the mind of an investor of average prudence. But this . . . is the ideal to be aimed at . . . and for this purpose to secure the utmost publicity is the end to which new legislation on the formation of companies should be directed.'

Our Victorian forebears did not envisage that investment in public companies would be the sort of activity indulged in by the honest poor. Then, as now, investment in an enterprise of a public nature was looked upon by many as being the prerogative of the monied classes and in particular, the emerging, upwardly-mobile, bourgeoisie. This is not to say that there was any discouragement shown to the lower orders of the practices of savings and thrift. Far from it. These were values which were preached to the children of the working classes from birth, mostly, it must be said, by the Church, but reinforced by a paternalistic State. While it may have instilled a sense of financial self-reliance, its overriding motive was to minimise the burden of the maintenance of the poor and indigent upon the parish.

It was recognised that in order to protect the savings of those of limited means, and to encourage habits of thrift and moderation, special protections could be enforced to encourage those most desirable of practices; and so developed the paternalistic approach towards investor protection. This degree of Government protection can be witnessed in the regulations of the Trustee Savings Banks and later, the Post Office Savings Bank. It is a matter of historical record that successive Governments have provided for the protection of the less financially sophisticated, both for reasons of their greater lack of understanding of complex financial matters and to provide them with security of their capital.

Subsequently, Building Societies, in order to maintain a degree of security for the deposits of their investors have been confined to investing their funds in those areas of investment which pose the least risk. This requirement is enshrined in the 1962 Building Societies Act although it restates fundamental principles first outlined in the Act of 1874. This has been interpreted by modern observers to be based upon the rationale that Building Societies received deposits from persons whose means were insufficient to enable them to obtain independent advice as to the most profitable disposition of their available savings. It is too early to say whether recent changes in Building Society legislation will alter the degree of protection offered to unsophisticated investors.

The principle of informed disclosure has been adopted by other countries for the protection of investors. In this book, reference will be made many times to the American organisation called the Securities and Exchange Commission, which is the Federal body with the primary responsibility for administering the securities laws in the United States. In the introduction to its excellent handbook, entitled *The Work of the SEC*, the American philosophy of investment responsibility is outlined. It states:

'It should be understood that the securities laws were designed to facilitate informed investment analyses and prudent and discriminating investment decisions by the investing public. It is the investor, not the Commission, who must make the ultimate judgement of the worth of the securities offered for sale. The Commission is powerless to pass judgement upon the merits of securities; and assuming proper disclosure of the financial and other information essential to informed investment analysis, the Commission cannot bar the sale of securities which such analysis may show to be of questionable value.'

It is possible to see quite clearly that there is an historical tradition of protection for investors. This protection also encourages a degree of prevention against scandal within the markets themselves. It would appear to be insufficient simply to protect current investors, without protecting the reputation of the markets in which these investors place their funds.

So, how do Governments maintain public confidence in their investment markets which they value so highly? In his speech to the Bow Group in July 1984, the Chancellor of the Exchequer, Nigel Lawson, said:

'Whatever the system of regulation that is applied, the investing public needs to be assured that wrongdoers and fraudsters will be speedily and effectively brought to book under the law.' Later, in the same speech, he said:

'It is just as important to have a system which makes it as difficult as possible for fraud and malpractice to occur in the first place.'

In these two small quotations which I have taken from a lengthy speech, Mr Lawson identified the two most important elements which comprise the only effective means of combating dishonest and criminal activity in any field. Yet, within a year, John Wood, the Principal Assistant Director of Public Prosecutions, speaking to the American Bar Association at their annual meeting in London, was making the following harrowing admission:

'We in this country are extremely concerned about what appears to be an explosion in white-collar crime, brought about partly because sentences for bank robberies are very high, while sentences for white-collar crime are ridiculously low.'

John Wood was, at the time, in the best position to make such a statement as the responsibility for the administration of prosecutions for major fraud came under his jurisdiction. His choice of the words 'an explosion in white-collar crime' could not have been more apt.

In its reported statistics for the year 1984, the Metropolitan and City Police Company Fraud Department (The Fraud Squad) had commenced 1963 new investigations of fraud. It is not possible to quantify what percentage increase this figure represents over the previous year's new investigations, as those statistics are, for some reason, unavailable. However, it is possible to calculate that at the end of 1984, the Fraud Squad were still investigating 594 cases, which represented an increase of approximately 33% over the figures for the year ending 1983.

When the money at risk comes to be examined, the sums involved at the end of 1984 show an increase of 133% over the sums at risk for the year ending 1983.

The crime figures for allegations of fraud in 1984 indicated a dramatic increase over the previous year and one of the factors in that increase is the perception of fraudsmen of the lack of likelihood of their being caught.

A second element in the fraudsman's calculation is the likelihood of conviction in the event of capture and, then, the likelihood of a custodial sentence. This last element is important because it is the possibility of an immediate prison sentence which is the major determining factor in the attitude of the criminal, after he has been apprehended and charged, and it is this aspect to which John Wood referred in his speech to the American Bar Association. A very successful solicitor who specialises in the defence of professional criminals explained his philosophy to me.

'If you've got a client who's wanted, then the best thing you can do is to get him to surrender himself while you're present. That way you get to hear all the allegations and you can ensure that you're present while he's interviewed. Say they suspect him of an armed robbery. After a while you get a feel for the sort of evidence which is going to be accepted by a jury and if they've got a good case against him, and he's got the sort of form which is going to mean a lengthy prison sentence, then at least you can discuss the potential value of a guilty plea with him. Judges like guilty pleas and they are encouraged to reflect that in sentencing. If you think that it is likely to shorten his sentence, and if he's a pro, most times your client will accept your advice. Most of my clients look upon prison as an occupational hazard, but that doesn't mean they dislike it any less.

'Now, a fraudsman's different. For a start, the issues involved are much more complex. In a lot of cases, the DPP won't prosecute at all, because of the complexity and the costs involved. Robbery, by and large, is a very simple matter and, in most cases, it boils down to whether the jury believe the police evidence, but fraud cases contain a wealth of possibilities. For a start, your client is almost invariably on bail. In most cases, there is so much documentary evidence that you can almost always find something the police have overlooked and use this fact to suggest that they haven't done their job thoroughly. The trials last much longer and are usually fairly uninteresting to the average onlooker. I suppose the chances of conviction are much the same as any other offence, in the end, but the big plus factor from your client's point of view is that he is very unlikely to receive a custodial sentence, even if he is convicted. If he does go to prison, he is most unlikely to receive the same sort of sentence he would get for a robbery. The fraudsman will always give it a run, because he has nothing to lose by fighting a charge and everything to gain.'

The attitudes described here are those of a practising solicitor who has spent years defending professional criminals. They do not alter in any way the fundamental premise that the greatest disincentive to crime is the possibility of getting caught.

The potential for being successfully apprehended, in fraud cases, is different from certain other major criminal offences. Fraud investigation is, with the exception perhaps of Long-Firm fraud, almost exclusively, a reactive activity, in that the investigation usually commences long after the fraud has been committed. It is rare for the investigation to commence while the fraud is still taking place. Police or the other investigative agencies are normally introduced after the damage has been done and this introduction can be days, weeks or even months later. In one case I investigated, the allegation was made to police almost two years after the alleged offences took place, the interim period having been taken up with the liquidation of the company and the arguments between the directors and the creditors concerning the whereabouts of the assets.

One of the important aspects of modern police philosophy is the provision of good criminal intelligence, aimed at the prevention of crime and the frustration of criminal activity. The Commissioner for the Metropolitan Police, in his Strategy Report to the Home Secretary for 1985, stated, as his first priority for 1986 and beyond, a concentration of resources to reduce criminal opportunity through crime prevention and, to achieve that end, he sought to identify those areas of criminal activity which were perceived by the public to be worthy of policing priorities.

A geographically representative National Opinion Poll survey conducted in August 1985 for the Metropolitan Police indicated that the greatest public fear was having their home broken into and property stolen. This was closely followed by fears of criminal damage, violence, and rape. The outcome of the research into public perceptions and fears has resulted in a force goal for 1986 and beyond of concentration upon the offences of robbery, burglary, drug misuse, racial attacks, vandalism and auto crime and it is towards these priorities that the Metropolitan Police will direct its resources. If, as it appears, resource allocation is to be determined by public perception of criminal priority regardless of whether that view is based upon justifiable fact or merely uninformed opinion, it is an irreconcilable decision. Lord Hailsham, in a recent speech in the House of Lords has said that the public's perception of the levels of fear of crime is not justified by the actual risks and it was necessary to develop ways of harnessing that degree of public concern with commonsense. If that is the case, then why is it that nowhere in the Commissioner's report can I find any reference to fraud as a major cause for concern? It is almost as if fraud did not exist as a criminal category, either in the public's perception or in the Commissioner's sense of justifiable priorities.

In the report entitled *The Incidence, Reporting and Prevention of Commercial Fraud*, compiled by Dr Michael Levi of Cardiff University and published in March 1986 it is observed that, 'neither the Department of Trade and Industry nor many police forces routinely compile statistics on the cost of fraud as is done with other property crime. However, commercial fraud recorded by London Fraud Squads represents almost three times the total cost of all other property crimes in London.'

The study goes on to estimate that UK companies could be losing up to £1 billion annually through fraud and fraud-related criminal activities and while this figure does not necessarily illuminate my particular subject, which is investment fraud, it amply illustrates the point that among criminal activities, fraud is considered to be a very low profile priority when the values at risk are compared with the resources allocated to deal with the problem.

Why should this be? The Prime Minister has only recently called a much publicised meeting of senior police officers, Home Office advisors, and leaders of Britain's security industries to establish a common policy of crime prevention. The urgency of this meeting was emphasized by the dramatic increase in the figures of losses sustained by the public in what are termed 'property crimes', and, perhaps more pertinently, the enormous sums of money being paid out by Insurance Companies in settlement of theft and burglary claims. Much of this seminar was aimed at providing more facilities whereby the public can protect themselves from the activities of criminals, particularly as the available figures suggest that the public are most concerned with the likelihood of sustaining criminal loss of their property.

The public perception of fraud is construed by senior policemen as being a very important indicator in the priority of allocation of resources to combat the problem. The number of police officers deployed on the investigation of allegations of major fraud, throughout the country, totalled 588 in 1985, according to the figures published in the Fraud Trials Committee Report (The Roskill Report). This figure represented an increase of only three police officers from the total number employed on the same task in 1982.

In 1983, the manpower of the Metropolitan Police Fraud Squad was reduced by 10% in line with the Commissioner's stated aims of making more men available for the investigation of the more high-profile offences such as street offences and burglary, yet an analysis of the statistics of reported allegations of fraud indicates an increase of 520%

between the years 1982 to 1984 in the Metropolitan area of London alone.

Faced with statistics such as these, it becomes necessary to examine the root causes of the apparent lack of concern among senior policemen for the problems created by fraud. If the criterion of investigative priority was the value of loss incurred, major fraud would rank among the most serious of criminal activities. Ironically, it is just this aspect, ie the value involved, which as we have examined, is the major consideration in the mind of the investor, when he is deciding whether to invest in a particular enterprise. Unhappily, society adopts an ambivalent attitude towards fraud.

'I mean, it's not as if anyone gets hurt,' is a common feeling, expressed by a number of people to whom I have spoken. Another view was:

'The only sort of people who get ripped off are the insurance companies and the banks. What the hell, they can afford it.' 'They can afford it' appeared to be a common attitude. In many cases, there appeared to be an almost grudging admiration for the workings of a particularly complex and successful fraud. 'I've got nothing against a good con-man. If he can have it off, then good luck to him.'

These views were expressed, not as might be expected by persons with criminal records or connections, but by three working men who would never consider committing any overt or deliberate criminal offence themselves. All three are family men, with young children, who would, in other circumstances, express very strong views about child molesters or persons charged with offences of a sexual nature.

It seems almost as if our perceptions of fraudsmen are coloured by their portrayal in films such as *The Sting*, in which the heroes are painted more in the style of Robin Hood type characters, 'more sinned against than sinning', rather than adopting any recognisable villainous characteristics. Attitudes like those expressed above are common throughout all levels of society. Despite the reported losses in the region of £225 million and an alleged personal misappropriation of £39 million, there are some people in the City who look upon the activities of Peter Cameron-Webb and Peter Dixon at Lloyds as being 'nothing really wrong, old boy! Old PCW didn't really hurt anyone, so jolly good luck to him. I hope he gets away with it.' It is as if fraud has become so institutionalised a practice that somehow our moral perceptions have become distorted when we talk about fraud as opposed to theft, criminal deception, forgery or false pretence. In an economy where the prime criterion of efficiency is expressed to be that identified by market forces, it becomes hard to define the dividing line between monetarist efficiency and illegality.

A very good example was recently described to me by an accountant who specialised in auditing companies' annual financial reports. We were discussing the proposals to make auditors responsible for reporting allegations of fraud or financial misconduct if they discovered them during the course of an audit. My friend was completely in favour of the suggestion but he pointed out a very practical draw-back. He said:

'Look at it like this. When I was employed by X and Co., accountants, we were employed by a major company to conduct their annual audit. The annual audit fee for this job was in the region of £50,000 for our firm. During the course of the audit, we discovered some fairly sizeable areas of "financial concern", which we naturally reported to the directors and made certain qualifying remarks in our draft final report. When the time came to discuss the report with the directors, the qualifications were on the report. The first thing they wanted to discuss, however, was our continued retention in the following year as their auditors, pointing out to us that Y and Co. were prepared to conduct the audit for a smaller fee. The outcome was that we were retained as their auditors for the following year, the report was re-written, and the qualifications, after further consideration, were removed.'

The concept of moral integrity has become so devalued in recent times, it is hard to see who will take the lead to restore real meaning to the phrase 'My word is my bond', so that it no longer translates as 'my word is my bond, so long as it is financially advisable for me to keep it.'

Coupled with this apparent lack of public concern for the activities of the fraudsman, is the attitude of the police themselves. Chief officers of police have to spread their annual budget to cover a multitude of problem areas and it is almost inevitable that some problems will assume a political hue which require a greater degree of active attention than others. Chief officers are only human after all and possess all the normal human characteristics, chief among which, in career officers of senior rank, is a highly refined instinct for political survival.

The investigation of fraud does not enjoy a high profile of interest among detective officers. Indeed, it is looked upon by many to be somehow different from 'normal' police duty. This is partly due to the fact that many fraud investigations can involve long-term attention to figures and paperwork, which require long hours of duty tied to a desk, sorting papers. This immediately places fraud investigation outside the 'active' ethos, so beloved by most detective officers. There is still a tendency for some senior officers to be imbued with this philosophy and to consider fraud investigation as being 'inactive' and therefore, by definition, not 'real' police work.

A second element which is perhaps complementary to the action concept is the early arrest theory. Detective officers are taught that their primary duty is to place the facts of any given case and the person who has allegedly committed the offence before the court. Once that duty has been performed, it should not be their concern if the person charged is subsequently acquitted by the court. However, this priority can sometimes be used by the less than conscientious officer to justify sloppy and slipshod work, while maintaining the 'active' concept.

'My job is to nick 'em and charge 'em. If they get let off by the juries, that's not my problem.'

This was a not uncommon attitude among certain officers, which might or might not have enjoyed a degree of practical reality when applied to the majority of relatively minor offences commonly dealt with at District level. At the Fraud Squad however, such an attitude would be completely out of place as most allegations reported to Fraud Squads are of a highly complex nature. I am aware that there is a tendency among the smaller forces for the Fraud Squad or Commercial Branch to receive all fraud allegations, but generally speaking, all specialist fraud units deal with matters which are complex and can involve considerable sums of money.

There are a large number of technical legal problems which arise when a man is charged with a criminal offence. It is, therefore, particularly inadvisable in cases of major fraud to charge a defendant before the investigating officer is certain that he has completed all the relevant enquiries. I am only too well aware that this most desirable of alternatives is not always possible. The defendant might attempt to flee the country or to interfere with the course of the investigation, in which case it may be necessary to bring him before a court at the earliest opportunity, but in many cases, the necessary degree of investigative time can usually be allotted to the case.

Another factor which plays a part in the diminishing of the importance of fraud investigation is the likelihood of a non-custodial sentence being passed upon a defendant in the event of conviction. Policemen view sentencing as an important and integral part of their work, taking the view that if a man is sentenced to a long term of imprisonment for an offence, then this in some way represents society's justification and approbation of their actions. Police are not encouraged to court publicity, so a long sentence, handed down by a judge with a reputation for severe sentences, is considered as 'a way of the court saying "thank you"'.

Fraud, as we have seen, does not attract heavy sentences, whereas bank robbery does. Therefore, in police concepts, bank robbery is a more important crime than fraud. There has always been a degree of professional rivalry between officers from the Robbery Squad (the Flying Squad) and the Regional Crime Squads, both of whom tend to deal with similar types of defendant and criminal activity and who are the best examples of the 'action' methodology. Neither group would be prepared to equate their particular mystique and group loyalty with officers from the Fraud Squad, who are perceived, in the words of one particular senior officer I knew, as being 'nothing more than a bunch of paper cowboys'.

Bearing all these aspects in mind, it is hardly surprising that the Commissioner of the Metropolitan Police and his professional colleagues do not deem it necessary to advance more resources to the investigation of major fraud, surrounded as they are by senior advisors who have similar views to those described above. There are men in the Fraud Squad of relatively lowly rank, who possess considerable degrees of expertise in the investigation of highly complex financial frauds. This knowledge has been acquired over a period of time and, usually, by the individual officer concerned devoting his private hours to study of his subject, for nothing more than a wish to become professionally competent at his job. There are also a cadre of men there who have absolutely no wish to be there at all and who share the view that a posting to the Fraud Squad is akin to being cast into outer darkness.

There is, or was, no policy of permanent staffing among the technically competent, regardless of how much a man might wish to stay and develop even greater competence, and this has led to a constant intake of men at the Fraud Squad who need to be trained in the peculiar ramifications of the work carried out there.

It is, therefore, ironic that although the police seem unable to move forward in their approach towards dealing with major fraud, this has not deterred the criminals who have discovered that crime can pay and pay handsomely with minimal risk to the perpetrator of lengthy prison sentences. A large number of previously successful criminals have moved into the area of company formation, off-shore banking, inter-company transfer, and all the other ramifications of company director-ships. Assisted by highly qualified accountants and solicitors, they have diversified their criminal activities, under the guise of successful businesses, a fact which comes as no surprise to their underworld counterparts in America who have been engaged in similar activities for many years and who are now so much a part of the national business fabric, that it is hard to differentiate between the genuine corporate identity and the criminal front.

So what is the picture that confronts us?

We see a capitalist society that requires public confidence to be maintained in its financial markets, in order to continue to attract those investors its system needs, both to create future employment and to fund the invisible earnings factor on which our economy is so dependent. Yet, in order to maintain that confidence, we have had a system of investor protection which was cumbersome, antiquated and insufficiently provided with effective means of enforcement and which did not provide the necessary disincentives to professional criminals from taking part in ever bigger enterprises of a fraudulent nature. The lack of perception in the official mind of their real danger to society means that the resources made available to investigate them are shrinking in comparison with the growth in their size and scope of operation. This has a direct effect upon the likelihood of their apprehension, conviction and subsequent sentence, which, as we have discussed, are the only meaningful preventative factors in relation to the activities of the professional fraudster.

Some commentators might be prepared to describe the scenario I have outlined here as 'a chain of events in which the discovery of one difficulty, leads on to a set of new problems involving increased difficulty.' (Webster's Dictionary)

I just call it 'a vicious circle'.

CHAPTER TWO
The Pin-Striped Revolution

At the start of the previous chapter, you were exposed to the very serious risks involved in reading investment magazines, in an attempt to illustrate the wide variety of investment services on offer. Investments are offered to the private client in a wide variety of media and the market is expanding rapidly. Now, you may have said to yourself: 'that's all very well, but how does this apply to me? I can't afford to put spare cash into these schemes and I don't own any shares.'

The market place for investments does apply to you however and whether you are an investor in specific investment areas, such as shares, or you hold a Building Society account or you are making contributions to a company pension scheme, you and your money are an integral part of an enormous, multi-national system of financial management, whose administration can have far-reaching effects upon your life style.

So, what is it that the investment advisors want to offer you and what do they want from you?

The answer to the second part of the question is easy, they want your money, and as much of it as they can persuade you to give them. The answer to the first aspect of the double question is not so easy.

British investment techniques and the markets which exist to service their needs have undergone a dramatic revolution, possibly the most radical in their history. The outcome of this violent upheaval has changed the face of financial dealings in the City of London, which has had a knock-on effect on the financial services in the rest of the country. These changes are reflected in every High Street and their effects are fundamentally altering the services being offered to a largely unsuspecting public by the sort of firms which advertise in those investment magazines you looked at.

The sort of services now on offer will be supplied not only by the established investment companies but by less established businesses which are developing to take advantage of the new markets and last, but by no means least, by the fraudsman, who views developments and changes as a new challenge to his skills. It is useful to examine his methods and techniques in an attempt to learn how to avoid him when you see him coming and how to identify him when he disguises his activities under the façade of commercial respectability.

Now, the concept of revolution does not normally go hand in hand with the traditional image of the City of London. It is hard to imagine that inside that pin-striped commuter on the 8.10 from Surbiton, beats the heart of a radical revolutionary, dedicated to the overthrow of the establishment. Yet that is exactly what has happened. All right, the traditional image is perhaps a bit too predictable, a little too obvious and the players in this game are more likely to be parking their BMWs and Porsches than taking the suburban train, using tailors on 5th Avenue as much as Jermyn Street or Savile Row and talking to Wall Street as often as Throgmorton Street but whatever the surface image, inside they are pressed from the same mould and took part in the same revolution.

You wouldn't have seen barricades in Cheapside, manned by radical foreign exchange dealers, and I doubt whether they sang the 'Red Flag' in the Long Room but what has been termed the 'Big Bang' was as much a revolution as was the misnamed Industrial Revolution of the eighteenth and early nineteenth centuries.

The City of London has experienced a number of radical influences in its long history and has absorbed them all. The Black Death, the Peasants' Revolt, the Great Plague, the Great Fire and more recently the Blitz, each has contributed to making the City what it is today and their separate monuments can still be observed, if you know where to look.

The City of London has always been the traditional centre to which Kings and Governments have looked for money, to encourage foreign trade, to subsidise exploration, to finance social change, to pay armies to fight wars, or, more mundanely, to borrow money to pay their debts. During the troubled times of the fifteenth century, one of the first acts of whoever had recently assumed power was to reassure the City fathers of their continued enjoyment of their ancient charters and privileges.

Through the years, the City has developed traditions and practices which have moulded the way in which business has been conducted and, in many ways, some of these traditions may seem anachronistic to modern eyes. Yet it was the very existence of these traditions which made the City what it became and gave it its reputation for fair dealing. Business involving considerable sums of money was conducted on nothing more than a handshake and a gentleman's good word and reputation. 'My word is my bond', the motto of the Stock Exchange, was no idle boast and summed up the situation very neatly.

Sir Peter Tapsell MP, in his speech to Parliament on 16 July 1984 during the debate on the Gower Report described the Stock Exchange as: 'An institution that has grown up over the centuries. Moreover, it has served the country extremely well and helped us win every war from the time of Louis XIV to the Falklands.'

'Well,' you may ask, 'if it's such a good system, why is it being forced to change?'

It is a question that a number of people have asked and Sir Peter Tapsell amplified their concern earlier in his speech when he said: 'Everyone who reads a financial newspaper and anyone who enters a City luncheon room will know that the City is in a state of revolutionary flux and is deeply worried about its future.'

Like most revolutions, things didn't happen overnight and the seeds for the changes were planted as far back as 1974; indeed, if Sir Peter is right, their roots go back even further to 1970. One of the fundamental traditions which marked out the London Stock Exchange was its unique separation of the functions of Stock Jobbers and Stock Brokers. This was an important distinction, important from a British point of view anyway, and their separation was an inherent part of the way in which the British traditionally dealt in stocks and shares. In order to maintain the distinction and to encourage financial independence Stock Brokers had, for at least the last seventy years, earned their remuneration by a system of fixed commissions below which no member of the Stock Exchange was permitted to deal.

There were other important Stock Market traditions which minimised the shareholding that foreign companies could own in member firms and the way in which members were admitted to the Exchange, and during the late 1960s and the early 1970s, certain senior Civil Servants began to pursue a theory that a number of the practices indulged in by the Stock Exchange were in fact acting against the wider interests of British financial dealings.

It was during this time that certain economists were identifying the need for a greater degree of internationalisation of financial dealings and it was perceived by some that the old traditions of the London Stock Exchange were unnecessarily restrictive in their scope and prevented a wider degree of international participation. At the same time, it was felt by others that the rules perpetuated an 'exclusive club' system which maintained dealing costs at an artificially high level, had denied access to outsiders for too long and which concentrated quite considerable power in the hands of a select few, to the detriment of a greater degree of social mobility, considered, in the perceived wisdom of the time, to be eminently desirable.

Whatever the truth for the reasons behind the development of the philosophy, and it may be felt that like so many other socio/political developments in the last twenty years, the real reasons became swallowed up in the rush to create change for change's sake, a number of influential Civil Servants expressed a wish to see the abolition of fixed commissions for Stock Brokers.

Eventually, the idea was adopted enthusiastically by the then Secretary of State for Prices and Consumer Protection, Roy Hattersley, who referred the Rule Book of the Stock Exchange to the Office of Fair Trading, to ascertain whether the rules contravened existing Restrictive Trade Practices legislation.

Examine the effects of the proposed abolition of fixed commissions however, because it is from this point that so much of the City revolution flowed. It appears that the reformers of the time wanted to get rid of an artificially maintained price level, believing that this would encourage a more competitive industry, but at the same time, wanted to retain all the benefits of the enforced distinction between jobbers and brokers for the degree of investor protection which the 'single capacity' system afforded. But did they realise the long-term effects of their proposals?

Sir Peter Tapsell: 'The thing that worries me about it is that I don't think that anybody did think it through and it grew very quickly, almost by accident. The Office of Fair Trading did not like the minimum commissions of the London Stock Exchange and, in my view, largely as a political measure, Mr Hattersley, under a previous Labour Government, referred the Commission Rule Book of the London Stock Exchange to the Office of Fair Trading, which was a straightforward traditional Socialist attack on the City.' He went on to say:

'The Office of Fair Trading, which in my view is an unduly theoretical body, is obsessed with a rather academic approach to what it regards as free markets and I regard their activities with considerable scepticism. The Office of Fair Trading were extremely hostile to the minimum commission rule of the London Stock Exchange and, as you know, the case dragged on for a very long time. I don't think the Office of Fair Trading was an appropriate body to be examining the matter. It should have gone to the Monopolies Commission, who are in a position to look at the wider implications of abolition. The Office of Fair Trading were never interested, as far as one can see, in the wider implications of the abolition of minimum commissions, they just regarded it as a restraint on trade and wanted to get rid of it.'

This is a very traditional City view shared by many. Sir Nicholas Goodison, the chairman of the Stock Exchange, described the referral to the Office of Fair Trading as 'a political decision taken in too much of a hurry'. He too pleaded for the matter to be referred to the Monopolies Commission and taken out of the hands of the Restrictive Practices Court, but even with a Conservative victory in May 1979, the matter was allowed to rest.

By now, you're probably saying to yourself: 'Well, so what, what difference does it make if dealing fees become cheaper? If anything, it's a good job, because it will make stock broking more competitive.'

The view of the traditionalists however, which was quickly taken up by a number of other experts within the industry, was that the abolition of fixed commissions would sound the death knell for the concept of single capacity, the traditional distinction between jobber and broker, and this, they argued, would create a dealing revolution within the City. The argument, known as the 'Link' argument, went roughly along the following lines. Stock brokers, when they acted for their clients acted as their agents, ie they had a legal duty to get the best possible deal they could for their clients, whether they were buying or selling. They did not own any stock themselves but merely acted as a go-between for their clients and the persons from whom they bought or to whom they sold the stock concerned, who were the stock jobbers. The stock broker earned his income from the commission he charged his client to deal for him and that commission had been fixed at a mimimum price, below which no broker could deal.

The jobbers on the other hand acted as principals, or wholesalers in the market, holding lines of stock in which they dealt. They did not charge commissions but earned their living from the difference in price at which they were prepared to buy and sell.

The distinction between the two sides of the industry was held to be in the best interests of the client because of the agency argument, which required the broker to obtain the best possible price for his client, without being permitted to profit from his client's affairs except by the agreed commission paid by his client for the transaction. Thus both participants were seen to have 'single' capacity within the market.

Abolish fixed commissions, ran the argument and you destroyed the capacity for stock brokers to earn a living. Sir Peter Tapsell:

'I immediately pointed out that there would be very large-scale repercussions from that decision but it was denied from the Treasury bench by ministers. They said, "Oh no, we are only interested in getting rid of minimum commissions, we want the separation of functions to continue in the Stock Exchange." Remember, only the previous session we had imposed separation of function on Lloyds in a special Act of Parliament and ministers, and, to some extent I think, the Council of the Stock Exchange didn't appreciate that if you abolished minimum commissions, it is extremely unlikely that the separation of functions could survive; and the reason why the separation of function couldn't survive is that without minimum commissions, there would not be sufficient profit to be made unless firms were going to deal on their own account. They wouldn't be able to earn enough commission to support their very large research staffs that the big firms have built up, simply from commission from clients. They would have to follow the American example and start speculating on their own account, and from that, the entire City revolution has flown.'

Now, it may well be that the decision to abolish minimum commissions is the catalyst by which the City revolution has been precipitated, but don't think that we can simply look upon this one factor as being the sole cause of the phenomenal degree of change which has come.

There has been a general move towards de-regulation since the late 1970s, coupled with a greater degree of international financial dealings. This has been brought about partly by the arrival in London of more than 450 foreign banks which were part of a far greater movement, world-wide, to deal with the growing market in foreign currency deposits held outside the home country, which you may have heard referred to as the Eurocurrency market. In addition the countries of the industrialised western world suffered a tremendous financial jolt during the 1970s when their dependence upon imported Arab oil brought home to them the dangers of financial isolationism. The flow of capital between nations which had grown because of two unexpected oil price increases and has added to pressure upon the UK to adapt her financial markets in order to bring them into line with other major financial markets.

In his speech to the Bow Group on 3 July 1984, Mr Nigel Lawson said:

'The Government cannot expect the City to adapt, unless it is willing to make changes itself, in particular, to remove impediments ... successive Governments had maintained exchange controls ever since the war. They constituted an artificial barrier to the efficient working of financial markets, while being of little or no practical use in staving off exchange rate crises. Accordingly, we abolished them in 1979, within six months of taking office. It was a bold step and an imaginative one. To the chagrin of our opponents, events since then have shown our confidence in the free working of markets to be fully justified. Freedom from bureaucratic controls on capital movements has allowed the City of London the freedom necessary to provide a full range of services in international markets.'

Geographically, London stands at a convenient mid-way point in time zones between New York and Tokyo. These are the two largest financial markets in the world but they are divided by very inconvenient time barriers. London is the natural strategic link between the two countries. Financial dealings are a twenty-four-hour process and as one market closes another opens. From this factor stems the natural move of foreign companies towards the creation of dealing facilities in other countries to continue the trading process.

Once the concept of global trading becomes accepted, to remain internationally competitive, it doesn't matter where in the world you have your dealing office because international communication is no longer timed in days, hours or even minutes, but in micro-seconds. The technological revolution has meant that a dealer in New York, watching prices on his dealing screen, relayed from London, can pick up a phone linked to London and deal in whatever stock he wants within seconds. In an industry where time is literally money, the development of communication technology has opened new horizons previously closed to entrepreneurs.

So, the revolution now begins to assume both an historical perspective and an impetus for change, but this still does not fully answer the question of what the future holds for the City of London.

In July 1983, the new Secretary of State for Trade and Industry, Cecil Parkinson, negotiated a compromise deal with Sir Nicholas Goodison which resulted in the withdrawal of the case from the

Restrictive Practices Court, in return for certain agreed alterations to the rules of the Stock Exchange. These were that minimum commissions would be phased out by the end of 1986, that non-members of the Stock Exchange would be free to serve as non-executive directors of member firms, that certain lay persons would join the Council of the Stock Exchange and that a new, independent appeals body would be established. In addition, it was agreed that single capacity would remain.

Sir Peter Tapsell's views concerning the impossibility of maintaining single capacity proved to be correct however and in April 1984, the Stock Exchange approved the establishment of International Dealerships, which were member firms dealing in foreign stocks, in a dual capacity role. This was shortly followed by the publication of what came to be called *The Green Book*, a discussion document in which the Stock Exchange effectively proposed the end of single capacity dealing and outlined certain other changes including the removal of the limitation of outside shareholdings in member firms and the sale of assets to new members. These proposals were, to some extent, forced upon the Stock Exchange by the agreements busily being entered into by the larger member firms with banks and foreign concerns.

Politically, it became necessary for the finalisation of the plans to be completed and in July 1984, the Trade Secretary, Norman Tebbit, insisted that the Stock Exchange should expedite the matter, for very pressing reasons.

In tandem with the changes in the markets, the Government had in July 1981 commissioned a far-reaching review of investor protection which had been undertaken by Professor 'Jim' Gower. It was probably the most important and influential examination of investor protection undertaken in this country for fifty years and had formed the basis of the Government's White Paper, published in January 1985, entitled *Financial Services in the United Kingdom*. Gower's report formed the basis of the proposed legislation which was intended to provide the safeguards for the investor of the future and it was necessary that the Stock Exchange should have completed and introduced its changes before the legislation received Royal Assent.

As you might have guessed, while time, which I have so conveniently condensed into a few lines, was marching on, the leading participants in the industry had taken stock of the changes that were coming and had started to make their arrangements to be in a position to compete efficiently when the dust from Big Bang had settled.

The new form of dual capacity dealing will involve the blurring of the distinctions between the roles of principal and agent and it is from that area that the real problems will emerge. Many commentators have identified the primary concern as being the immediate conflict of interests which will be created by the merging of the two separate capacities.

Let us look at a couple of hypothetical examples to see how this conflict of interests might work in practice.

Mr X is a stock broker in a large dealing concern with a considerable number of clients, both institutional and private. He is approached by one of his institutional clients, a pension fund manager, who wishes to sell a block of shares in a company which is not performing as well as it might and is believed to be experiencing management difficulties. Where under single capacity, the broker would have sold the shares at the best price he could have obtained for them to a jobber who dealt in those particular shares and simply have charged his client a commission fee for so doing, the broker will now find himself in a position where to keep his institutional client happy, he will be forced to negotiate a very competitive commission rate, or else his client will simply go elsewhere and use the services of another broker who will deal more cheaply.

Institutional customers have a considerable amount of influence as they have enormous sums of money to spend and stock brokers are not in the business of antagonising clients who regularly deal in large quantities of shares. The stock broker is placed in the unhappy position of having to take the shares on his own book, in the hope that he can find a buyer for them. His institutional client is not going to be prepared to wait for his broker to find the buyer, however, he wants to be paid now.

The broker is caught on the horns of a dilemma. If he pays his client with his own firm's money, he will be left holding a line of shares which could collapse in value at any minute. However, there is a solution available. Among his other functions, the broker acts for a large number of private clients, many of whom discuss their investment strategies with him. He recommends the shares he is holding to a number of his clients, who buy them, thus removing the broker's exposure to a possible sudden down-turn in the value of the shares. A few weeks later, the shares do indeed fall in value, the private clients taking the loss. Has the broker done anything wrong? If you listen very carefully, you will probably hear the screams of outraged stock brokers all over the country saying that such a practice would never happen.

Well, don't take my word for it, listen to what Sir Peter Tapsell had to say:

'It stands to reason if a firm has a particular position in a commodity, or an interest to advance, that however honest the people in the firm are, they are likely to be influenced, if only subconsciously, by their interest. It's only human nature, if you've got something to sell and somebody rings you up and perhaps takes the initiative entirely by ringing you up and saying "do you think that I would be wise to buy 'A', I've been thinking of buying 'A'." If you happen to have a lot of "A" in your storeroom and you're having to pay interest to finance it, and you're anxious to find a buyer to get it off your books, it's really asking more than can be reasonably expected of human nature for people to turn away potential buyers of "A".'

In order to provide the degree of financial support necessary to enable stock brokers to buy the long lines of shares they are required to take under their management, new business arrangements have been forged between stock brokers, stock jobbers and merchant banks. It was too much to expect stock brokers to become jobbers in their own right, without the jobbers saying, 'in that case, we demand the right to deal directly with clients'. The major banks did not want to turn down the opportunities thus provided for expansion into areas of securities dealing, hitherto denied to them as anything more than minority shareholders. This is not simply a phenomenon being experienced in London, however, as in the race to become global players in the new international markets, banks and large securities dealing institutions are forging links and creating ever larger mega-institutions, dedicated to dealings of all kinds on a global twenty-four-hour basis. With the removal of traditional divisions between competing aspects of the financial market, we are seeing the development of the 'financial supermarket' dedicated to the provision of services of all kinds, under one corporate identity.

Creating the new conglomerates will not simply be a matter of historical inevitability. It will take a lot of time, effort and probably some expensive mistakes before the British can say that they have created a realistic investment banking alternative to the Americans. The Americans are bigger than us, they have more available capital, and they have a ten-year head start on us in this kind of 'financial supermarket' mentality.

The Americans experienced the effect of the change in the balance of power among practitioners after abolishing fixed commissions in

1975. The immediate effect was to alter the commissions charged to institutions dramatically; they dropped like a stone, although the private clients did not receive any immediate benefits. This led to a considerable degree of shakeout among the smaller dealing firms who, not being possessed of the larger institutional accounts which provided the volume of turn-over could no longer afford to compete efficiently, and the larger companies increased their share of the market at the smaller firms' expense. The important point was that profits from commission earnings became less important than the profits that competing firms could generate from dealing and underwriting on their own account. One effect was to increase redundancies among the large number of highly paid securities analysts. One story I read recently said that every third taxi driver in New York these days used to be employed on Wall Street in an advisory capacity. The long-term effect of the American experience has been the emergence of the specialised trader at the top of the management pyramid, at the expense of the adviser or analyst, and there is no apparent reason why a similar change should not occur in London.

Such new corporate conglomerates can only increase the likelihood of a greater degree of conflict of financial interests. It is this aspect that our traditional methods of dealing sought to regulate, but which will now depend on other types of internal controls to protect the interests of clients. Where you have one company which finances the marketing of a new security issue and conducts the marketing exercise, yet maintains private client accounts at the same time as undertaking large-scale institutional management, the potential for conflicts of interest is enormous. What protections can be enforced to ensure that the disparate sides of the business function are not seen to conflict with each other?

One method is quaintly referred to as 'Chinese Walls'. This has been described as:

'An established arrangement whereby information known to persons in one part of a business is not available, directly or indirectly, to those involved in another part of the business and it is accepted that, in each of the parts of the business so divided, decisions will be taken without reference to any interest which any other such part or any person in any such part of the business may have in the matter.'

You may agree with me that such a definition could only have been created by the sort of tortuous mind possessed by a Civil Servant or Parliamentary draughtsman.

Can anyone realistically believe that any firm is going to contemplate a situation whereby they might find themselves losing a substantial amount of money, but which they will not discuss among themselves, preferring to run the risk of loss. Take as an example the situation where a large organisation is making the market in a share of a company. Their marketing division is actively selling the stock to established customers, while the corporate management division is observing the performance of the company's finances. Aware that the company is about to announce record losses, which will have a sudden and possibly terminal effect upon the share price, are we expected to believe that the marketing boys will not be told: 'Push the sales of X as much as possible and don't buy back any shares. If anyone wants to sell, tell them to hang on. We don't want to be left with any more of these shares than we have to.'?

Alternatively, is it reasonable to suppose that any company will turn down the opportunity for profit, simply because a Chinese Wall exists? An example might be where the investment banking division of a large company is investigating the financial costs to a client of a take-over bid for another company. The fund-management side of the firm is well aware that the value of the take-over target is going to shoot up when the bid is announced. Their function is to earn as much as possible for their client funds and investment trusts. Are they going to ignore the profit potential or are they going to indulge in a little insider dealing, and earn a lot of money for the company by so doing?

Sir Peter Tapsell, in his speech to the House of Commons on 6 July 1984 said:

'I do not know why Chinese Walls are so called but I have visited the Great Wall of China. It has this characteristic. It has never kept anybody in or out.'

Another spokesman was quoted recently in the *Financial Times* as saying, 'the problem with Chinese Walls is that they have chinks in them.'

So, what is the future for the securities market in London? Dominated by foreign money, most notably, American and Japanese, its primary control could be removed from the hands of the London institutions and the Bank of England. There is little argument that the Americans can and will effectively control the securities side of the market, followed closely by the Japanese. Merrill Lynch, the American financial giant, and Nomura, the Japanese securities house, have already been admitted to membership of the Stock Exchange. Other companies have applied for membership. The financial muscle of these and other companies means that they can literally dominate and control the twenty-four-hour market in certain selected stocks, and their advice to clients is bound to influence supply and demand for certain stocks in the market. The President and Managing Director of Nomura said recently:

'Japanese investors are becoming increasingly interested in investing in the UK, having been very pleased with their investments in such British shares as British Telecom, Cable and Wireless, Reuters and Jaguar.'

Add to this a future where such shares as British Gas, Trustee Savings Bank, and the other hitherto publicly owned companies which the Government intends to sell on the world's markets, fall in ever greater quantities into foreign hands and it is not hard to understand the degree of concern expressed by some commentators for the future of British interests in these companies. While these shares continue to enjoy popular support in Tokyo and New York, they will maintain their price. However, the holders of large quantities of these shares will be motivated by profit and nothing else. They will not be prepared to maintain their holding if the profit potential in the share starts to slip and they will sell quickly, depressing the price of the share even faster. The end result of these sales will be felt here in Britain, not in Japan or America, and it is this concern that Bryan Gould was expressing when he said:

'With the internationalisation of the City, the ability to move money around is so much greater and you are going to be dealing with much bigger financial institutions whose real loyalties are not going to be to the British economy at all.'

At the start of this chapter I said that this revolution is going to have far-reaching effects upon the lives of all of us, even those of us who may not ever have thought about buying a share. The question is twofold, why and how?

The why is easy: as I said before, the answer is money, or perhaps more directly, cash. Your cash, and as much as you can be persuaded to part with. This enormous market thrives on a constant diet of cash money of all descriptions. If you starve it of its basic food, then like any other animal, it will die. But how do you encourage High Street Man to part with his cash, to fund these vast operations? What new methods can be offered and how can they be advertised? Traditional methods belong to the past and the advertising executives and the marketing men are frantically dreaming up new concepts to attract new customers to the new markets.

There is nothing special or particularly sacred about money, unless of course, you don't have any. It's a commodity like anything else which can be bought and sold. It's a subject which has been surrounded by mystique and an elevated sense of importance for too long, and it has been in the interests of those men who traditionally have made their living from manipulating your money to maintain this air of exclusivity.

Have you ever been to a bank for an interview with the under-manager because your overdraft had become a bit extended, or because you wanted a loan to build an extension on your house, or buy a car? Do you remember what it felt like, hanging around in the lobby, while they kept you waiting, until you were finally ushered into the presence. Then, in the hushed atmosphere, your file was examined and you were put through the third-degree as to exactly why you wanted this money. Do you remember how insignificant they made you feel, and the implication of the risk they were taking by advancing this sum to you?

It was all part of the mystery, designed deliberately to make you feel humble and unworthy and therefore, doubly grateful, when they granted you the loan or extended your overdraft. Believe me, if it wasn't for people like you and me, banks would go out of business.

When you boil it all down, banks are nothing more than money-lenders and they are now beginning to realise it. Have you noticed how their advertising has changed? Gone are the up-market, high-tech, hard-sell routines and in have come the soft sell, the sweet smile, the pretty face with the 'How can I help you?' approach. Another lesson the banks have learned is that they can no longer afford to be so cavalier in their attitude towards pulling the rug out from under clients' feet, if they get into short-term difficulties. Their tendency in the past to advance money when cash was slushing around in their vaults, only to turn off the flow without notice at the slightest chill wind from the Treasury has made them a lot of enemies, particularly amongst farmers, many of whom were encouraged to borrow substantial sums of money by the banks on the strength of their land values. This was fine while land prices remained buoyant. Too much investment by non-farming elements and investment institutions pushed land values way past their real limits. Now, land is dropping in value as a lot of institutions are pulling out. The value of land no longer supplies the support for the debts incurred by farmers who borrowed money to enlarge their business base, and the banks have been stepping in and foreclosing on debts, forcing farmers out of business and families from their homes.

These are enemies the banks cannot afford to maintain. They know that they are going to have to compete in the financial climate of the future with the Building Societies, who have been offering a very similar range of customer services for some time. The Building Societies are now marketing personal pension schemes which are going to offer direct competition to the Insurance companies. The trend towards the concept of the financial supermarket in the High Street has gathered momentum as all three services have observed the profit potential to be earned from the private house-owning market. A main plank in the Government's platform to enlarge the property-owning franchise, the purchase of a house represents not only the single biggest financial transaction that most people undertake in their lives but also an opportunity to enlarge the financial services sector of the company advancing the purchase money. A mortgage is but the first step and it makes sound financial sense to be able to provide for the other financial requirements at the same time. Mortgages require life insurance backing and in some cases bridging loan facilities are needed. It is not surprising, therefore, to observe the move by a number of financial service institutions into the Estate Agency market.

As competition develops it is inevitable that the other financial conglomerates are going to want to be able to provide a range of financial services, to support their more traditional roles, supply their customers with a more efficient service and thus attract new users to their facilities.

In America, it is possible to deposit cash with a single financial service, who will perform an extensive range of functions for the client. Merrill Lynch, one of the world's leading financial service companies and a recent new admission to the London Stock Exchange, will give their clients a cheque book and a credit card. Their clients can use these services, while their account remains in credit. The account however, is a trading account, with which Merrill Lynch are trading stocks, securities, commodities, financial futures and performing a number of other financial services for their client. The cash deposited with Merrill Lynch will earn interest for the client while it is not being utilised by way of margin deposit, but the customer can settle bills or maintain credit facilities by using the plastic made available by the company in return for the use of his money.

How long will it be before similar services are on offer in the United Kingdom? Not very long, by all accounts. Already the Building Societies will offer their clients a cheque book and a cash card. They offer an additional facility in that they open on Saturdays, a fact which is being acknowledged by the banks, many of whose branches are now offering Saturday opening. The banks are also extending their share dealing services, realising that the growing trend towards the purchase of new securities represents an important market which they do not want to miss. Traditionally, the banks have provided a securities service for customers, but buying through your bank manager has always been construed as an expensive way of dealing. However, the continuation of a bull market in securities coupled with a greater public awareness of share dealings has meant that banks are now competing for these additional services. 51% of the new shareholders in British Telecom had never bought shares before and the trend is growing, particularly in view of the Government's commitment to further privatisation.

The Insurance companies, never ones to miss an opportunity, are now extending their range of facilities and services into the High Street shops. Menzies, the booksellers and retail newsagent chain have recently formed a link with a leading Insurance broking concern to offer free, in-store financial services to customers. Advice can be obtained on savings, investments, insurance, pensions, loans and tax-planning.

The Midland Bank has forged a link with a certain supermarket chain where their banking facilities will be open on a six-day week basis, a service which is receiving very extensive advertising on television.

A leading firm of stock brokers, Quilter Goodison, has opened a share-dealing facility in Debenhams in Oxford Street. British Home Stores have opened a chain of what they call 'Money Shops', inside their stores, which maintain links with a major financial service company and a Building Society.

But why stop here? Woolworths are offering estate agency facilities with their property shops. A firm specialising in estate and property management has been granted a licence to deal in securities. A leading American financial service company is moving into the British mortgage market by offering British mortgages as a form of securities, which will mirror the concept of mortgage-backed securities already on offer in America.

By the time this book comes to be published, the range of financial services on offer will have expanded dramatically and will have completely changed our perception of ordinary financial dealings. Will the end-user however be any better served as a result of this revolution? What are the risks involved? The present public love affair with share buying could come crashing down if this country enters a prolonged bear market, yet there can be little doubt that many new investors have not appreciated the dangers which exist in share buying. A MORI poll of those people who bought shares for the first time in British Telecom established that 45% of those polled, an alarmingly high percentage, believed that they were as safe investing in BT as they were in leaving their money in the Building Society. Incredibly, 8% of those polled thought BT was safer than the Building Society.

Sir Peter Tapsell sounded a cautionary note on this topic. He said:

'I am not such a completely committed enthusiast of share owner-ship as you might expect from a stock broker because I think again that academics and theorists talk about share ownership with an enthusiasm which is not always sufficiently tempered with caution and realism. The fact is that equity shares are inherently volatile in value, I wouldn't use the word 'speculative' necessarily, but it doesn't follow that they are always suitable for widows and orphans . . . The fact is that people who buy shares must remember that what goes up can also come down and we are nearing the end, in my view, of the longest bull market in equity shares in the history of the stock exchanges of the world, and if large numbers of people with very small savings are encouraged to put their money into equities towards the end of their working lives, they might find that in three or four years time, they had a 20% loss of their capital, and they wouldn't like that at all. My own view is that those sort of people are much wiser to have their money in a well-run unit trust than trying to build up private portfolios of their own.'

With a self-effacing smile, Sir Peter added, as an aside:

'That, I may say, is not a view which is personally held by stock brokers or in the Conservative Party.'

This is a problem which confronts the Government at the moment. They are faced with the inevitable changes which are taking place around them in international financial dealings, whether they want them or not, and it is their responsibility to ensure that Britain plays her part in the markets of the future. In order to tap the sources of capital necessary to fund this new, free-wheeling de-regulated industry, the Government must encourage wider share and property ownership, encourage new forms of financial investment and generally encourage more people than ever before to spend their disposable income in markets hitherto considered to be beyond their reach. At the same time, however, the Government cannot be complacent about the degree of danger which attaches to the speed with which these changes are taking place.

Dennis Skinner believes that the Conservative Government will do little to combat the effects of existing fraudulent activity in the market or do anything about the potential fraud in the future, which he believes will flow from the City revolution. You may say that Mr Skinner represents an extreme view but there are others of a more traditionalist background who have also counselled caution and sounded warnings.

Sir Peter Tapsell, in his speech to the House of Commons on 16 July 1984 made the following point:

'I suspect that we shall lurch from scandal to scandal as a result of moving into dual capacity, particularly as it is to be internationalised.'

I was very interested in this remark, and in my interview with him I asked Sir Peter if he would expand his views on this point of 'potential scandal'. He said:

'Whether in the long run the general community will be well served by having these huge new financial conglomerates, where you get banks and merchant banks and foreign banks all mixed in together, with a British stock-broking firm, I very much doubt. I think it's going to be extremely difficult to regulate, I think that the authority of the Bank of England will be greatly undermined and I think a great many of the people who will be operating in future on the London Stock Exchange will have different traditions from those in which my generation has grown up and I think you will get a lot of scandals and when these scandals break, the Conservative Party and the Government will be held responsible for them.'

CHAPTER THREE
What Goes Up Must Come Down

Subscribers here by thousands float,
And jostle one another down;
Each paddling in his leaky boat,
And here they fish for gold, and drown.

With these words, Jonathan Swift described the public mania for stock speculation during a period of our history in the eighteenth century when public companies were floated on an almost daily basis to cash in on the speculative fever which gripped England. This whole episode came to an end with what we have come to call the great South Sea Bubble.

Public speculation in fantastic enterprises is not an unknown phenomenon and the propensity for the uninitiated to place their money into a scheme about which they know little or nothing has been a common factor of many financial failures over the centuries. The willingness of people gladly to part with their cash to the promoters of enterprises of little pith or no merit, remains unchanged, despite the passing of the years, and reinforces the wisdom of the writer of the book of Ecclesiastes when he said that 'there is no new thing under the sun'.

This aspect of our behaviour will be better understood when we have discussed the Over the Counter market, but the time has come to look at the world of the stock broker and the jobber, or, as we should now learn to call them, the broker/dealer.

Up to now, we have looked at what is likely to emerge in the future but we have spent little time in examining the history of the Stock Exchange and the traditions of those men and, latterly, women who have made this arena the source of their livelihood.

The development of trading in stocks began to adopt a more settled and centralised market late in the eighteenth century in London. Thitherto it had been the practice of those persons who traded in the stock of companies to meet together in the coffee houses which surrounded the Royal Exchange. One of the most popular was known as Jonathon's, in Change alley, and a large number of dealers met there to transact business. As their numbers grew, they looked for premises in which to accommodate their business and in 1773 they moved to premises in Sweeting's alley, which became known as the Stock Exchange Coffeehouse.

As business developed, it rapidly became clear that even larger premises were required and in 1801, the sum of £20,000 was raised in 400 shares of £50 each and a site in Capel Court, Bartholomew Lane was acquired. The new building opened in 1802.

Membership of the Stock Exchange was restricted to two distinct types, jobbers and brokers. Prior to Big Bang, the stock broker was prevented from forming trading partnerships with jobbers, although as we have discussed previously, this state of affairs has been changed. The reasons for this prohibition were quite simple: it was considered to be in the best interests of the client to separate the functions of the man who was the wholesaler and the man who bought on behalf of the client. However, this traditional system has ended and we should look forward to the future rather than backwards into the past.

The other method of share dealing which has been allowed previously has been that adopted by a number of off-exchange dealers, who were not members of the Stock Exchange. Admission to a member firm of the Stock Exchange meant that the individual applicant became subject to the regulatory oversight of the Council of the Stock Exchange and subject therefore, to the strict rules regarding admission, capitalisation, conduct of business, etc., and no other qualifying condition was required. Non-members were not prohibited from dealing in stocks and shares, but were required to be Licensed by the Department of Trade and Industry. These participants were known as Licensed Dealers in Securities.

It is not my intention to discuss the regulations for Licensed Dealers at length but suffice it to say that in general terms, a Licence to deal in Securities could be obtained by any adult person, upon application, after the payment of a modest fee, and, in the event that he wished to obtain a Principal's licence, the deposit or guarantee of the sum of £500.

The Act of Parliament which dealt with these aspects was the Prevention of Fraud (Investments) Act 1958. The Act established a presumptive right to a licence, which means that any person making application was entitled to be granted such a licence, unless the Secretary of State felt that there were circumstances which would render the granting of a licence undesirable.

The licence once granted was renewable annually, refusal of renewal being governed by similar provisions as those dealing with refusal of the grant of a licence.

The main grounds for such refusals or revocations were that the applicant or licence holder had failed to supply information prescribed by the Department, had been convicted of an offence under the Act or had ceased to carry on a business of dealing in securities. A licence could also be refused or revoked where the Secretary of State was satisfied that there were circumstances likely to lead to the improper conduct of business by, or which reflected upon the method of conducting business of, an applicant, licence holder or person associated with him.

The practical effect of the rules in the past has been that virtually anyone could apply for and be granted a licence to deal as a Principal as long as he had not been convicted of fraud and could raise £500.

You may say, 'This is no bad thing, when, as we have seen, the licence could be revoked at any time if the licence holder did not conduct his business properly.' We shall see how well the Department of Trade protected investors when we discuss the case of David Langford.

There has been one other way in which individuals could deal in securities without being either members of the Stock Exchange or Licensed Dealers and that was by becoming members of a Recognised Association of Dealers in Securities. We shall deal with this aspect in greater detail later when we discuss the activities of a man called Neal Bruckman. A Recognised Association of Dealers in Securities has been what we shall come to refer to more and more as a Self Regulatory Organisation (SRO).

Licensed Dealers and members of Recognised Associations, when dealing for clients were still required to use the services of stock brokers when buying the shares in which they wished to deal, if the particular shares were those quoted on the Stock Exchange. They ordered the shares through a broker and paid the broker's commission. They then passed on the shares to their clients, and charged them a further commission for so doing. Alternatively, they were able to charge the client a 'turn' for the shares as opposed to a commission rate. Licensed Dealers could deal either as principals or as agents and they were a good example of what we shall come to call in the future, the broker/dealer.

The rules relating to Licensed Dealers have now been swept away by the new regulations governing the activities of authorised dealers in investments. All dealers and advisors must now be members of a recognised Self Regulatory Organisation and subject to their rules of conduct, or be authorised directly by the Securities and Investments Board.

Licensed Dealers were not merely restricted to shares quoted on the Stock Exchange. They were the moving force behind the fastest growing development in securities dealing, the over-the-counter market. However, before we discuss the various types of share market in detail, perhaps it would be useful to look at the products they deal in: shares.

A share has three technical values. It has its face value, its intrinsic value and its market value. Its face value does not alter, its intrinsic value depends upon its capital foundation and its market value depends upon public anticipation of profitability. This third element can influence a share price resulting in its being under or over valued and it is in the manipulation of this market price where considerable harm can be caused to the share, the company, the market on which it is traded and the economy which operates that market and which in turn looks to that market for support.

Let us examine the way in which a new share is brought to the market in order to illustrate certain technical aspects of share dealing and to explain some of the areas of malpractice which can occur. Any City expert will probably accuse me of ignoring technical areas of market dealing, and I shall admit to the charge. It is however not part of my brief to write a technical manual and anyone who wishes to read such a book can find an enormous range of very helpful literature in any public library.

The basic method of introducing a company's shares to the public is by way of what is called a 'floatation', and they can come on to the market by way of an offer for sale. The first buyer is known as a subscriber, the subsequent purchaser is merely a buyer, although both are shareholders.

The company will already have discussed with their bankers how much money they want to raise. Their bankers, in most cases one of the highly select and experienced merchant banks who specialise in these activities, will have advised them on the best means of marketing their shares and will have arranged to underwrite the issue. This means that the bank have guaranteed that they will 'insure' the issue by making up the difference between the amount of money raised by the public offer and the amount required by the company, should the public issue fall short of the projected amount.

Thus it is that the shares will be offered to the public showing two prices. The first will be the face value of the share and the second will be the value that the bankers have placed on the share, the price at which they feel the public will be prepared to invest. The number of shares being offered multiplied by the price of the share to the public equals the amount of money the company wishes to raise.

The offer must be introduced by way of what is called a prospectus, which is a document which will contain a considerable amount of detail about the business, its plans, proposals, and current structure. In the United Kingdom it is permissible to include financial projections based upon past earnings by way of a report from accountants. (This is not permitted in the United States.) The prospectus will run to many pages and it must contain the following details:

The identities of the directors and the benefits they will receive from their directorships;
The profits being made by the promoters of the share issue;
The amount of capital the company wishes to raise;
The company's previous financial record;
Existing contractual obligations, commissions and preliminary expenses;
Voting and dividend rights of each class of share.

The purpose of these details is to enable the necessary information to be communicated to the potential public investors so they may decide whether or not they wish to subscribe for the company's shares.

In most cases, the prospectus must be published in at least two national newspapers. These advertisements contain coupons on which the public can make application for such shares as they wish to buy. After the publication of the prospectus, the public are given a period of time within which to digest the details of the offer and to decide whether they intend to subscribe for the shares.

Once all the applications for shares have been received, and the issuing house will have announced a date by which time all applications should have been received, the staff of the issuing house then sort out the applications to ascertain how many shares have been subscribed for.

In the event that the public has no confidence in the new issue, the share will be 'undersubscribed' which means that the underwriters will have to make up the difference. They will then be landed with a large amount of stock which they will have to get rid of in what is called the after-market and which will have a depressant effect on the share price thereafter.

Merchant banks do not usually make a habit of underwriting too many flops. It's too expensive. Part of their particular expertise is in deciding the offer price of shares in order to make them attractive to the share-buying public. In most cases, if the bank have done their job properly and the public's interest in the share has been properly stimulated, the issue will be heavily oversubscribed and the issuing house will then be faced with the responsibility of allotting shares to applicants.

If a potential investor has decided that he wants to purchase 1000 shares in a particular floatation, and the offer is oversubscribed, he may find that he is eventually allotted 200 shares or even fewer. Once the issuing house has decided the basis upon which it intends to allocate the shares, the successful applicants will be sent allotment letters, containing details of the number of shares they have been allotted.

Once all the shares it has been decided to issue have been allotted, then the shares will be registered in the names of those persons who have purchased them. These names and addresses are held by the Registrar of the company's shares, and the register is a public document which anyone can inspect.

That, in very basic terms, is how a share is brought to the market. As soon as the share commences dealing on the first day of trading, its price, ie the price at which the public are prepared to buy and sell, is recorded and reported by the Stock Exchange. During the first few days of the issue's life, trading in the share may be quite hectic. People buy shares for different reasons, intending to use them for different purposes, and it may take a few days for the general trading price to find its natural level. During this period, a number of things can happen to the share and its buyers and it is this aspect of share dealing that we are going to examine next.

Buying shares through the Stock Exchange sounds as if it should be

WHAT GOES UP MUST COME DOWN

a fairly uncomplicated process, once you have finally decided to buy. However, as you might have guessed, it is not as easy as it might first appear. For a start, you don't have to pay for them straight away and you can sell them again before you have paid for them. Coupled with that, you can sell them without owning them in the first place, although you will not get paid for them immediately and you will have to deliver them later. Being a British system, these rules do not apply to all securities. When you bought this book, nobody said it was going to be easy!

Let us assume you have decided to buy some shares in that well-known company, Amalgamated Widgetts. You have been following their share price and you have decided that they offer a good investment. You have decided to use the services of a stock broker recommended by a friend and you give him a call. The price of A.W. is currently quoted on the Stock Exchange at 150p per share. It is your intention to invest approximately £1500 in A.W. shares and you instruct your broker to buy 1000 shares. How much is this transaction going to cost you?

Your broker manages to buy 1500 A.W. shares at 152 pence each. This has cost you £1520.00. Your broker now adds his commission charge to that bill. Brokers, as we have learned, used to have a fixed scale of charges, below which they could not trade. Their charges began at 1.65% for bargains under £7000. They reduced in size when very large numbers of shares were traded, but this aspect is unlikely to concern us. In the previous chapter, I described the American experience when their minimum commission rules were abolished, noting that negotiated commissions did not mean any great saving to the private client. I believe that the same result will occur in Britain, and therefore, for the purposes of this illustration, I am going to assume that your stock broker's commission rate will remain what it was prior to Big Bang. So, at 1.65%, your broker will charge you £25.08 commission. In addition, you will be required to pay VAT at 15% on the brokerage commission which will be £3.76 and last but very much not least, the Government will charge you stamp duty at 1% on all share purchases, which will be £15.20. Your total purchase price will add up to £1564.04.

Already you can see that you have had to pay £44.04 more for your shares than you calculated. Your shares are going to have to rise at least 3% in value for you to break even and bear in mind you will have to pay broker's commission on any sale outside the account period, plus the dreaded VAT, and you can see that you need to see the price move upwards in excess of 5% before you start to make any money.

As I told you, you do not have to pay for your purchase straight away. Share dealing is conducted in an account period, during which you may buy and sell as many times as you like. Normally speaking, account periods are of a two week duration, with the occasional three week period to keep matters orderly. These account days are worked out annually and the dates of each account period are quoted in the financial pages of all major newspapers. You will be required to pay for your purchases on the first Monday ten days after the last day of dealing in the account.

You will have received a contract note from your broker within a few days of the transaction, showing the details of the transaction, and towards the end of the period, you will receive a statement from him, showing how much you will have to pay. So, theoretically, if you bought your shares on the first day of the account period, you would then have another twenty-one days before you were required to pay for the shares.

During this time, anything can happen to the price of your shares. Let us assume that you have decided to buy them for a long-term investment plan you are operating because you wish to earn dividends from them. You intend to hold on to the shares, so you will settle your broker's account on settlement day and sit back and wait for your share certificate to arrive. This will normally take from four to eight weeks, depending on how efficient the share registrar's office is at clearing all the details. It is one of the American criticisms of our system that there is no central clearing house for share transactions, which the Americans perceive can lead to abuses of the system.

Share certificates are evidence that you are a shareholder in the company. They are a valuable document and you should ensure that you look after them very carefully. When you come to sell the shares, you will be required to surrender the certificate, so if you lose it you will experience considerable difficulties in getting a replacement.

Let us look at another scenario. Instead of holding on to the shares for a long period, you decide, a few days after having purchased them, that you want to sell them. The price has risen dramatically, following news that A.W. have signed a major export agreement to supply widgetts to another country. The price of A.W. shares has risen to 170p per share, which is the price quoted in the *Financial Times*. Bear in mind that you have not paid for them yet as we are still within the account period.

It matters not. You ring your broker and instruct him to sell your holding. Again, the quoted price may not be the one you finally receive and your broker is lucky to get them sold at 169p per share. That will realise the sum of £1690. Now, here comes the real incentive to deal 'within the account'. By so doing, you will only pay one lot of commission, which you do on the opening transaction, which you will remember was £28.84, including the VAT. In addition, you do not have to pay the stamp duty, which will save you another £15.20. Your broker will send you an additional contract note identifying the transaction.

At the end of the account period, your broker will send you a statement showing your original purchase price which was £1548.84, plus your sale price which was £1690.00. In addition, he will send you a cheque for £141.16, which is your profit on the transaction. You have made a profit without paying out a penny of your own cash. You may rest assured however, that no broker will deal for you before you have deposited a sizeable sum of money with him to cover any transactions you may wish to undertake.

Some hardy souls, who possess a taste for life in the fast lane, sell shares they do not own. This is known as selling 'short'. How does this work, and why?

Let us assume that your understanding of the market has become so acute that you decide that the share price of A.W. is grossly overvalued. It has enjoyed a considerable amount of public popularity and its share price has spiralled upwards, fuelled by a considerable degree of public sentiment and uninformed belief in the value of the company. You, however, have no reason to think that the company is as healthy as the share price would indicate. There has been a general decline in the need for widgetts world-wide and new technology has made their use obsolete. In addition, they are an elderly company who have not changed their manufacturing technique for years. Recently you have noticed a small snippet in the newspaper that a fiery young radical union activist has just been appointed General Secretary of the widgett makers union. All in all, you feel that there are potential problems ahead for A.W. and that the price of their shares is about to come a cropper.

You know that their annual figures are a few months away from being reported but following your evaluation of the company and its affairs, you feel that the price of the shares is due to fall in the very near future. You instruct your broker to sell 1000 A.W. shares. What you have done is to enter into a contract to deliver 1000 A.W. shares within the account period to the person who has bought them from you. Your account with your broker will show the price which you will be paid for the shares on the accounting day. In the interim period, you hope that the price will fall sufficiently to enable you to buy the shares you must deliver at the end of the account period to the person who has bought from you and still make a profit.

Sure enough, your hunch is proved to be correct. There is a sudden announcement of a break-down in wage negotiations between the union and the management of A.W. An all-out strike is called and violent picket clashes take place outside the factory gates. During the days that follow, it becomes apparent that the company is financially overstretched. The share price starts to fall drastically and by the end of the account has dropped 30p per share. On the last day of the account, you instruct your broker to buy the 1000 shares you require to be delivered to your purchaser and the deal is completed. You have just made £300, minus whatever brokerage commission you would have been charged.

Had your timing proved to be incorrect, however, you would still have been required to deliver the shares at the end of the account period, and you would have had to purchase them for delivery at a loss to yourself. This is why selling short is such a risky operation.

The Americans have a saying about short sales, which goes:

'He who sells what isn't his'n pays it up or goes to prison.' I think it sums up the situation quite succinctly.

Up to now, we have used an illustration which assumes that you intend to deal through a stock broker, who, you will remember, is a member of the Stock Exchange and subject to their rules. The share we have been discussing, Amalgamated Widgetts, is quoted on the Stock Exchange and is traded on the floor of the Exchange.

In order for a share to be admitted to a full Stock Exchange listing the company seeking admission must be able to satisfy a number of stringently applied criteria. It takes a considerable amount of money and expertise to bring a company to market, or to 'go public' as it is commonly known, and many companies do not possess the normal entry requirements for a full Stock Exchange listing. To obtain admission to a full listing, the company must be able to show an independent existence and a trading record for the previous five years. If a company can satisfactorily show that it has existed for five years, unaided by public subscription, then it is a reasonable bet that it has or should have a product which, with sufficient investment and prudent management, will represent a valuable investment medium for the potential public investor.

There are a large number of companies however, who are looking for investment to help them expand and who may possess all the likely qualifications to be a potential investment opportunity but which cannot be admitted to a full quotation because they do not possess the necessary qualifications. The shares of many such companies were traded informally but prior permission had to be obtained from the Stock Exchange's Quotations Department before brokers traded in these unquoted stocks. These dealings were restricted to what were called 'matched bargains' which meant that the brokers had to find a buyer who wanted to buy stock at the same price as the seller was prepared to sell. It was a cumbersome operation and did not properly reflect a dealing method suitable for the growing demand for such stocks. There was, in addition, a perceived demand for a more simple and cheaper share marketing method and in November 1980, the Unlisted Securities market (USM) was created, primarily to provide a regulated environment for the rapidly growing number of stocks being traded off the official stock market.

Entry qualifications were made less demanding; for instance, where a company sought entry to the main market, a minimum of 25% of the company's equity had to be offered for sale to the public. On the USM, a company had only to offer a minimum of 10% of their equity. USM applicants were not required to provide certain documentation which was mandatory for applicants for a full listing, such as an accountant's report on record. In practice, many USM shares do include such a report. The USM applicant needs only show a three-year trading record and financial reports in their prospectus can show older figures than those required for full listing applicants.

One of the aims of the USM was to enable developing companies to seek public investment to assist their growth, with the aim of transferring from the USM list to a full quotation when they were eligible. In reality, the USM and the main market are traded by the same brokers and jobbers on the floor of the Stock Exchange. Some dealers specialise in USM stocks.

The important thing to remember about the USM is that investment in such stocks represents a higher rung on the risk/reward ladder. As we have seen, fewer shares need to be released and institutional investors account for ownership of approximately 70% of those shares which are traded, so the remaining shares tend to show a greater degree of volatility than main market shares. When the price of USM stock moves, it can move very dramatically in a short space of time. While this may provide a welcome source of profit, if you have got the market direction right, it can also prove to be a source of loss if you got it going the other way. Generally speaking, these rapid price movements have a tendency to take place in the early days of the life of the share. When they settle down, they tend to stay fairly steady and, in some cases, slowly drift downwards. Some commentators estimate that about 25% of the shares on the USM are trading at below their issue price.

One aspect of the USM which is worth looking at however is the fact that it represents an attractive venue to foreign companies to get a public quotation. Certain American companies have applied for listings on the USM because it offers them a much cheaper and quicker method of becoming listed than they would experience in America. In America, the Securities and Exchange Commission has very strict rules about the way in which it regulates companies coming to market. American companies are not permitted to make financial projections about the likely profitability of their company, based upon previous figures. They are also required to file a full company profile with the SEC before they can issue their prospectus. In general, the SEC operates a stricter control over the admission of companies to a full listing and it may be wondered why an American company would wish to seek a USM listing in this country rather than comply with the rules required of it in its own country. One reason must surely be that the company perceives that the regulations in this country governing the marketing of companies are less stringent.

Some reporters have suggested that the introduction of a number of foreign companies to the USM means that a greater degree of responsibility is placed on the shoulders of the issuing houses to ensure that home-based investors do not get misled by the claims made on behalf of the aspiring entrant. One can only hope that the issuing houses will be ready and willing to shoulder this awesome responsibility.

Now, however, we come to the area of the share dealing market which truly represents an area of considerable concern for regulators. The Over-the-Counter market, or, as its more cynical observers would call it, the 'under-the-counter' market is the third tier of share trading and one which many commentators would like to see far more closely regulated.

We have seen how companies requiring capital investment have been brought to market and the rules which are applied to ensure that those companies which obtain a listing can show a track record of trading. This is done to maintain investor confidence. We have also looked at the degree of relaxation of the rules applied to USM companies in an attempt to provide a means of obtaining venture capital, while at the same time ensuring a degree of regulation. The OTC market however, provides little or no regulation regarding the sort of schemes which can be marketed and represents an area where the unsophisticated investor treads literally at his peril. I make no apology for this statement, believing that the OTC market is an area which is best left to those with a taste for speculation rather than realistic investment.

I have no doubt that my comments will attract the wrath of the market makers and OTC dealers who will point out that they can offer a genuine alternative to the services offered by stock brokers. This may be true up to a point and in some circumstances the OTC market represents an attractive medium for young companies seeking venture capital. The activities of its market makers offer a practical lesson in the way that broker/dealers will act after Big Bang and it is instructive to examine their methods to see if we can glean any information which will assist us in the future. In the next chapter we shall examine at length some of the less happy experiences reported by investors who have dealt in OTC stocks. Suffice it to say that there have been so many such examples that without the acceptance of radical regulatory proposals, the developing market could represent a real threat to investor confidence.

The OTC market, as it has come to be commonly known, is, in reality, a trading operation which has developed separately from the activities of a small and highly specialised marketing operation conducted by a firm called Granville and Company, which for a number of years has conducted dealings in the shares of very selected companies, on a matched-bargain basis only, and which first coined the phrase in this country. Granville provides a highly specialised service which is useful only to companies whose products may be of such a small but unusual nature that they represent a valuable investment medium for sophisticated investors but which are prohibited from obtaining a quotation in the ordinary course of events.

The bulk of OTC stocks are brought to the market by individual authorised dealers who attempt to make a market in their own, and in other stocks. Their aim is also to provide a venture-capital-raising service for new companies. Their activities are viewed with concern in many areas of the City for a number of reasons. Virtually all the new companies are small enough to be badly affected by unforeseen setbacks. One major upheaval can result in a company foundering. Very few of them have an established track record which a potential investor can study to ascertain their realistic worth. The market on which they are traded has had no meaningful regulation, although this factor is changing and will be different in the future. There is no realistic pricing structure as there is rarely sufficient depth or volume of trading to provide such a model. Yet, without a doubt, the OTC market provides a very realistic illustration of the trading arena of the future.

In America, the OTC market is a large, vibrant trading medium, operating under strict regulatory controls. In the UK, the OTC is a relatively small operation in comparison with its American cousin, yet already it has been the source of a considerable number of complaints from hapless investors.

One of the factors in the attraction of the OTC market for the private investor is the existence of a Government inspired tax incentive called the Business Expansion Scheme (BES). Briefly, the Government has said that it will allow an individual investor to claim relief on investment in recognised schemes up to £40,000 per annum. In other words, an investor who places money with a new company, ie the subscriber, will be allowed to claim tax relief at his highest rate on the amount he has invested in the new enterprise.

Now, this represents a valuable incentive for wealthy investors to invest in new companies. In addition, the allowance is not available for investment in the shares of companies already admitted to either the main index or the USM. This means that the investment potential will be channelled into enterprises which are being brought to market via the OTC.

There are conditions attached to this offer however. The individual shareholder must retain his shareholding for five years, otherwise he will lose his tax allowances.

The BES was an inspired attempt to utilise the development of a small market to encourage people to invest money in emerging companies which would not otherwise attract investment. It was hoped that by providing this sort of financial incentive, investors would be prepared to utilise some of their investment potential in new companies and thus provide jobs and stimulate further growth. It was deemed reasonable to require investors to leave their money with the new companies for a minimum period of five years in order to provide a degree of financial security during the early formative period.

In reality, however, the desirable social aims of the scheme were rapidly overtaken by the activities of the financial entrepreneurs who quickly identified a means of providing an investment forum which would encourage public investment but where subsequent failure of the enterprise would not come as any great surprise.

This is not to say that some companies have not benefited from the BES. They have, and jobs have been created thereby, but in many cases the companies brought to market have been floated solely for the benefit of obtaining tax reliefs and for no other reason.

When a company is brought to the OTC market, it starts off in exactly the same way as any other company and issues a prospectus, identifying its aims and its projections. Needless to say, OTC prospectuses are not as detailed as those required for a main index quotation. The company usually has no trading record to speak of and in many cases represents nothing more than a bag of promises for the future.

The authorised dealer who is introducing the company takes upon himself the responsibility for making the market in the shares. He will be the person from whom you buy and to whom you will sell if you want to deal in the shares. The prices he quotes will be both buying and selling prices and the disparity between them can sometimes be quite dramatic. This only confirms the fact that shares are worth what investors are prepared to pay for them.

Let us suppose that you have been impressed with the prospectus which has been issued by Crapshoot Enterprises and are considering investing in their scheme to turn base metals into gold. In order to buy their shares, it will be necessary for you to ring the dealer who is making the market in these shares. We shall assume that they have not rung you already, extolling the virtues of this latest opportunity.

You will pay the price at which the dealer is prepared to sell to you. You will not pay any obvious commission fees, because the dealer is making the market himself, and therefore holds a line of the shares on his own book. He is dealing as a principal in the contract and is free to charge any price he likes. In this instance you have to become your own jobber and ring around the various dealers to see what prices they are quoting for Crapshoot Enterprises.

However, in many cases you will find that the shares are only being marketed by one dealer, in which case you will have to pay his price if you want to buy the shares. You will, in due course, receive a contract note showing the details of your dealings and within a few weeks, you should receive your share certificate. There is no account period for OTC shares, you will pay for them as a cash transaction.

A few weeks later, having kept a close eye on the share price of Crapshoot Enterprises, you are delighted to see their share price has risen quite dramatically. You might be forgiven if you decided to profit from your good fortune. You ring your dealer and ask what price your shares are trading at. Do not be surprised if he attempts to persuade you not to sell. This is a share which is 'going through the roof', you may be told and you would be 'unwise to part with it now'.

Nevertheless, you are insistent that you wish to take your profit and you ask for the dealing price. The figure quoted is vastly below your anticipations. You query the figure which you have seen reported in the columns of the Sunday newspaper. 'No, there is no mistake,' you are told, 'that is the figure at which we are prepared to sell. If you want to sell however, this is the price at which we are prepared to buy back.' It may not come as too much of a surprise to learn that in some market makers' offices, only a select group of experienced staff are permitted to answer incoming calls from clients, on the basis that most people ringing in want to sell.

You have already learned the first lesson. If the Licensed Dealer is the only person making the market, then you have no one else to turn to, in the event that he does not offer you a realistic price. If the price of the shares starts to tumble, then you literally have nowhere to turn at all. The dealer will suddenly announce a suspension of dealings in the share and you are left with a piece of worthless paper. There is absolutely no guarantee that you will be able to sell your shares.

In a bull market, that factor might not represent quite such a threat but in a bear market, where share prices generally become depressed and go into a decline, holding OTC traded stock will represent a major financial handicap. A number of commentators have warned against the present OTC market's ability to survive a major bear market influence.

Yet, the share-buying opportunities offered by certain OTC market makers continue to flourish and expand, which indicates that little has changed in the myriad ways of public gullibility. En masse, humans have a tendency to behave in irrational ways. This fact has been minutely recorded in a remarkable work published in 1841 entitled

Extraordinary Popular Delusions and the Madness of Crowds written by Charles MacKay. In this book, MacKay records mankind's overwhelming desire to speculate in investment methods, when even the most simply enquiry would indicate the offer to be worthless.

His study of the South Sea Bubble records the fantastic story of an attempt to float a company whose objective was to assume responsibility for the National Debt in return for a monopoly on trading with South and Central America. The scheme was fuelled by rumour and uninformed opinion concerning the inexhaustible supply of mineral wealth in South America. The value of the shares rose steeply and as they rose, so further tranches of the National Debt were 'purchased'.

Every class of society was involved in the mania which ensued. More and more investment schemes were marketed to satisfy the apparently insatiable desire of the public to invest their money. Included among these were companies formed to create a machine capable of perpetual motion, or for 'carrying on an undertaking of great advantage but nobody to know what it is'.

Throughout this period, the value of the shares in the South Sea Company continued to rise, until eventually the rumours and promises ran out of credibility and the whole bubble burst. Thousands were ruined. Isaac Newton alone lost £20,000, a phenomenal amount of money by the standards of his time. A phenomenal amount of money by modern standards for that matter.

The fact is that once investors become imbued with the notion of buying securities with the sole aim of a quick sale at a profit, instead of buying those securities for the merits of the enterprises they represent, then the value of the stock quickly becomes overinflated and the market within which they are traded is put at risk. The Wall Street crash of 1929 resulted in part from a mania of speculative dealings using paper worth to finance further purchases of securities, whose paper values were realised again to finance further purchases, and so on.

I intend to close this chapter with a quotation from Charles MacKay's book, in the hope that his words do not have the prophetic quality which I fear. He said, when discussing the aftermath of the South Sea Bubble: 'The English learned that nations, like individuals, cannot become desperate gamblers with impunity. Punishment is sure to overtake them, sooner or later.'

CHAPTER FOUR
It's Only Money . . . ! ! !

My concern is that the British financial services sector should be both competitive and a 'clean' place in which to do business, and moreover, that it is seen to be so.

This unequivocal statement was made by the then Secretary of State for Trade and Industry, Mr Norman Tebbit, in his opening speech of the debate on the Gower Report, to the House of Commons on 16 July 1984. In those few lines, Mr Tebbit expressed the two fundamental concerns which govern the administration of financial markets. Firstly that they should be, in his words 'clean' and secondly, that their cleanliness should be a well-known fact among the investing public.

By 'clean', I have taken Mr Tebbit to mean that the markets should not simply eschew downright fraud, which anyone can recognise, but also the conduct of certain participants, whose practices which, if allowed to continue unchecked, would bring the markets and those who seek to practise in them into grave public disrepute.

To my knowledge no one has successfully attempted to create an all-embracing definition of fraud and I am certainly not going to be foolhardy enough to try. Of one thing, however, we can be certain. One of the elements of any definition of fraud which might subsequently be formulated is that of secrecy or deceit, closely linked with damage or harm. It is for this reason that I intend to include in this book illustrations of acts which might not in themselves be widely assumed to be 'fraudulent', in an easily recognised way, but which are, nevertheless, secret or deceitful and which cause untold harm or damage.

The first category of fraudsmen are those whose activities are most easily understood to be criminal. They are the professional 'con-men' who start with the sole intention of defrauding such individuals as may be persuaded to part with their money. The schemes they propose, the companies they create and the investment opportunities they offer are totally bogus. There is no difficulty in the public mind in branding these operators with their correct title, which is 'thief'. The criminal law abounds with charges and criminal proceedings which can be applied to their behaviour and activities, always assuming they can be caught.

The second category is much more difficult to identify. They are what I have learned to call 'slippery slope' fraudsmen and, in using that definition, I have openly borrowed from Dr Michael Levi, who first propounded the phrase in his excellent book, *The Phantom Capitalists*. These are men who in the process of operating a business, lawfully in the beginning, slowly but inexorably slide down into unlawful behaviour, to keep their business going. I doubt if any of these men start out with the intention of defrauding their clients but events overtake them, and in an attempt to claw their way back into solvency, they attempt to buy time or stave off their most pressing creditors, by telling lies, creating deceptions and using clients' monies for purposes other than those for which they were invested. Eventually they find themselves swamped in a morass of lies and untruths, with a mountain of debt and a long line of creditors.

Yet they should be the ones whose damaging behaviour could so easily be prevented, if the laws which exist to administer their activities were more efficiently enforced. There does exist a considerable body of legislation to regulate the conduct of companies and their directors. In many cases, if the provisions of the Companies Act were more stringently applied, particularly with regard to the various financial reporting provisions concerning annual accounts, many of these financial failures could be prevented.

There are criminal sanctions which can be applied against these persons but they are harder to formulate and the crime often more difficult to prove. In addition, the person charged is looked upon, in many cases, as being simply the victim of 'bad luck' and not as a thief, and losers are sometimes reluctant to give evidence against such people.

The third group are the most difficult to define, because their behaviour does not fall easily into categories which are instantly recognisable as dishonest. They may be highly successful, yet their actions are 'dirty' and do not belong in the 'clean' market place. They are deceitful, and they cause harm and damage to the reputation of the market itself, despite the attempts made by the market to protect itself. Included in this category I place the actions of those who use their businesses to facilitiate the 'laundering' of the proceeds of crime and the activities of those organised criminal groups who use the markets to hide and disguise their criminally obtained funds.

If it is not in the interests of civilised countries to permit criminal behaviour, then why should it be any less important to deny criminals access to means of retaining their profits? All countries which claim to be governed by the rule of law pass strict laws preventing the handling of stolen goods, in some form or another. Why then are we so mealy-mouthed about our attitude towards the proceeds of the sale of unlawful drugs, or the results of bullion robberies or tax evasion simply because they are dressed up in the guise of 'investment capital', and placed through the market?

During a discussion with a London commodity broker, I learned his particular attitude towards knowingly dealing with the proceeds of organised crime. He said:

'In this business there is no such thing as clean money and there is no such thing as dirty money. There is only money.'

When I pointed out that in dealing with that money he was assisting the activities of organised criminals, he simply shrugged his shoulders. He was paid, he told me, to bring in business for his company, not to adopt moral positions.

With attitudes like that, and I doubt very much whether he would have been the only man in London to take that view, it is perhaps not hard to see how difficult is the task of those whose job is to uncover and combat the activities of major criminal groups throughout the world.

The first activity I intend to discuss is what is known, commonly, as staging. You will by now have come across a number of animal terms which are used when talking about the securities markets. First we met bulls, and not long after we were talking about bears and now stags. There is absolutely nothing wrong with staging. It is a time-honoured tradition which has existed as a City practice since before God knows when. The practice of staging, however, has led to some peripheral activities which may or may not be 'dirty', depending on your point of view.

You will remember, when we talked about the way in which a share was brought to the market, we discussed the methods by which potential shareholders could apply for shares. You remember how I said that any person could apply for as many shares as he or she liked and, if the offer was oversubscribed, the issuing house would apportion blocks of shares as fairly as they could, which could mean that an applicant might not get as many shares as he had applied for. Well, the stag evolved to take advantage of this situation. In principle the stag is a speculator who does not intend to take a long-term interest in the share but merely hopes to take a very short-term profit from the movement of the share, in its early days. Once an issue is announced, it doesn't take long for those in the 'know' to ascertain whether the issue is going to 'go'. The stag then attempts to buy as many shares as he can with the sole intention of selling them within a few days, still within the account, and taking a profit. In those issues where great public interest is expected to be engendered, the stag knows that applications are going to be scaled down by the issuing house. This will mean, using a simplistic illustration, that if he applies for 100 shares, he is likely to receive 10. He knows that he isn't going to make much of a profit on stagging 10 shares, so instead, he applies for 1000, in the hope that if he is scaled down, he will realise the 100 he originally wanted.

That aspect of the stagging game is considered to be acceptable by most people because the stag has applied for the shares in his own name and has taken the risk that if he has got the issue rumours wrong, he will be allotted the 1000 shares he applied for, and he will have to pay for them before he receives them, his cheque will be banked and he will be left holding a line of shares which very few people want and which he cannot sell at the profit he anticipated.

This practice, as I said, is widespread but is restricted, by and large, to those people in the 'know'. These people are usually the employees of the issuing houses, the dealing firms and their friends. Stagging among such persons is looked upon as a 'perk' of the trade.

Sir Peter Tapsell: 'When I first entered the City, everybody, and when I say everybody I am thinking particularly of the young clerks, stagged. It was a way of making a little money in the early days.'

The issuing houses have the experience to spot the over-large application being submitted by the potential stag and if they suspect that they have received just such an application, the tendency is for that application to be scaled down considerably. Once the major blocks of shares have been distributed among the major applicants such as the pension funds, the insurance companies and other institutions and the larger applications have been dealt with, the balance of remaining shares is then split up among the small applications. This is usually done by way of a ballot, and the stag who suspects that his one large application is going to be rumbled then adopts another method of application. He submits a large number of 'multiple applications', hoping that this will give him a better chance in the ballot.

The issuing houses do try to keep a watch on the same name turning up time and time again on share application forms and if they should discover a name constantly appearing, that application can be disqualified.

Well, the stag has adopted another method to combat that problem. He submits a large number of applications, using false names. This practice is frowned upon because it means that the stag is effectively cheating the other applicants in the ballot. The practice continues however and was probably most widely reported in the British Telecom issue. Now, this was an episode which caused a great degree of soul searching, when it was first announced that the Government intended to restrict the number of shares any one individual could apply for during the sale of British Telecom. The reasons are very simple.

It has been part of the Conservative Government's manifesto and plans for the future that certain profitable, state-run industries would be 'privatised'. By this they meant that those industries would be turned into public companies, and their shares offered to the public. Removal of State involvement, wherever possible, from businesses which could attract private investment, is a general, long-term, Conservative policy and one which they have advocated for many years. At the same time, there is a school of thought which is firmly of the belief that there are certain socially vital industries which are too important to be left to the whim and caprice of private enterprise and which should be controlled and paid for by the State and run for the benefit of the State as a whole and not for the mere profit of a small sector.

I have no doubt that there are good arguments to support either case. What is certain, however, is that the Government knew that in selling off British Telecom, and other profitable State industries, they would immediately attract the opprobrium of their opponents in Parliament, who would accuse them of pandering to the vested interests represented by the City of London. They had already been criticised severely over their sale of Britoil and they were intent on making the sale of Telecom as fair as possible.

They were anxious to avoid the activities of the stags and others in the 'know' making a quick killing during the early days of the placing, which would mean that the shares which were quickly sold in the first few days would swiftly find their way into the hands of the institutions

and would mean that the small investor would be left with little or
nothing from a share placing which was potentially very profitable
indeed.

The Government have said many times that they are anxious to
enlarge the 'share-owning franchise', to create an 'equity-owning
democracy'. This philosophy would have come under heavy fire from
political opponents, if the public sale of shares in BT, at the time the
most potentially profitable vehicle to be 'privatised', was seen to be a
financial jamboree for the stags, at the expense of those new, potential
shareholders which the Government claims it wants to attract. Allowing this particular issue to be heavily stagged would have meant that BT
had simply become another juicy plum to be snapped up by the
Institutions, once the stags had taken their immediate profits during
the early days.

The Government was facing growing criticism in Parliament and in
public over its apparently cavalier attitude towards unbridled profiteer-
ing in certain City Institutions, at a time of raging unemployment and
what had become known in broad terms as 'City fraud'. For the
Government the real danger was that their stated aim of encouraging
wider share ownership would be perceived to be an empty promise,
expressed more with the cynical intention of diverting criticism of a
policy which enriched its friends in the City, than in achieving a
desirable political objective.

British Telecom became a *cause célèbre*. It was marketed using the
most modern techniques of mass communication and a highly
sophisticated team of marketing consultants, and the message reached
a wide audience. Many people, for the first time in their lives,
considered buying shares. It was an issue that caught the public's
imagination, as it was intended to do, and the message it carried was
expressed loudly and clearly.

'No person may individually apply for more than 800 shares.'

As you might expect, the public took an awful lot of notice of this
warning, the stags went to work with a vengeance. This time, however,
it was not simply those 'in the know' who submitted multiple applications. Thanks to the efforts of the marketing men, now everybody was
'in the know' and the applications rolled in.

Parents submitted applications in the names of their children, their
pets, even relatives who had been dead for years. Solicitors' and stock
brokers' clerks worked round the clock filling up applications in the
names of clients, both real and imaginary. The Government issued

stern warnings against making multiple applications and still the application forms rolled in.

When the dust finally settled, it was estimated that the British Telecom issue added 1 million new participants to the list of public shareholders in the country.

To no one's surprise, many multiple applications were discovered. The problem was what should be done about them. It was well known that many multiple applications had slipped through the net and many applicants were now enjoying the benefit of their disguises.

The matter was referred to the Fraud Squad, and the City collectively held its breath. It was unthinkable, in a game which had been played for so long, that the rules would suddenly be changed. It was certainly very ungentlemanly to bring in the 'Old Bill', who don't understand the niceties of City behaviour and would certainly go tramping around some very delicate flower beds in their big size twelves.

In the end, a number of minor players were summonsed for various offences relating to the submission of multiple applications using false names and were dealt with in the Magistrates' Courts, receiving the equivalent of a financial slap on the wrist. The City was able to breath again as honour had been satisfied, the Government had shown it meant business, and their firm action would certainly teach the stags not to do it again.

What did not emerge from this episode however was a clear set of guidelines regarding the behaviour of others in the City who had undoubtedly profited from the BT issue. Did the Government's intentions apply to every member of the public? It would seem not.

One of the ways in which underwriters ensure as wide a distribution of shares in a new issue as possible is to 'ask' other banks and business houses to take a percentage of the new shares, to be placed with their institutional clients, in order to raise part of the required capital. These banks are in a very special position to be able to assess the worth of an issue and they are not in business to recommend 'duds' to their institutional clients.

The British Telecom issue took place in November 1984 but it had been the subject of considerable City comment for months before, coupled with an expensive publicity campaign. It was generally perceived by informed City investment analysts to be 'a goer' and there was no doubt in their collective minds of the potential success of the issue. They were absolutely correct in their analysis, the public shared their view and the issue was over-subscribed several times.

As part of the administration of the issue, the Merchant Bank Singer and Friedlander were 'asked' if they would take a parcel of BT shares worth approximately £5 million, to be placed among their institutional investors.

In October 1984, a month before the issue date, Singer and Friedlander, as part of their responsibilities to their institutional clients, examined the worth of the BT share issue and, apparently concerned as to the success of the floatation, decided to minimise the risk to those they advised, by absorbing some of the shares among their private clients and their own directors, particularly those directors whose own portfolios were managed within the bank on a discretionary basis.

One of the directors and chairman of the bank, Mr Anthony Solomons, was allocated 50,000 BT shares, $62\frac{1}{2}$ times as many shares as he would have been permitted to obtain in the course of an application in the ordinary way. When the news of this apparent overcautiousness on the part of the bank became public in September 1985, there was an outcry. An enquiry was conducted by the auditors Peat Marwick Mitchell, who confirmed that there was nothing 'improper or irregular' in the allocation of the shares to Mr Solomons. Another spokesman is reported to have said that Mr Solomons had behaved 'perfectly properly'.

The Department of Trade and Industry had already investigated a number of allegations that certain persons in the City had received large quantities of BT shares in similar fashion and had largely been unsuccessful in establishing the truth of such allegations. To a Government committed to enfranchising a wider body of shareholders, the activities of such persons must be seen, to use an old phrase, as being 'an unacceptable face of capitalism'. It is certainly not the sort of behaviour which qualifies as being 'clean' and we must hope that future issues of profitable, privatised companies will be more rigorously policed to prevent similar irregularities happening and to prove that the rules of the game apply to everyone. If you happened to be one of the many who missed out in the BT issue, now you know why.

The public offering of shares in the Trustee Savings Bank represented another test of the Government's intentions to crack down on multiple applications. The offer caught the imagination of the public in a larger way than BT did and considerable efforts were promised to prevent the stags and the institutions from taking too great a bite at the cherry. The stags are nothing if not versatile and they thought up other ways to try and get more than their fair share. One method reported was that of a stag who placed advertisements in a newspaper offering a 'fee' of £25 to any TSB customer who would transfer their priority applications to him. The shares would have been issued in the customer's name, but would have been transferred to the stag.

Other activities reported were that employees of stock brokers Simon and Coates had indulged in stagging the shares of Windsmoor. Later, in a classic type of understatement which usually identifies a description of City wrongdoing, the employees involved in the stagging were described as having been involved in 'errors of judgement'.

Another practice which is closely allied to stagging is Insider Dealing (ID). Stagging is an attempt to get as many shares as possible before a new issue. ID is the practice of trying to buy as many shares as possible of an existing issue about which the buyer has specific information which he knows will affect the price of the share, once the news becomes public. Let me explain.

One way of pushing up a share price is to announce that the company is to be taken over by, or is about to merge with, another company. Take-overs are conducted therefore in great secrecy and require a considerable degree of discretion on the part of those concerned. A take-over need not necessarily be resented by the target company but, in general, take-overs are resisted because it usually means that the target company will be split up.

Let us return to our earlier illustration, Amalgamated Widgetts. By now, A.W. has become a highly efficient operation, led by a dynamic management team. It is extremely profitable and has expanded its range of products. Its closest competitor, Consolidated Gadgetts, is a company which manufactures widgetts but in addition, manufactures gadgetts as well, and as everyone knows, gadgetts represent an important part of the widgett market.

The management of A.W. have decided that they would like to get into this highly specialised and profitable area of the market. Their financial advisors have made a close study of C.G.'s structure and have conducted an analysis of its share price and its inherent worth. The present share price of C.G. is 100p. For obvious reasons, however, they do not wish to pay any more for the shares than they need to and in the weeks prior to the announcement of the take-over bid, they will be quietly biding their time, hoping that the share price of C.G. will stay at 100p. For obvious reasons, any publicity at this time will affect the price of the shares of C.G. and the plans for the take-over are a jealously guarded secret. Now, it doesn't take a great stretch of the imagination to realise that anyone who knows that the take-over bid is about to be made can buy shares in C.G. himself, knowing that when the bid is announced, his shares will start to increase in value dramatically, and that he will make a huge profit.

This practice is called 'Insider Dealing'; it is widespread in the market despite protestations from the practitioners to the contrary and it is illegal. It is governed by the Company Securities (Insider Dealing) Act 1985 and is, unusually, a fairly simple piece of legislation. Its fundamental provisions are that no individual who is or has been within the past six months, connected with a company, may deal in its share on a recognised Stock Exchange, if the individual is in possession of unpublished, price-sensitive information. The provisions extend to connected individuals, such as a relative or a friend of the connected person, and extend further to include connected companies and advisors. I said that the practice is widespread, and I make no apology for that statement. It is another example of behaviour which brings the reputation of the market into disrepute and attempts to deal with it are, frankly, derisory.

You may say: 'What's so wrong about it, good luck to you if you can get the information.' It is not difficult to see how this attitude could be adopted, which makes it harder to explain why the practice should be recognised for what it is, which is dishonest.

Capitalist societies depend for their survival on investment. The means of raising that investment and administering the share dealings of public companies are carried out in the investment markets. It is in the interests of those societies to attract as many individuals as possible to invest in those markets to maximise the free flow of capital. Capital markets depend upon the willingness of private investors to speculate for profit and speculators in search of profit bring liquidity to such markets. Nobody gambles knowingly on a fixed roulette wheel and no speculator is going to put his money into a market where only the locals have any chance of making a profit. He will take his capital elsewhere to a market where the odds are better. Once this happens, those areas of industry which come to the City for investment capital will be unable to obtain the money they need to expand, and they will die.

Insider Dealing concentrates the profitable information among a small percentage of those 'in the know', at the expense of the majority of those outside, and is the sort of behaviour which gives those whom the market wishes to attract the impression that the market is rigged in favour of a selected few.

If you doubt that ID is widespread, consider this. In 1985, take-over bids worth £9 billion were organised and in 1986, that figure will be even higher. An analysis of the shares which became the subject of take-over bids reported an average price rise of 54% prior to the bid being made. This must almost inevitably be due to the fact that the bid plans have been leaked and that shares are being bought in anticipation of the announcement.

The Sunday Times, in an article in March 1986, reported an interview with a broker who said: 'Twenty years ago, everybody did it.' Undoubtedly this is true but what has become of greater concern is the apparent inability of the regulatory authorities to do anything about the practice.

In an article in the *Financial Times*, a representative of the Stock Exchange's surveillance department said:

'Time and again, our investigations have run up against the brick wall of an off-shore company whose true ownership we cannot discover. We can track down the small insider deals which are done in this country, but the big fish go off-shore.'

The Stock Exchange Surveillance Department is certain that there exists a series of organised groups within the City, comprised of members who work for a variety of City institutions, all of whom would, at one stage or another, be party to the information concerning a particular take-over bid. These people would include merchant bankers, fund managers, accountants and solicitors. These people will create an off-shore company in the Caribbean or in Liberia which will offer complete secrecy as to the identity of the beneficial owners of the company. They will not co-operate with any investigation; indeed, certain off-shore areas have local laws expressly prohibiting any divulging of confidential information. The share dealings will be placed through brokers by these companies, and they will adopt very aggressive tactics in their buying methods. Today, the off-shore company is prepared to let everyone know what it is doing, secure in the knowledge that the true identity of its beneficial owners will not be discovered. They are prepared to pay cash for their purchases and will even pay a higher price for the shares.

Of the 139 bids announced in 1985, only a small number were not heralded by a sharp increase in the price of the target shares prior to the announcement of the bid.

Insider Dealing is easy to identify and very difficult to do anything about. In the past, prior to the passing of the 1980 Companies Act, which first made the practice illegal, the Stock Exchange would investigate allegations of ID and, if they found sufficient evidence, they would 'name' the person concerned. The perception was that in naming a man, even though the evidence would be insufficient to found a prosecution, the resultant public ridicule of the cheat would be sufficient to act as a further deterrent. Since the practice became a criminal offence, the Stock Exchange has been prevented from 'naming' suspects, on the basis that they must now pass their information to the relevant authorities for proper investigation.

At the present time, the Department of Trade and Industry has the responsibility for conducting investigations into ID allegations. Their record is singularly unimpressive in this field as in so many other areas in which they operate.

Consider this, in the last six years, the Surveillance Department of the Stock Exchange has investigated 284 allegations of ID, of which it has referred 93 allegations to the DTI. Of those cases, the DTI has prosecuted five, resulting in three convictions. The Stock Exchange believes that it has forwarded sufficient evidence for the DTI to act. The Department on the other hand is reported as saying:

'Tell the Stock Exchange to send us proper evidence and we will take action. We've gone as far as we can.'

The Stock Exchange has expressed some concern however at the attitude expressed by the Director of Public Prosecutions in failing to prosecute allegations in which the Stock Exchange believed it had provided overwhelming evidence. The Director of the Stock Exchange Surveillance Department, Bob Wilkinson is reported in *The Sunday Times* as saying:

'It was made clear that we should only send those cases where there is a chance of securing a conviction.'

Insider Dealing is a major problem for the future and one area where those responsible for ensuring the cleanliness of the market will be stretched to the limit, and a conviction rate of little more than 1% is frankly, risible.

I have previously stressed the American nature of the markets of the future and ID is a regular feature of investigations conducted by the Surveillance Department of the Securities and Exchange Commission (SEC). Suffice it to say at this stage that they are infinitely more successful than their counterparts at the DTI.

Talking about American methods, however, leads us neatly on to discuss the activities of two kinds of market practitioner whose activities cause the SEC considerable concern and who will become a much more common feature of the British markets of the future. Bear in mind that we are still talking here about the need to maintain 'clean' markets, so neither of the following two market methods is considered to be 'dishonest'. These activities are related to each other and both have a subtle similarity to Insider Dealing. They are called 'Risk Arbitrage' and 'Greenmailing' respectively.

The last few years have seen the growth of a series of take-over situations in financial markets both in the US and in Britain. The skill in take-overs lies in being able to predict the degree of opposition which the take-over bid will arouse in the target company and the amount of resistance they will put up. If they are antagonistic to the bid, then they will fight it with all their might and may even make an appeal to another company, with whose management style they are more attuned, to assist them in fighting off the bid from the predator.

The longer the fight goes on, the more uncertain becomes the eventual share price, and the more likely it becomes that others will seek to profit from the dealings in the share. Messy take-over bids result in messy battles, from which neither side usually emerges with any credit. Shabby firms of private detectives are hired to scuff around in dustbins, looking for any evidence which can be used to smear or expose the leading directors of companies involved in take-overs. The Guinness take-over of the Distillers Company provided some of the more elevating examples. There is no doubt, when two City mega-giants decide to battle it out for overall control, the public are treated to a series of instructive lessons in character assassination, duplicity and double standards worthy of a Borgia.

As the battle for control of the target company's shares rages, the predator company hopes that it has properly predicted the final price it will have to pay for the shares in order to secure control. Companies planning take-overs will spend a considerable amount of time with their financial analysts, evaluating the worth of the target company, to decide the price which they are prepared to pay for the shares they need to buy. They will also spend a lot of time with their bankers discussing the ways in which they intend to raise the finance necessary to pay for these shares. For obvious reasons, the investment bankers, financial analysts, lawyers and their respective staffs, will all know of the potential take-over, and it is from among the ranks of these persons that by far the greatest number of insider dealing actions emanate.

These take-over battles have also helped to produce the Risk
Arbitrageur. Arbitrage is the name given to the practice of buying and
selling the same commodity at the same time, in two different markets,
in order to make a profit from a differential in prices which may have
occurred. Risk Arbitrageurs have coined the name because their
practice is to buy shares which have become the subject of take-over
bids as soon as a bid is announced, in the hope that they can sell them
later at a profit. These particular practitioners deal in huge sums of
money and in immense blocks of shares, because the profit differential
may be very small in terms of price on one share, but multiplied by the
huge numbers in which they deal, can represent substantial profits.

The concept of risk arbitrage is very much an American
phenomenon at the moment because of the way American institutions
tend to react when take-over bids are announced. Americans are much
more litigious than their British counterparts and fund managers in the
States and other investment institutions are reluctant to take too great a
degree of risk with funds entrusted to their management care. If they
are holding a large quantity of stock in a particular company which has
become the subject of a take-over bid, they are much more likely to sell
their holding at an early stage of the battle, in order to lock in their
profit, rather than risk an action from unhappy fund members if the bid
fails and the price of the shares collapses. It is these huge blocks of
shares which the American arbitrageur is prepared to buy in the hope
of making a profit later in the bid, when the price has risen even further.

Their activities have come under a considerable amount of scrutiny
in recent months, particularly by the Surveillance Department of the
SEC, because of the potential damage that they can cause to the
orderly running of a market. These concerns were amplified with the
arrest and conviction of an investment banker, Dennis Levine, who was
charged with a number of offences of Insider Dealing, as a result of his
involvement in a number of take-over preparations. During the
enquiries conducted by the SEC, the role of the 'arbs', particularly in a
number of highly publicised take-overs, came under the spotlight, and
the investigators did not like what they found, particularly in the
growing cosiness of the relationship between the 'arbs' and the
investment banks which are vital to a successful take-over.

The arbitrageurs would like us to believe that they spend a lot of time
and money conducting their own financial analyses into companies
which they believe are ripe for take-overs. Having identified a company
which they feel is a potential take-over target, the 'arbs' then begin to

buy shares in that company so that when the take-over bid is suddenly announced, they are already in position to be able to benefit from the rise in prices which the bid has precipitated. Simple, isn't it!

Needless to say, risk arbitrage has become a highly profitable activity, even among the major financial houses, and many of them are creating arbitrage departments to take advantage of the increasing number of arbitrage situations created by the spiralling popularity in mega-take-overs.

What has caused concern to the SEC is the number of times the arbitrageurs 'get it right'. Deals don't always go through successfully and there are occasions when a bid fails in a spectacular fashion. One arbitrage manager was recently quoted in an article in the *Financial Times* as saying: 'We've been on an incredibly lucky streak.'

Now, I'm prepared to believe that he might be right and that the 'arbs' do spend a lot of time looking through the historical records of thousands of companies, to discover one which might be suitable for a take-over bid. I might be prepared to believe that they buy the shares in sufficient quantities just before a bid, about which they had absolutely no knowledge whatsoever, is announced and then make an enormous profit. I'm prepared to believe that financial houses will risk millions of dollars of client monies on this equivalent of 'find the lady', without having any inside knowledge at all, and I'm prepared to believe in the tooth fairy and that the moon is made of green cheese.

What is perfectly clear is that human nature is such that investment banks will do all in their power to maximise their profits from underwriting the financing of a take-over battle. When millions of dollars are at stake, the banks would like to be in a position to know how many shares are likely to be bought up by free market speculators, before they commit themselves to financing such a bid. If they can obtain assurances from the 'arbs' that they will purchase the shares, by letting them know in advance what companies are likely to become take-over targets, then their decision becomes so much easier.

The 'arb' is a phenomenon which will become more common in the UK as we develop our new markets. There is a school of thought that insists that they provide a valuable service to the market by injecting liquidity into the stock markets and permitting institutions to sell large holdings of stock quickly and efficiently. There is another school of thought that believes that they are the logical extension of the activities of insider dealers. The SEC certainly feels that the 'arbs' are undesir-

able and would like to curtail their activities. Their success against Ivan
Boesky is an encouraging portent for the future.

In discussing arbitrageurs, we have drawn closer towards the
concept of price manipulation, although I admit that in principle, risk
arbitrage is not a price manipulative activity in itself. Price manipulation of a share is a concept that all observers can easily accept as being
dishonest, as it directly interferes with the free working of the market.
If the price of a share is being artificially manipulated by an individual,
it gives a false value to the share and that false value can radically affect
other share prices. For this reason, share manipulation is illegal in
America.

The other activity which I referred to earlier is the practice of
'Greenmailing'. Now, this is an activity which is much harder to
identify but which is indulged in by certain financial predators in an
attempt to influence the price of a share in order to profit from its sale.
It can most simply be described as a take-over bid which is intended to
fail. Again, it is primarily an American concept and has grown out of the
rules which surround the public acquisition of company stocks.

We have discussed the way in which companies can be taken over by
buying a controlling interest in their shares. This procedure, as we
have seen, is a public affair, with everyone concerned knowing about it.
This is because it has been deemed desirable that companies should
not become the subject of secret take-overs. In certain cases recently,
you may have read of companies' take-over bids being referred to the
'Take-Over Panel', an institution which studies the effects that a
proposed take-over or merger will have on the industry as a whole and
has a right to permit or refuse such a bid to proceed.

In America, once an individual has acquired approximately 6% of a
public shareholding in a company, he must announce his holding to the
SEC. In Britain, the same individual holding a similar percentage of
shares in a public company must report his holding to the share
registrar of that company. This is so that the Board of Directors of the
company concerned can know who is buying their shares and can keep
observation on any proposed take-over attempt.

Greenmailing is the practice of buying shares in a company until one
holds the required percentage for public announcement and then
making the announcement in a highly public way, indicating one's
intention to make a take-over bid for the company. This has the effect
of driving up the price of the share as the speculators, attracted by the
potential of a take-over bid, buy into the stock of the company

concerned. The board of the target company almost inevitably resist the take-over and the usual acrimonious public slanging match takes place. The greenmailer will do his utmost to ensure that the publicity is conducted as noisily as possible, with ever-spiralling offers being made for shares. When he has decided that the time has come to call a halt to his adventure, he will instruct his lawyers to enter into negotiations with the board of the target company. In many cases, they will be prepared to make an offer to the greenmailer to buy his shares from him, at a handsome premium, in order for him to go away. Reluctantly, he allows himself to be persuaded to accept this profit and to forego the prospect of owning the company and subsequently makes the announcement that his take-over bid has failed.

The natural outcome of this announcement is to drive the price of the share downwards as the speculators realise that there is to be no great profitability arising out of a successful take-over. Even at this time, the greenmailer and his friends have been active. They have entered into stock put options, which means that they are predicting that the price of the shares will fall. When the failure of the bid is announced, they pick up a second profit on the way down.

The great difficulty with such activities is in proving that the take-over bid was not a genuine one from the start. It is not wrong for companies to make take-over bids and there is no guarantee that a bid will be successful when it is made. Trying to prove, however, that a specific bid was made with the sole intention of failing, simply in order to profit from the artificial price-hike thus created is next to impossible. There can be no doubt in anyone's mind that such behaviour is dishonest, being deliberately manipulative. The long-term damage that such activity causes to the share concerned is incalculable.

Why is it called greenmail? Because it is remarkably akin to blackmail but it is paid out in 'greenbacks'.

In the summary of the Roskill Committee's report, the Committee made the following observation:

'If the Government cherishes the vision of an "equity-owning democracy", then it also faces an inescapable duty to ensure that financial markets are honestly managed, and that transgressors in these markets are swiftly and effectively discovered, convicted and punished.'

The sort of behaviour we have been discussing in this chapter is that which brings the reputation of the market itself into disrepute. The persons who indulge in this sort of activity are not concerned with the long-term future of the companies in whose shares they trade. They are not making any investment in or contributing to the fabric of the society in which they live. They are simply looking for the easiest way to make a quick profit. Their actions are nothing more than speculation, they are nothing more than gamblers and the market merely a casino. Like all gamblers, they seek to shorten the odds against losing by attempting to gain an unfair advantage over others who invest in the market and in doing so they resort to cheating and trickery, thus ensuring that the market is not a 'clean' place to do business. Should anyone still be under the mistaken impression however that these activities are restricted to minor participants in the marketplace, a thorough examination of the activities of the main parties involved in the so-called Guinness affair, as reported by the popular press, should help dispel such an illusion.

Their activities are included in this chapter because they involve the markets in which the investor of the future will be expected to place his money. It is right to describe the methods of these cheats in order that those people who are unsophisticated in market practices can at least know the sort of activities which are adopted by other, less ethical players in the game so that they can be fully informed before they make the decision to part with their money.

Those who try to gain an unfair advantage over others in the financial markets, whether by making multiple share applications using false names, or using inside information, are merely using the financial markets as a 'posh betting shop'. Their activities benefit society not one jot. That is not to say, however, that they should be prevented from indulging in such a gamble. In a free society, it is right that any person should be permitted to gamble with their money, if they so wish. I doubt if I am alone, however, in believing that if they wish to gamble on the stock market, the least society should do is ensure that they play by the same rules as everybody else.

CHAPTER FIVE

Robbing Peter, Paying Paul

In the previous chapter we discussed the activities of those who seek to take an unfair advantage of the market to make profit for themselves. Theirs is the sort of behaviour that causes the greatest degree of difficulty in the minds of regulators and legislators because their actions imitate so closely the ordinary practices of the market and are indulged in by so many market participants that eventually unfair activities become looked upon as the norm. When this happens, those involved can usually find some academic who will excuse their practices by saying that they bring liquidity to the market, thus enabling the ordinary business of the market to operate in an efficient and unhindered environment. It is just this sort of City doublespeak that seeks to confuse relatively simple issues by giving them an air of quasi-respectability.

The Securities and Exchange Commission in America has absolutely no difficulty in identifying these practices as being unhealthy for the market and makes great efforts to control them. We shall look at their activities in more detail when we compare their role with that proposed by Government for the Securities and Investments Board in Britain.

In this chapter, I want to talk about the sort of things that can happen to individual investors who may venture into the marketplace and the traps that can await the unwary. This chapter deals with the activities of what I called the 'slippery-slope' fraudsmen. These men have caused great problems in the past and their activities, more than anyone else's, have been influential in the findings of those commentators whose investigations lead to the introduction of the Financial Services Act. Whether these kind of operators are now merely an historical memory remains to be seen.

Let us assume that you have just become that most happy of persons, the sole beneficiary of the will of a long-lost uncle. In his will he left you his entire portfolio of shares.

Let me assure you that this scenario does happen and, when it does, the rewards can be extremely valuable. On the other hand you might find yourself holding some worthless bonds whose sole value rests in their being framed and used as an unusual conversation piece. To find out whether you have suddenly discovered a way to tell the boss what you have always really thought of him, you have to get the portfolio valued.

There used to be a number of ways in which this could be done, through your solicitor, your bank or by finding a stock broker or a licensed dealer in securities. As we saw, a licensed dealer was a person who held a licence granted to him by the Department of Trade and Industry. This procedure has now been superseded but the relevant individuals still exist. Bear in mind that these practitioners are now subject to a host of new rules and administrative requirements. What we are discussing here is what happened before the rules were changed.

For the purposes of this chapter I am going to assume that you went to a licensed dealer who was recommended to you by a friend. Today you would use an authorised dealer instead. The function remains the same, only the title has been changed. He might have told you that your portfolio contained some interesting shares, some of which were valuable, some of which were slipping in value and some of which ought to be sold as quickly as possible. He valued the portfolio for you as being worth in the region of £10,000 but said that some of the shares should be sold and their proceeds re-invested in other, more profitable shares. He would have described for you a variety of ways in which your portfolio could be spread, in order to take advantage of different types of investment and to spread the risk. He recommended buying some shares for their dividend potential, some for their growth potential and some for their speculative potential. This practice had a number of names but we shall call it portfolio management.

The first cause for concern in so many of these cases was that many of these dealers were undercapitalised. Capitalisation requirements were non-existent, the proof of the liquidity of the company being controlled by its requirement to file an annual return at Companies House, showing, among other documents, its audited accounts.

Many companies failed to make their annual returns on time, indeed, some companies failed to make returns for two or three years, yet without those returns, an individual seeking to make enquiry as to the solvency of a company had no means of ascertaining the true position of the company's finances.

A licensed dealer was permitted to earn such fees from his dealings for his client as were agreed between the client and the dealer, before any transactions were undertaken. These were the only sums of money that the dealer was permitted to take from the client.

Now in the case of portfolio management, the client's monies would be held by the dealer and accounted for to the client. When the dealer made a purchase on behalf of the client, the sums concerned would be debited to the client's account. Any subsequent sales would be credited to the client's account and a monthly statement sent to the client showing the dealings carried out and the balance on the account.

Inevitably, we found that a client's monies were inextricably linked with those of other clients and those of the dealer himself, in one large, omnibus bank account. The funds for the running of the company, paying the rates, the salaries of the staff, etc., were the responsibility of the company and should have been paid for out of the monies of the company. Dealers had no lawful right to pay those bills with the funds of their clients. Yet this is exactly what used to happen in so many cases.

Imagine the situation where a licensed dealer has a large number of individual clients, all of whom have sums of money deposited with him. This may not necessarily cause a problem, as long as the dealer is (a) scrupulously honest, (b) well capitalised and (c) extremely efficient. In some cases it was almost inevitable that at least one of the above criteria was missing. More usually two or all three criteria could not be identified.

The way most 'slippery-slope' frauds started was when the dealer suddenly found himself being heavily pressed by a creditor and rather than have to admit that he was unable to pay the money, the dealer would 'borrow' the sum from his other clients. Most of them did so, in the first instance, with the intention of re-paying the money as soon as possible, and had no intention of depriving their clients of their investments.

These good intentions soon evaporated, however, for as we all know, the road to hell is paved with them and very quickly, the dealer would find himself 'owing' the client's account a considerable sum of money. The clients themselves would be unaware of this state of affairs and you can rest assured that the dealer would have made sure that they remained in this blissful state of ignorance.

The dealer would be faced with an insoluble problem. He would now owe the clients so much money that he would be unable to make proper repayment, without the company collapsing. This would lead in turn to an investigation of the affairs of the company and possibly court proceedings and ruin. And so, the inevitable slide into criminal behaviour began.

The pattern that then emerged usually followed predictable lines. New clients would be solicited and new investment schemes proposed, in order to encourage the in-flow of more cash funds. These new funds would be used to pay off existing and most pressing creditors and then new clients solicited, and so on and so on. The Americans call this type of fraud a 'Ponzi' scheme, named after Charles A. Ponzi who defrauded thousands of investors in the 1920s using such a technique. Some of the investment schemes offered were of a type that involved the client tying up his funds for a considerable period of time, from six months to a year. This way, the dealer would have more time in which to solicit more clients to provide the necessary funds to pay the earlier investors when their repayment date came due.

From these early beginnings, the next stage was to 'invest' a client's funds in stocks which would lose money. This method was particularly popular in those instances where the dealer exercised discretion in the management of the client's portfolio. You will recall the 'account' period, within which shares could be purchased and sold. A technique which proved very popular among some of the more unscrupulous dealers was to find a share which had the potential to perform badly and then to create false contract notes, showing heavy purchases of those shares, a day or two before they began to decline in value. This first contract note would be followed, within a few days with another showing the sale of those shares, the end result being a considerable loss of money to the client, which could then be deducted from his debit balance on the dealer's books.

To all intents and purposes, the dealer would have been shown to have made an error of judgement in his choice of stock, which he would have taken steps to rectify as soon as possible, to minimise the risks to his clients. Rarely if ever would a dissatisfied client ask to see proof of the purchase of the shares in the first place, having taken the contents of the contract note at face value. It hardly ever occurred to the clients that the securities had never been bought at all and that the contract note was simply a document intended to deceive.

Now, this procedure could not be used too often in case the client did become suspicious, but the ever-inventive mind soon found other ways to relieve the client of his money.

Licensed dealers would operate their business in one of two ways. If dealing as an agent, they would charge the client a commission on each transaction. They would then owe the client a fiduciary duty, in the same way as a stock broker did, to act in his best interests, taking as their earnings the agreed commission fee. Alternatively, they could act as a principal, and charge the client no commission at all for the deal, but mark up the cost of the security bought to the client and mark down the sale price.

One technique which was widely used in the market by many practitioners was the practice of 'churning' the client's account. Churning can be defined as being: 'Excessive trading of a client's account simply for the purpose of generating commission.'

This was a method whereby the dealer would identify a stock which was behaving very erratically over a period. Erratic behaviour does not necessarily mean that the price was yawing widely all over the index, but simply that there was a considerable degree of activity in the stock. He would, if he were taking a commission on each transaction, proceed to buy and sell quantities of this stock on a regular basis, taking commission on each transaction, regardless of whether the client made a profit or a loss. He would be able to justify his actions by saying that he believed that the stock was one which, while being speculative in nature, was nevertheless an attractive investment opportunity and that he was closely monitoring the behaviour of the stock, and trying to take advantage of upward movements, while minimising losses, thus justifying a large volume of trading.

The fact of the matter would be that at the end of the transaction period, the client may have made a profit on trading, but he would have suffered a considerable loss on commission payments. It would be very difficult to prove that a broker had not acted in his client's best interests if he could show that he had made his client a trading profit, regardless of the fact that his client had paid through the nose for the privilege.

Another technique which was quite commonly observed was the practice of late booking. This method used the existence of the account period to enable the dealer to decide when and to whom to book a particular block of shares. The first record a client receives identifying his contract position is the contract note which the dealer sends him. Late booking described the practice of holding on to a line of stock to ascertain in which direction the stock was moving. If it made a profit, then the stock would be booked to the dealer's personal account. If it went down, it was booked to the client's account and the loss spread between the clients, the date on the contract note being adjusted accordingly.

Another variation of this technique enabled the dealer to lock in his position in order to create losses for his clients while being able to show that he had bought the securities concerned. It was a particularly valuable tool in the armoury of the dishonest dealer which enabled him to cover up large discrepancies in his client accounts and make a profit for himself.

This method was slightly more complicated than simple late booking and involved buying and selling the same number of shares at the same price at the same time. The dealer would identify a share which was moving busily in price, indicating that it was the subject of active trading, and he would buy a line of shares in the stock, early in the account period. At the same time, he would go short, or sell an equivalent amount of the same stock at the same price. Some stock brokers would transact both these contracts themselves. Others might be less happy about such a transaction and would decline to accept such instructions. It did not matter as most licensed dealers would deal through more than one stock broker and could place either contract with separate brokers.

These stock deals would be identified in the books of the stock broker in the name of the dealer, or any nominee name the dealer cared to use. In 'short' transactions, the seller is required to deliver the stock at the end of the account period, either at a loss or a profit to himself. The dealer would not sit back and await developments. During the account period, he would carefully monitor the movement of the price of the stock and when it had moved sufficiently he would then close both contracts.

If the share had gone up in value, his buying contract would have increased in value, while his short contract would have lost in value to the same degree. The profitable contract would then be booked to the dealer's personal account, while the loss-making contract would be booked to the clients' accounts, and the loss shared among them. Alternatively, if the price of the share declined during the period, the dealer would book the short sale to his own account, giving the clients the purchasing or 'long' contract. Whichever way the market turned, the dealer could not lose and the clients could never win. The dealer could not be accused of not having gone to the market, because he would always be able to prove that he had entered into the transactions lawfully. At the same time he would be able to say that he had acted with his client's best interests at heart, by closing the loss-making contract within the account, thus minimising the losses to the clients. It is no offence to be an incompetent dealer.

The techniques outlined so far occurred most commonly where the dealer was granted 'discretion' by the client to deal on his behalf. Discretionary accounts were very common and existed, for the most part, where clients were inexperienced or unsophisticated in financial matters and looked for professional advice in their affairs.

Inherent in this relationship, which involved the client signing a contract absolving the dealer from liability for acts of negligence, lay the principle of a fiduciary relationship. The dealer was required by law to act in his client's best interests and give the client the best execution possible. He was not permitted to make a secret profit at his client's expense and was obliged to disclose to his client any such monies. In return, the dealer would be paid an agreed commission.

The practice developed for many dealers to adopt what were known as 'principals' contracts', in which the dealer negotiated with his clients the right to deal as a principal in all dealings. Some cases involved the dealer telling the client that in so doing, he avoided the necessity to charge VAT on the commission earnings, which was true. The client was told that instead the dealer would adopt the stock himself, charging the client a premium for buying and selling the security. The big carrot in this offer was that the client would not be charged the VAT on the commission and thus readily agreed to be bound by the principal's contract.

Once this contractual relationship existed, however, the client could no longer rely on the protections offered by the law of agency, because he had entered into a separate agreement allowing the dealer to act as a principal. The dealer could now legitimately charge what he liked to the client, the client's only protection being the principle of 'Caveat Emptor', or 'Let the buyer beware'.

In many if not all cases, these and other practices only came to light, when the dealer's company had been placed into liquidation. This happened most commonly when a dissatisfied client, whether an investment client or a trade creditor, tired of waiting for his money and, not believing any more promises to the future, petitioned the court for an order to wind up the company. Less often, the dealer himself would attempt to place his company into voluntary liquidation and then the facts might or might not emerge, depending upon the honesty of the liquidator.

Liquidation of the company's affairs presented another insuperable hurdle to the unhappy investors in the company. Under the law as it then stood, once a client had parted with his money to the dealer, the dealer owed the client a contractual duty to deal with his money as per the agreement made between them, but there was nothing wrong with the dealer placing those funds into his company's bank account, thus inextricably mixing them with other monies in that account. If, unhappily, the company were to be wound up within a few days, the last client's funds would become part of the proceeds of the winding-up and would become available to the liquidator of the company called in to settle the affairs of the company.

The likelihood of a client's funds being available for such a procedure was slim, in any event, as the last client's funds simply went to reduce an existing overdraft position and were dissipated before they arrived in the account. However, you would be forgiven for sympathising with a client who said, 'I parted with my money in good faith, I've got nothing out of my venture, and I want my money back. I don't see why I should help pay out other creditors to whom I owe nothing.' In the absence of a segregated client account, the answer would be, 'Tough'.

One simple answer to this problem would have been a legal requirement that all dealers should maintain segregated client bank accounts, which would prevent the mixing of client and company monies. It is a requirement which has been mandatory in America for years and has operated there without difficulty. The existence of such accounts will not deter the deliberate thief but they will minimise the risks involved in 'slippery-slope borrowings'.

While writing this chapter, I was interested to see the reaction of the financial industry towards the draft proposals from SIB regarding the requirements of segregated trust accounts for client funds.

The Stock Exchange apparently believes that the requirements will impose an 'intolerable administrative burden' on its members and that such accounts will not prevent criminal activities by fraudsters. It also believes that clients are best protected by the existence of the Stock Exchange's compensation fund.

The banks have requested immunity from legal action in the event that such trust funds are improperly removed from a trust account held at one of their branches. Well, they would, wouldn't they!

The Securities and Investments Board, while recognising the controversial nature of these requirements, are insisting that they become a practical reality and they are resisting the banks' demands. It will be fascinating to see what happens.

So far, I have described some of the many methods used by unscrupulous dealers to cheat their clients and it may be thought that I have adopted too wide a set of terms of reference. Many authorised dealers would be able to say that, while the methods described in this chapter are well known to them, they take great pains to ensure that their dealers and associates do not behave in these and other ways. Many stock brokers would make the same comment.

I have tried to make it clear throughout this book that my remarks are not addressed towards every practitioner in the industry but towards those persons whose activities have become the subject of criminal investigation. The fact which I found to be of greatest fascination was the almost inevitable similarity of method used by such persons, which led to the suspicion that such activities were not simply restricted to those practitioners who had the misfortune to become the subject of an investigation. I began to see the truth behind the old detective's adage that to uncover a course of action once could be put down to misfortune; find the same behaviour twice, and it could simply be a coincidence; find it three times and you've got a conspiracy.

To illuminate some of these activities, I am going to turn to the case of a licensed dealer called David Langford, whose downfall neatly illustrates some of the techniques I have covered; and further describe how, with proper supervision by the relevant department, he could have been effectively prevented from committing the criminal offences to which he eventually pleaded guilty.

Early one morning in February 1983, a park attendant in Torquay was checking the safety fences around the notorious clifftop at the quaintly named Daddyhole Plain. The spot is famous for its spectacular views of the surrounding coastline and it is infamous for the occasional suicide attempt. The sheer cliff face drops steeply away from a dangerous, crumbling edge, and falls for a considerable way. Beneath the cliff top are a number of deep cracks and fissures, in which small trees and cliff plants grow in abundance, effectively masking anything which might fall from sight.

While making his rounds, the attendant found a small wallet containing bank cards and other correspondence belonging to David

Edward Langford of Chiswick, London. They were found on the very edge of the cliff, partly hidden by some grass. Indeed, it says much for the keen eyesight of the attendant that he spotted the small brown wallet at all. He handed the wallet into the police in Torquay and reported its finding at Daddyhole Plain.

The police officer on duty rang Chiswick Police Station in London to report the finding of the property and asked the Metropolitan Police to inform the loser that his property had been recovered.

'What did you say the name was?' asked the London officer in a surprised voice.

'D. E. Langford,' replied his Devon and Cornwall colleague.

'That's funny,' said the Chiswick policeman. 'His wife's at the counter now, reporting him as a missing person. He didn't come home last night and she hasn't heard from him.'

At this stage, David Langford had a thirty-six-hour start on the police and he used it to good advantage. He dropped out of sight so effectively it was as if he had never existed.

The previous day he had kissed his wife and said goodbye to his two young daughters and had left his substantial suburban home in Chiswick, to drive to work at his office, less than a mile away. His wife didn't expect him home at any special time as he always worked late, but when she looked at the clock and found it was after 9.00 pm, she felt a small tremor of concern. She checked his diary and found that he had been expected at a meeting in Aldershot with a business colleague that morning. Surely the meeting couldn't still be going on. She rang the man and found him at home.

'No, David hadn't turned up for the meeting, hasn't he come home?'

David Langford didn't come home for three months.

Two days later, a car park attendant in Exeter reported a suspicious car to the police which had apparently been abandoned. The police ran a check on the registration number and found it registered to David Langford, who was also shown as being a missing person. They took the car to Exeter Police Station, where a few days later, police from London examined it. In the car were found more personal documents, cheque books, and credit cards, but of David Langford there was no sign.

The police from London were conducting an investigation into allegations involving the fraudulent conduct of Langford's investment consultancy in London. Numerous worried investors were ringing the office to try and find out what had happened to the business and, more

importantly, their money. By now however, the offices were locked and
the documents were at the Fraud Squad.

After a lengthy consultation with their colleagues in Exeter, the
Scotland Yard detectives left to commence a nationwide search for the
missing finance advisor. David Langford was no longer a missing
person but a wanted man.

The story of David Langford and his various company affairs is a
classic example of a man who inexorably rolled down the 'slippery
slope' despite all his good intentions. I do not and never have believed
that he set out to be a criminal or deliberately to defraud his clients, but
he eventually became so immersed in financial problems that he could
find no other way of maintaining his business.

He operated by dint of his possession of a principal's licence granted
by the Department of Trade and Industry. He ran, latterly, a company
trading under the name of Langford Scott and Partners Ltd from premises in Chiswick High Road and this business existed to trade securities
and later, traded options, conducted portfolio management and advised
individual clients on their financial liabilities to the Inland Revenue.

Langford specialised in one particular field of money management
which proved to be extremely attractive to older clients who had
become concerned about their dwindling resources. He offered a
facility for what became known as 'Bond Washing'.

During periods of high inflation, people on fixed incomes, such as
non-index linked pensions, found that their incomes were becoming
whittled away by the effects of inflation. It became necessary for them
to find a means of investing in areas where they would be able to
maintain the level of their income. At the same time, it was imperative
that these clients should find a means of investing in securities which
would be safe, as the loss of their capital would represent a considerable threat to their livelihood.

Langford offered these people a system whereby they could invest
substantial lump sums of capital in Local Authority Bonds. Being
offered by local authorities, and maturing annually, they were
perceived to be a very safe form of investment and they generally
carried a good rate of interest. The proceeds of the sale of such bonds,
however, were considered to be income and, as such, were subject to
taxation at whatever rate of tax the investor paid.

Paying tax at higher rates could well render these bonds unattractive
because the income from them, after tax, might still not provide the
financial return required. Langford had discovered a way of circum-

venting this provision by selling the bond approximately halfway through its life span and then immediately rolling over the proceeds into a new bond. That way, he explained, the client was able to persuade the Inland Revenue Authorities to assess the gain from the sale as a capital gain, which could provide a saving in tax payments and thus make the investment more attractive. Some of Langford's clients found this scheme represented a valuable addition to their portfolio and a number of them placed quite considerable sums of money with him for the purpose of investing in Local Authority Bonds.

In the beginning, Langford did buy the bonds through his stock brokers, and sent the clients contract notes, showing the bonds purchased on their behalf. He did not, however, send them the bonds themselves, explaining that they would have to be surrendered when the time came to sell them and that they were better kept with him for safe keeping.

Initially, at the end of the six-month period, the bonds were sold and their proceeds accounted for to the clients. The capital sum was then rolled over into another bond, the client receiving a cheque for the balance remaining. As long as the client received a contract note and a cheque every six months for his earnings from the bonds, there was no reason, theoretically, for him to become suspicious.

The point about these clients is that they were not speculators or gamblers. They were looking for the safest, most securely profitable way they could find to do nothing more than keep their incomes stable. They could be forgiven for believing that their money was in as safe an investment as they could find.

What they did not know was that Langford was in deep financial trouble due to a series of unfortunate, highly speculative investments, which had resulted in considerable losses, both to him and his clients' accounts. These losses were, frankly, irreplaceable, and had arisen out of a wild attempt to recoup his fortunes in an orgy of speculative investment in the shares of two companies which collapsed before he could gain a controlling interest in them. Had he been successful in his attempts to gain control of them, the story might very well have had a different ending.

Coupled with this financial difficulty, however, was a far more serious and potentially damaging situation. Langford was under investigation by the Department of Trade and Industry for the way in which he had operated a previous company. This company had been officially wound up, following Langford's failure to pay certain investors, and the investigation had revealed considerable discrepancies in his existing company's dealings. Langford had already been the subject of a lengthy investigation when his second company collapsed and he went on the run.

We have discussed the different types of licence which could be granted to a dealer in securities, the principal's licence and the representative's licence, and how each licence needed to be renewed annually. The Secretary of State may refuse or revoke a licence where a holder has failed to supply information prescribed by the Department or where he is satisfied that there are circumstances likely to lead to the improper conduct of business by, or which reflect upon the method of conducting business of, a licence holder or person associated with him. During the ensuing paragraphs, it will be instructive to bear those provisions in mind.

Langford, together with a man called John Scott, had been operating a company called Quane Investments Ltd, which had held a principal's licence since February 1976. In October 1980, Quane ceased to trade although Langford continued to place business through his stock brokers in the name of Quane, this business being that which had originated through Quane, prior to its demise.

On 25 November 1980, the Licensing Branch of the Department of Trade and Industry granted a principal's licence to Langford Scott and Partners Ltd, for one year. This was a company owned jointly by Langford and Scott. Subsequently, the Licensing Branch issued a representative's licence to Scott and on 3 April 1981, they renewed Langford's representative's licence. At this time, the Department did not know that Quane had ceased to trade.

Quane had effectively ceased to trade because it owed the capital sum of £40,000 to a client who had invested in Local Authority Bonds (LABs), and this man had subsequently demanded the return of his money. They were unable at this stage to repay the sum owed and the dissatisfied investor had commenced proceedings to have the company wound up.

These proceedings were completed on 13 May 1981 and the following day, the Official Receiver's office (OR) telephoned their departmental colleagues in the Licensing Branch to inform them that Quane Investments Ltd had been placed into compulsory liquidation. Now, at this time the Licensing Branch were apparently aware of the connection between Quane and LSP and they ascertained that there had been 'considerable dealings' between the two companies. Later on 29 May 1981, Scott resigned from the company.

On 2 June, a Senior Executive Officer (SEO) in the Licensing Branch referred the Quane file to his Principal who noted the liquidation and instructed that the case should be pursued with the Official Receiver's department. It was apparent at this time that Quane had been ignoring correspondence from the Licensing Branch prior to its liquidation, and the Principal queried whether any machinery existed for maintaining surveillance on companies which had dealer-linked directorships with other companies. Later that day, the SEO passed the file down the line to a subordinate, a Higher Executive Officer (HEO), instructing him to make the relevant enquiries as to the existence of such a system.

On 5 June 1981, a letter was received in the Companies Division of the DTI, another branch of the same department, sent from the Stock Exchange, which enclosed a letter from an unidentifiable firm of stock brokers, indicating that they had been receiving dealing instructions from Quane subsequent to its official winding up. After enquiry, on 17 June 1981, the Companies Investigation Branch (CIB) requested that the Insolvency Service (IS), yet another branch of the same department, maintain liaison with the Licensing Branch (LB) over the proceedings concerning the winding up of Quane Investments Ltd.

On 22 June, the Licensing Branch Principal was asked by his departmental senior whether the information from the Stock Exchange raised any questions regarding LSP's fitness to hold a licence. This query was referred to the SEO to be linked with the previous minute of 2 June 1981 and was passed in turn by the SEO to his HEO.

On 25 June 1981, the IS asked the OR's department to be kept informed of the process of the liquidation of Quane Investments Ltd.

On 24 July, some eight weeks later, the HEO replied to the request of 2 June saying that there was no collation system identified by the Principal and suggested that such a system might be advisable. The SEO acknowledged the minute and asked if there had been any further information on the liquidation.

The HEO left this request until 27 August 1981 when he rang the OR's office to find out what was happening. He was told that a report on the affairs of Quane was forthcoming and would deal with the relations between Quane and LSP, and that there was evidence that creditors of Quane had been paid with sums of money, deposited with and subsequently misappropriated by LSP, such sums being the property of other clients. This evidence consisted of an admission made by Langford to the OR's department when he was interviewed on 3 July 1981.

On 1 September 1981 the HEO informed his SEO, who, in turn, formed the intention to refer to the case at a meeting with CIB on 17 September 1981. It is unclear whether any such reference was made at that meeting.

Whatever else was or was not clear by 1 September 1981, in the light of subsequent events one fact stands out with crystal clarity. Langford had admitted misappropriating clients' funds from the accounts of a company operated by him, which sums had been used to pay an outstanding creditor of another company operated by Langford, now in liquidation.

This information was available to the Insolvency Service, or at least the Official Receiver's department, and it had been made known to the Licensing Branch. What better evidence could there have been to satisfy the Secretary of State that Langford's conduct revealed circumstances likely to lead to the improper conduct of business by him? There were a number of options open to the DTI with that information to hand, so what did they do?

They sent LSP their renewal application forms, reminding them that they had to be returned to the Department not later than one month prior to the date of expiry. They also made a standard enquiry of the Companies Records Office (CRO), to ascertain the date of the last set of accounts filed by LSP.

These annual accounts are the only way an enquirer can ascertain the financial status of a limited company and are thus an important document in the public records of a company. They were informed by the CRO that the last set of accounts filed by LSP covered the financial year ending 31 March 1979. In other words the only public information regarding the financial status of LSP was two-and-a-half-years old.

The CRO reported this fact to LB on 23 September and on 2 October 1981, the official from the OR's office rang the SEO in the Licensing Branch, enquiring about the LSP licences. He told the SEO that the OR's report would be critical of LSP and said that they intended to 'throw the book' at them. He reiterated the allegation that client funds of LSP had been used to discharge the Quane debt and that he would be forwarding a copy of the report to the Licensing Branch for their information.

The report was issued on 16 October 1981 and incorporated a very close analysis of Quane Investments Ltd and itemised twenty-three criminal offences which the examiners alleged were disclosed by their inspection of the company's affairs. These offences were alleged to have been committed by Langford and Scott, singly and jointly and included offences under the Companies Acts, the Theft Act and the Perjury Act. Included in these offences were two which alleged misappropriation of property belonging to a client of LSP which had been allegedly used to satisfy a debt of Quane.

The report was submitted to the Legal Branch of the DTI for them to consider what further action to take and a copy was sent to the SEO in the Licensing Branch, on 13 November 1981, with a covering minute which said that the report was submitted on an 'In Confidence' basis.

The Licensing Branch had received LSP's renewal application on 10 November 1981, some two weeks after the official deadline, and on 17 November 1981, the SEO passed the OR's report and the application to his Principal, with the recommendation that there were sufficient grounds to refuse to renew LSP's licence. The Principal agreed and further recommended to the DTI's solicitors that Langford's representative's licence should be revoked immediately.

What happened next has all the hallmarks of a Whitehall farce.

The DTI solicitor to whom the papers were passed criticised the Licensing Branch for their delay in submitting the papers on the basis that refusing to renew the licence so close to its renewal date would effectively mean putting LSP out of business, without giving them a chance to state their side of the case. The solicitor also said that the Department could not use the OR's report because of its confidential nature and concluded by saying that the only means to stay the matter would be for LSP to be required to provide an explanation for their failure to submit the application for renewal within the time required by law. The solicitor also asked the Insolvency Service if there were any facts arising from the report which they felt could be discussed.

He finished his minute by stating that he had not personally opened the envelope containing the report and instructed that no one else within the Licensing Branch should look at it.

Confronted with allegations of serious wrong-doing supported by evidence of admission by the director concerned, the solicitor responsible for making the decision to refuse the renewal application chose to turn his back on the evidence and pretend that he hadn't received it.

Langford's explanation for the late submission of the application was that he had effectively forgotten it and on that basis the Assistant Secretary in charge of the Licensing Branch decided to forget about refusing the application on out-of-time grounds and instead, he and the DTI solicitor interviewed Langford about his affairs. In the interview, Langford attempted to lay the blame on his former co-director for much of the failure of the company and stated that he would make up the deficiencies of Quane's affairs out of his own resources. He ended by saying that he intended to take legal action against Scott.

On this basis, the licence was renewed. On 25 November 1981, LSP was granted a further principal's licence. Later that day the Assistant Secretary returned the OR's report to the Insolvency Service with a declaration that neither he nor the solicitor had read the contents, nor had he been made aware of any of the contents of the report by any of his staff.

By this time, some very high-powered meetings had been held in which it was generally decided that the contents of the OR's reports could not be seen by other officers in other departments of the DTI, on the basis, apparently, that if it became clear that the discussions at such meetings were to be known to other offices within the same department, it would 'discourage candour' on the part of directors of failed companies.

I doubt if many official examinations of directors of failed companies by the OR's department are marked out by the excessive candour shown by the luckless director, but there we are.

In any event, it was subsequently decided to ascertain the true situation regarding the OR's reports and instructions were drawn up for counsel to advise upon the whole procedure. This apparently complex duty took five months to complete. During this time, LSP was continuing to trade and one solicitor in the DTI's legal branch became concerned about the way in which LSP was apparently raising capital for the company and its connection with a discharge of a debt to outstanding Quane creditors. He stated that he believed that the Department should make a prompt decision about revoking Langford's licence since, 'if investors' money were to be lost due to the Department's failure to take revocation action soon enough, when they had sufficient grounds for doing so, they would be open to criticism'.

The Assistant Secretary wrote to Langford on 9 February 1982 asking to see documentary proof of the restitution payments which Langford claimed he had made.

On 3 March, Langford applied to renew his representative's licence and the Licensing Branch chose, for some reason, to wait until almost the last minute to see whether counsel's opinion on the availability of the OR's report would be finished, before deciding to renew the licence. The fact was that instructions did not even reach counsel until 26 May 1982, so again, a breakdown in communications within departments took place. However, Langford was told that his licence would be renewed, but he should first reply to the request for proof of restitution payments. Amazingly, Langford replied the same day, 31 March 1982, saying that he would be able to produce the documentary proof, at some unspecified date in the future, when his accountants had finished auditing his accounts.

On this basis, and with no other proof or corroboration of any of Langford's assertions, the Assistant Secretary noted Langford's letter with the immortal phrase, 'Good enough, I think,' and the representative's licence was renewed on 2 April 1982.

In March 1982, a retired gentleman from Swansea, whom I intend to call Mr Jones, although that is not his real name, was looking for a safe means of investing his golden handshake. He had been prematurely retired from his lifetime's employment with the closing down of the premises in which he had worked, a common enough practice in many parts of the country in these days, and he needed to find a means of maintaining a minimum income for his wife and himself.

A careful and cautious man, Mr Jones was not the sort to rush into things without giving the matter some thought and he had been looking around for various means of investing his capital in order to obtain the safest but most efficient return. He had been discussing with his friend, Mr Evans (again, not his real name) the possibility of putting some of his retirement funds into a bond-washing scheme which he had seen written up in an investment magazine. The beauty of the scheme was that it was totally legal, and enjoyed the grudging blessing of the Inland Revenue. Did his friend, Mr Evans, agree with his assessment of the plan?

Mr Evans suggested that, although the scheme looked good in principle, offering safety of capital with a little income on which to live, he and his friend should not place money with a man they did not know, without first meeting him and making an assessment of his character and his methods. It was agreed that Mr Evans would travel to London and would first of all satisfy himself that Langford was a man to whom they could entrust their money.

On meeting Langford at his offices, Mr Evans was undeniably impressed. A man used to a lifetime of hard work and thrift, he 'knew the value of a penny', as the old saying goes. He liked the apparent efficiency of Langford's office, set above a car showroom in Chiswick High Road. There did not appear to be any spurious or unnecessary equipment which would, Mr Evans felt, have been evidence of a spend-thrift lifestyle. There was no apparent waste and David Langford was a quiet and thoughtful man who listened carefully to Mr Evans' explanation of his visit.

Later, Mr Evans would say that Langford 'presented himself well' and, in addition, he possessed a licence, granted to him by the Government, which authorised him to deal with other people's money. Perhaps not unreasonably, Mr Evans and his friend Mr Jones believed that this fact was of paramount importance in their decision to entrust their money to Langford. As Mr Jones was to say to police later: 'You would think that they [the DTI] would be in the best position to know if he was a suitable person to hold a licence.'

Mr Jones, reassured by Mr Evans' visit and report, gave Langford the sum of £5000 in March 1982, for which he subsequently received a contract note, showing his ownership of a Local Authority Board. In late August 1982, Mr Jones parted with a further £5000 which was also apparently used to purchase a LAB, the proceeds of the first roll-over being paid to Mr Jones in the form of a cheque from LSP. Not long after this, Mr Evans also invested some thousands of pounds with LSP, to be invested in a similar fashion and he too received his contract note.

In August 1982, Treasury counsel opined that it would be lawful for the OR's reports to be communicated to other departments in order to assist in a better discharge of their functions, and a meeting was called to discuss the ramifications of such advice. Subsequently, on 17 October 1982, the Department finally instructed OR's representatives to report relevant information.

Also in August 1982, the Licensing Branch had written to LSP reminding them that their principal's licence expired in November and sending them the renewal application forms. Their standard enquiry at CRO regarding the current position of LSP's accounts revealed that they still only covered the period up to the end of 31 March 1979, despite previous reminders. Continued reminders had, by October 1982, produced a set of photo-copied accounts for 1980, which showed a loss, and a promise of the 1981 accounts 'when they were finalised'.

The Licensing Branch wrote to the Insolvency Service on 30 September 1982, asking them to provide another copy of the report on Quane as a matter of urgency, and on 18 October 1982, a new copy of the report was forwarded setting out the facts, together with the supporting evidence together with a summary of findings, which were:

a) Quane owed substantial sums of money to clients for which it was unable to account;

b) Langford had admitted failing to maintain company records;

c) Langford had admitted that Quane had given inaccurate statements to a client in connection with his investment;

d) Langford had admitted using LSP money to pay off this client;

e) Langford had made 'conflicting' statements to the Official Receiver.

This report was passed to the DTI solicitor on 20 October but the file did not reach the Licensing Branch until only three weeks remained for the decision as to the renewal of the principal's licence to be made.

Incredibly, the Licensing Principal decided that there was insufficient time to allow Langford to state his case if the decision was made not to renew his licence and that therefore, it was decided to renew the licence on certain conditions, despite the fact that they had still not received the information from LSP which they had previously requested concerning Langford's financial position, nor had they received his 1981 accounts.

Eventually, however, having examined the OR's report, the decision was taken to revoke LSP's licence, and on 7 January 1983, the Licensing Branch referred the papers to the Legal Branch with a request that they prepare the suitable notices of intention to revoke the licences.

The response from the solicitor's department provides the fitting final touch to this sorry tale. The lawyer concerned sent back a minute to the Licensing Branch, commenting that it would 'look rather odd' that the department had possessed the relevant information for some time, but had only recently renewed LSP's principal's licence and he asked for certain points to be clarified in order that they be incorporated in the letter.

While the two departments argued about the semantics of the draft revocation letter, Langford paid all his bills, paid his daughters' school fees, filled up his car with petrol and quietly slipped out of the lives of his family and his clients, leaving behind him a mass of bills, unpaid accounts, and some very angry Welshmen.

Mr Jones and Mr Evans were not the sort of people to take this sort of thing lying down, indeed throughout the investigation into the Langford case they were a constant source of assistance and support. They were unable to accept, at first, that they would not receive any official assistance in getting back their money and they continued to believe that eventually, the truth would come out. Both men wrote to their respective Members of Parliament and eventually the matter was aired with the Parliamentary Under Secretary of State for Corporate and Consumer Affairs, who having reviewed the facts, considered that the Department's actions had been reasonable in the light of the facts available at the time. He expressed regret for Mr Jones' predicament, but pointed out that it was no light matter to close down a business on the basis of 'unproven doubts and suspicions'.

By now, both men realised that they were on their own. Possessed however of an overwhelming determination to air the whole affair, they commenced a campaign against officialdom, which culminated in a complaint to the Parliamentary Commissioner for Administration, who is more commonly known as the Ombudsman.

This excellent gentleman enquired into the whole affair on the part of Mr Jones and it is from his final report that I have been able to obtain many of the facts, a copy of the document, for which I am extremely grateful, being given to me by a victorious Mr Jones. The Ombudsman in his findings has reviewed the actions of the various departments concerned in the affair. He finds some behaviour 'surprising', he finds other actions 'extraordinary' and he criticises the Department for 'their poor performance here and for their apparent lack of regard for the protection of the public interest.' He found other failings, which 'merited criticism', and considered the overall handling of matters by the DTI, particularly in their failure to follow up repeated requests for further information, as being ineffective and ill-judged. His most telling criticism illuminates the fundamental dichotomy that has always been at the heart of investor protection. He said, when dealing with the renewal of Langford's representative's licence in April 1982, that in failing to take any follow-up action the Department 'showed a lamentable lack of concern for the interests of those members of the public who, like Mr Jones, had a right to assume that the Department's licensing system offered them a reasonable measure of protection for their investments'.

David Langford eventually surrendered himself to police in the buffet on Paddington Station three months after he first went missing. He had spent the time living in a series of small hotels and bed-sits in and around the lovely old cathedral town of Hereford, under the name of David Edwards. He eventually appeared at the Central Criminal Court in November 1985 and was convicted of certain offences relating to his management of Quane Investments, together with his co-director John Scott. Langford further pleaded guilty to an offence in relation to his management of Langford Scott and Partners Ltd and was sentenced to one year's imprisonment.

Mr Jones and Mr Evans were reimbursed their entire investment, together with interest, by the Department of Trade and Industry, following the Ombudsman's findings, which goes to prove, I suppose, that if you are prepared to fight hard enough for what you believe to be true, you may just succeed. It took them three years, and there were times when we all thought that they might fail. When it was over, Mr Jones rang me to tell me the good news.

'It was a hard fight,' he said, 'and I'm glad it's over, but I'd do it all over again if I had to.'

I honestly believe he would.

CHAPTER SIX
Psst. Wanna Buy A Share?

DOGBERRY *If you meet a thief, you may suspect him by virtue of your office to be no true man; and for such kind of men, the less you meddle or make with them, why, the more is for your honesty.*

SECOND WATCHMAN *If we know him to be a thief, shall we not lay hands on him?*

DOGBERRY *Truly, by your office you may; but I think they that touch pitch will be defiled; the most peaceable way for you if you do take a thief is to let him show himself what he is, and steal out of your company.*

Much Ado About Nothing

As in so many other examples, Shakespeare's words, satirising the activities of the bumbling constable, Dogberry, find an echo in modern times. When we come to examine the behaviour of professional criminals in the investment markets and the efforts made by the regulatory authorities to combat them, we can see that Dogberry's twentieth-century equivalent is very much alive.

I said earlier that there were certain activities which everyone can recognise as being dishonest and thus would find no difficulty in describing them accordingly. This is true when we talk among ourselves but the problems begin when we try to make those descriptions public. In a hard-hitting editorial, Melvin Marckus of the *Observer* newspaper said:

'Writing about fraud is a delicate matter. It requires considerable expertise, not only financially but, more importantly, legally. The draconian libel laws in the UK, where truth is not necessarily a defence (the greater the truth, the greater the libel) hamper the reporting of fraud. Solicitors are only too eager to lend their services to the supposedly maligned, whatever the client's track record may be.'

In this chapter we shall look at the activities of professional criminals in the investment marketplace and examine their methods. Much criminal activity will, hopefully, be rendered impotent by the new laws and I feel that little purpose will be served by simply reciting a litany of previous 'stings' and 'cons'. I intend therefore, to restrict my attention to those activities which most closely influence potential investment in the markets of the future by persons who are unaware of the dangers, and which play the greatest part in bringing the reputation of the market into disrepute.

The influence of organised criminal groups within the investment market has long been recognised as a major problem by the American regulatory authorities. The Americans spend a considerable amount of time, money and effort identifying the activities of groups of organised criminals and attempting to prevent their unlawful behaviour. Wherever possible they do this by freezing their funds or sources of finance by court orders, in the belief that cutting off the supply of money will make the financing of further criminal acts more difficult. Proceeds of crimes such as robberies, the illicit sale of narcotics, or gold smuggling need to be laundered out of the reach of the Federal authorities, in order to disguise their true provenance. The annual report of the Commission on Organised Crime, an American watch-dog body set up to examine and analyse the activities of groups of organised criminals, recorded that such groups could expect to earn $100 billion in 1986 from their collective activities. The loss in tax revenue alone could amount to $6.5 billion, which would be reflected by an increase in consumer costs of construction, transport and refuse collection.

Laundering this money has become a financial priority for such criminals and their techniques for disguising the sources of their cash have become ever more sophisticated. These activities are not simply restricted to America, neither do they exist solely in the imaginations of fiction writers. As the markets of the world have come closer together as the time zones have contracted electronically, so the professional criminals have expanded their laundering methods, utilising the facilities offered to them by the large number of off-shore financial havens in the Caribbean, Panama, and the British off-shore islands. A team of detectives from Scotland Yard has recently uncovered evidence of a network of secret companies and bank accounts, maintained and operated in the United States, the British Virgin Islands and the Isle of Man, which is believed to have been used to launder the proceeds from the Brinks Mat gold robbery at Heathrow, and from drug smuggling and narcotics trafficking in the US.

Much of this money can be laundered through the financial markets in various kinds of securities dealings. In order to be truly successful, it becomes necessary to be able to replace 'dirty' money with 'clean' money, in such a way that the precise source of the funds in the account can not be identified. What better way for this end to be achieved therefore, than by encouraging private investors to invest in companies, owned, controlled or operated by professional criminals and traded on international markets?

For many years, these 'funny money' companies were not a common feature of the British marketing scene. Admission to a public listing was a complex and expensive affair, and one which required a considerable degree of proven trading record. The Council of the Stock Exchange maintained an enviable degree of oversight of companies being brought to the market and if applicants for listing were unable to show the requisite degree of competence or financial probity, they did not get admitted.

The problem has arrived with the burgeoning growth of companies seeking venture capital, coupled with the degree of encouragement of de-regulation in international capital markets.

The development of the third-tier market or over-the-counter market in the UK is the area of operation in which the greatest source of difficulty for the administrator and legislator presents itself. The aim of the OTC market is to provide a means whereby new companies can trade their shares in an atmosphere of enterprise and raise money for new business ventures, thus stimulating growth in the economy. To assist this aim, the Government has provided the Business Expansion Scheme as an incentive to investors to part with their money. The OTC market is a comparatively new phenomenon in the UK and still trades only a relatively small number of different stocks. Its American counterpart, on the other hand, is a large market, widely regulated by the National Association of Securities Dealers, which trades some of the most well-known, household company names. The third-tier market in the UK is in the process of introducing changes which will enable it to compete more efficiently with its American cousin, but it will be some time before it can be said to trade on equal terms. Nevertheless, as a means of encouraging investment in venture capital areas, the OTC market offers various opportunities to those persons who are prepared to part with their money in high-risk investments.

PSST. WANNA BUY A SHARE?

The first major difficulty is that the investor is being required to part with his money by investing in a concept which has no track record of which to boast and no proven history of success. The investor is being invited to take a leap in the dark in the hope that his investment will prove to be worthwhile. For this reason, one would be tempted to say, the investor should satisfy himself that the venture into which he is placing his capital has the degree of viability it claims. Yet here is the essential dichotomy. How does the investor establish the validity of the claims made by the capital seeker, when it is admitted that there is no product yet available for examination? How do you establish the difference between the company which has been set up with the genuine intention of seeking to make a profit and one which exists solely to fail once sufficient investors' funds have been solicited? In an atmosphere of growing de-regulation, how does society provide the necessary safeguards to protect the unwary and discourage the criminal?

I intend to examine the activities of one particular company whose dealings have caused considerable concern to the London authorities and which, it may be felt, could have been prevented if sufficient action had been taken at the right time.

In 1978, a Cayman Island based company trading under the name of Trafalgar Capital formed a British subsidiary company called Trafalgar Capital (UK) Ltd. The company remained dormant and did not trade until it was revitalised in 1984 and moved into premises just off Harley Street, before moving to its final offices in Mayfair. Its director was an American securities dealer called Neil Bruckman. Mr Bruckman had been involved in a number of securities transactions in the United States but had found that the United Kingdom with its lack of regulatory controls offered a far greater degree of opportunity for his particular brand of entrepreneurial flair and expertise.

On his arrival in London, Mr Bruckman applied to the Department of Trade and Industry for a principal's licence to deal in securities to be granted to Trafalgar Capital (UK) Ltd, and a representative's licence to himself. These were refused.

Undaunted, Mr Bruckman made application for admission to the Association of Stock and Share Dealers, an association recognised by the Department of Trade and Industry and an early form of Self-Regulatory Organisation. Being recognised by the DTI, its members were deemed to be regulated by the rules of the association and were therefore exempt from the licensing requirements of the Prevention of Fraud (Investments) Act 1958.

In his *Review of Investor Protection*, Professor Gower said, 'Recognition presupposes that the Department of Trade and Industry was satisfied that they were effective self-regulatory bodies but in most cases it is difficult to understand why.'

Having become a member of the ASSD, Bruckman looked around for a market and was successful in identifying the immense financial potential offered by investors in West Germany, Switzerland and other North European countries. They were anxious to take advantage of the booming market being created in England, about which they had read so much in financial periodicals. England had always possessed an enviable reputation for fair dealing and profitable enterprise and conducting business with an English stock broker had always meant dealing in absolute confidence, secure in the knowledge that the Stock Exchange was noted for its honesty and integrity.

Now, for the first time, the foreign investors were being offered a chance to become part of the exciting new market which was being developed in the UK and dealings in small, venture capital stocks, which offered great profit potential were being made available to them.

At about the same time, another company was being set up in Zurich, with branch offices in Dusseldorf and Munich. This company called itself Chartwell Securities AG and it began a high-pressure selling operation, dealing in OTC shares traded in the UK and in America. If the clients were in any doubt about the OTC markets, they were simply shown the impressive list of companies which do trade on the OTC in America and were told that although it was a new market concept in the UK it was under the control of the famous London Stock Exchange, which naturally guaranteed its excellence.

However, as the company was aware of its clients' natural caution in these matters, it was able to show that it enjoyed a business relationship with a London based broking company called Trafalgar Capital (UK) Ltd, a company which had been in business since 1978. Any prospective client who did indeed check, would have found these facts to be absolutely true. They would, had they but made a simple search of names of other companies dealing in securities, have discovered the name Chartwell Securities Ltd, a British based company established in London. What the inquisitive foreign client would not know is that there was no connection between the London company and the Zurich based company; the directors of Chartwell Securities Ltd were far from pleased at the use of a company name so similar to their own and they went to great pains to disassociate themselves from the other operation.

Chartwell Securities AG had as their directors a Kurt Meier, a Juerg Ratkovits and a Rochelle Rothfleisch, a New Yorker who was resident in France. Among other functions Ms Rothfleisch was the reported common-law wife of one Thomas F. Quinn. A letter sent to a potential investor in Chartwell Securities AG was signed by Thomas F. Quinn and a Thomas F. Quinn Jr was shown as being an executive marketing director of the company.

This could, of course, simply have been all a horrible coincidence, because the real Thomas F. Quinn is not the sort of man from whom investors ought to have been considering buying securities.

Mr Quinn had been disbarred from working as a lawyer in America following his conviction in 1970 on ten counts relating to the sale of $380,000 worth of securities in a company called Kent Industries Inc., which subsequently proved to be worthless. For these offences, Quinn was sentenced to six months' imprisonment and was disbarred. He had been barred previously in 1966 by the SEC from associating with any stock dealer or broker. In 1983, the SEC brought an action against Quinn for allegedly acting as an undisclosed underwriter of a company offering worthless stock called Sundance Gold Mining and Exploration Inc., and late in 1986, Mr Quinn signed what is called a 'consent decree' with the SEC concerning his dealings in Sundance. (A consent decree is a peculiarly American legal concept in which the person concerned neither admits nor denies the charges against them, but they promise never to do it again.) Perhaps the most edifying feature of Mr Quinn's previous exploits was his long history of association with organised criminal activities in securities dealing.

Having created his marketing group in Zurich, Quinn then proceeded to off-load some fascinating shares to the unsuspecting punters. What he needed was a first-class share which could be used to act as a bell-weather and which could be identified by anyone as a worthwhile investment opportunity, and then piggy-back the worthless shares on the perceived success of the good one.

He found it in a company called AC Scotland plc. This company was formed to take over the rights to the famous AC sports car marque and the intention was to start up a factory in Scotland which would produce a competitive sports car revitalising the famous name. The company had been brought to market by a dealership operating under the name of London Venture Capital Market Ltd, a subsidiary company within the Ravendale Group plc. In agreeing to underwrite the offer, LVCM undertook to provide the necessary finance needed by the company for its expansion plans. In October 1984, apparently unable to fulfil its financial obligations, LVCM sold its holding of AC shares to Neil Bruckman's Trafalgar Capital (UK) Ltd. These shares were then aggressively marketed by Chartwell Securities AG to literally thousands of foreign clients.

Having found the share which could be used to provide the basis on which to operate, the salesmen of Chartwell Securities AG went to work. Approximately 150 telephone salesmen were employed in offices in Germany, Switzerland and Lichtenstein, who spent their entire working day telephoning lists of potential clients offering them investment opportunities. It is estimated that they reached 8000 interested clients and raised in the region of £20 million.

Riding on the back of the popularity of AC Scotland plc, which did exist, and did have a product and a factory and employees, the swindlers foisted off some more exotic offerings, all of whose markets were allegedly made by Trafalgar Capital (UK) Ltd.

For starters, they offered an unusual investment opportunity in a company called North American Bingo. Created in Nevada in April 1984, it offered European investors the chance to share in the profits from the unlimited potential available from building bingo parlours on North American Indian reservations. Quite what fascination bingo held for the descendants of the survivors of Little Big Horn and Wounded Knee, no one seems to have ascertained. Nevertheless, the shares, and there were 66 million of them, were being offered to foreign investors at $2.50 each, a company valuation of $165 million.

Another share which seems to have enjoyed customer loyalty was one called Shelfbond Trust AG. This company employed a sales manager called Kurt Meier, who, strangely, had the same name as the chairman of Chartwell Securities AG. This amazing coincidence appears to have missed most customers' attention and it is easy to see why when the potential client would have been more interested in the profits to be earned from Shelfbond's control of a waste recovery plant in New York, or their controlling interest in another company called Swissoil.

Swissoil, which was being sold at $3.75 a share, was a Nevada company which went public in 1983, based, allegedly, in New York. It seems to have enjoyed a similarity with the company formed around the time of the South Sea Bubble, 'a company for the carrying on of an enterprise of great profit but no one to know what it is'.

Towards the end of November 1984, Trafalgar Capital (UK) Ltd was quoting market prices in eighteen stocks, and they were on the look-out for more British companies to market, to take over from AC Scotland plc. AC's shares were trading now at about 41p, a substantial rise of 28p per share in just over a month.

In a moment of inspiration, Bruckman commenced dealings in the shares of a company called Derby Vision plc.

Derby Vision plc is a share with a long and checkered family history and one which will repay a little examination. Its marketing represents the sort of activity which could prove so damaging to investors in the future and the identity of its promoters should be a matter of concern for those responsible for regulating the markets. If some of the names which occur in the next few paragraphs sound as if they come straight from the pages of *The Godfather*, I can only apologise.

In or about 1966, a mafia associate, Jimmy (the Weasel) Fratiano, was attempting to obtain financial backing to develop and manufacture a machine which would show horse and greyhound races via a video screen. Players would be able to bet on the outcome of the races, while watching them on the screen, by placing their stake into the machine before the off. Fratiano had enjoyed a colourful career with the Mafia, or as we should more accurately refer to it, La Cosa Nostra (LCN). He was subsequently arrested by Federal authorities and, realising that he was facing a lifetime's imprisonment for his crimes, entered into a deal with his captors and became an informant for the FBI, thus effectively signing his own death warrant. Fratiano's lifestory is told in the book *The Last Mafioso*, in which a description of the video machine first appears.

Little is known of the machine latterly, until 1979 when a company was formed in New Jersey to promote the enterprise, called Video Turf Inc. Video Turf Inc. was itself a subsidiary of another company which, in turn, became a subsidiary of a stable of stocks, operating under the name of Camseal Inc. The shares in this operation were being marketed by a small American brokerage called Marsan Securities Co. Inc., based in New York. Marsan Securities had been bought by Marsan Capital Corporation in February 1982, and the brokerage continued to make markets in various stocks until it ceased trading in October 1983.

Also in 1982 Marsan Securities became the subject of an investigation by the FBI to ascertain whether insider information had been used in certain transactions, and in the course of the investigation the FBI discovered that one of the major shareholders of Marsan Capital Corporation was one Robert Margolies. Robert Margolies had a history of involvement in LCN activities and had been identified as being a close business associate of, and courier for, one Anthony Salerno, a name which had become synonymous with all aspects of organised criminal activity. Salerno had been named as a member of the Genovese family by Joseph Valachi in his evidence to a Congressional Committee on Organised Crime as far back as 1963, and Salerno has subsequently been identified on numerous occasions in the New York press as a notorious member of LCN, even as late as 1985.

Another of the principals behind both Camseal and Marsan Securities was none other than one Thomas F. Quinn, previously disbarred lawyer and latterly, investment advisor.

In or before August 1983 Quinn had entered into negotiations with the Ravendale Group to bring to market a share called Video Turf Inc., indeed the negotiations were so advanced that a draft prospectus for the sale of the stock had been prepared. On 23 October 1983, of the 2 million shares issued for cash of the Ravendale Group of companies, a Mr Abraham Margolies was shown, in a document issued by Mr Singh of the Ravendale Group, as owning 500,000 shares.

It may come as something of a surprise to realise that Mr Abraham Margolies is in fact the brother of Mr Robert Margolies and, according to the same FBI report which identified Robert's activities, Abraham Margolies was also identified as being a financial associate of Anthony Salerno, and, in addition, was shown as being financed in his business activities by one Matthew Ianiello, who had been convicted of criminal contempt in 1971 for failing to tell the truth to a Grand Jury investigating allegations of police corruption in New York. On his own admission, in 1975, Abraham Margolies stated that he had known Ianiello for ten years and in 1977, the Chief of Organised Crime Investigation and Analysis Section of the New York Police Department, named Abraham Margolies as an individual who was 'part of the unique set-up of fronts utilised by Matthew Ianiello'. Ianiello was a publicly associated member of the Genovese family and on 30 December 1985, he was convicted along with others of racketeering, conspiracy to racketeer and fraud offences in New York.

All these facts have a degree of relevance when it is known that prior to 5 December 1984, Abraham Margolies was shown as being the holder of 5.8% of the share capital of Video Turf Inc. Video Turf Inc. had become something of a hot potato by the latter part of 1984 and the Ravendale Group abandoned its attempts to float the issue publicly. This was not, however, the end of the matter. Entrepreneurs of the kidney of Thomas F. Quinn are not so easily discouraged and hey presto! lo and behold, along came a new company entitled Derby Vision plc, which was the new parent company of the now discredited Video Turf Inc. The directors were shown enjoying the unlikely names of Mr Hy Ochberg and Mr Carl Porto.

Reading the prospectus for Derby Vision plc one might have been forgiven for believing that these gentlemen were a different breed, and had a background of solid financial probity. Mr Ochberg for instance was described as having a 'diversified background in corporate finance and securities dealing'. In 1980, Mr Ochberg pleaded guilty to two charges of violating securities laws in California following an investigation into currency investment fraud. In any event, Derby Vision plc showed Mr Ochberg holding 5.8% of the shareholding, Mr Porto held 5.7% and Abraham Margolies held 5.8%.

In December 1984, following the publication of a prospectus, Derby Vision plc was finally, and belatedly, brought to market by Neil Bruckman, marketed through that well-known business house, Chartwell Securities AG. In January 1985, Chartwell was sending unsolicited brochures extolling the virtues of Derby Vision, together with a package of press releases covering the activities of AC Scotland plc to prospective punters in Germany and Switzerland and the salesmen redoubled their efforts in an attempt to keep up with the demand for these shares.

Now, you might well ask yourself, 'How can these people sell this junk? Surely prospective investors are going to realise that it is a complete hype and tell them where to get off?' Under normal circumstances, you might well be right, but enter Mr Arnold Kimmes, long time friend, associate and business partner of Mr Abraham Margolies and Mr Thomas F. Quinn.

In a report of the Organised Crime Control Commission of California in 1978, the Attorney General of California identified Arnold Kimmes as a person who was directly linked to organised criminal activities in California. It was stated that Kimmes had three convictions for criminal activities and had served periods of imprisonment for fraud.

Kimmes, known to one and all as 'Charlie' became the office

manager and sales force leader of Chartwell Securities AG in Zug. This man had been trained in all the various techniques of separating the mug from his money and he knew all the motivations which will inspire a sales force. One method was for Charlie to pin $500 to the office wall, for the leading salesman of the day to collect at the end of business. Another method was for the salesman to stand on the table top, shouting down the phone to the prospective client, so that he was literally 'talking down to him'. Whatever the method involved, investors in Germany and Switzerland did not apparently need much persuading. The value of the shares rose dramatically, which is hardly surprising, considering Trafalgar was the only company making a market in the share.

What other shares did Trafalgar Capital (UK) offer to its luckless clients? Corrosion Research and Technology plc was brought to market, offering a coating which it was claimed would prevent corrosion. Of the sums raised by Trafalgar in the offering, 34% were retained by the company as expenses. Another offering was London European Airways plc which with its one Viscount aircraft operated a flight between Luton airport and Amsterdam. Even the OTC industry in the UK, not normally noted for its reticence concerning the activities of its participants, noted the spiralling increase in the value of LEA shares and warned potential investors in an editorial entitled *What goes up must come down*.

In the summer of 1985, police in West Germany and Switzerland, alarmed by the enormous volume of complaints being received from luckless clients who found that they could not sell their holdings despite the buoyant prices being reported, raided the offices of Chartwell on the Continent and closed them down. Trafalgar issued a statement disassociating themselves from the activities of the now defunct operation, particularly after it was discovered that the sales operation had sold more shares than really existed. They promised to examine all claims made by investors who allegedly held contract notes for the purchase of shares which they had never received.

In reality, the staff of Trafalgar were themselves getting ready to run. Their administrative offices in Aldershot, staffed by a team of temporary accountants, were desperately trying to reconcile the mass of client records. They were required to computerise all the records, a daunting task when the volume of dealing was considered. One accountant pointed out to one of the managers that the company was losing small fortunes in failing properly to debit the clients for the costs of

PSST. WANNA BUY A SHARE?

converting the foreign currencies which were being banked and subsequently converted into sterling or dollars. He was told that it was just another service which Trafalgar offered their clients and that he should mind his own business. This man, concerned at what he could see happening around him, left the job immediately and informed the police.

Another accountant had diligently stayed at his desk, reconciling the huge inflow of cash and the sale of the securities. His enquiries revealed that the company was hopelessly insolvent. In keeping with the ethics of his profession, he immediately demanded an interview with the managers in order properly to appraise them of the situation, believing it to be his duty to the company and its potential creditors. Present at the meeting was a Mr Thomas F. Quinn who, when confronted with the accountant's report and his suggestion that the company should urgently review its financial position, turned to the rest of the managers present and said:

'Who is this guy, I'll break his f...ing legs.'

Not long after this edifying exercise in financial management and ethical business dealings, Trafalgar Capital (UK) Ltd ceased to trade. The Association of Stock and Share Dealers suspended Trafalgar from membership of their association on 24 September 1985, which immediately removed their right to trade securities. Neil Bruckman, virtually a prisoner in his own offices, besieged by private detectives and television reporters, simply disappeared. He returned to America, where he was promptly arrested by the FBI following a lengthy investigation into the affairs of another of his interests. Bruckman is, at the time of writing, on bail for offences relating to these enquiries.

The company was placed into Official Receivership and, on 4 October 1985, Christopher Morris, an accountant employed by Touche Ross, was appointed as provisional liquidator. The first duty of a liquidator of a company is to ascertain what debts are owed to the company and what debts are owed by the company. At the first meeting of creditors where any realistic figures were available, in the early summer of 1986, Mr Morris was able to report that an estimate of Trafalgar's turnover revealed a figure of £38–43 million. In addition, it was estimated that the company's deficit was in the region of £8.2 million and that the liquidator had managed to identify assets of merely £1 million. Mr Bruckman was represented at the meeting by a solicitor who admitted that his client was then in the United States, facing charges of fraud. Through his solicitor, Bruckman promised to provide full co-operation in the liquidation, although quite how this co-operation was to be achieved, no one was quite sure.

Mr Morris was able to say that he had found the Trafalgar records of business in 'a disgraceful state', all the information being stored on computer disks, which required them to be transcribed, which was an expensive procedure. It further transpired that Trafalgar's affairs were, by this time under investigation by the DPP.

A large number of share certificates were discovered on Trafalgar's premises, including London European Airways, Derby Vision, AC Scotland, First Environetics Research Resources, Corrosion Research and Technology, Integrated Business Communications, North American Bingo, OTCI and Swissoil. The vast majority of the owners of these shares cannot be identified as most of the purchasers received contract notes only. Most of them never had the share certificates registered in their names.

The one fact that emerged from the meeting with the greatest degree of clarity was that Mr Bruckman, Mr Quinn and Mr Kimmes were not going to attend that or any other meeting, if they could help it.

I wonder why not?

What does emerge from this analysis is the fact that Trafalgar Capital (UK) Ltd was nothing more than a vehicle to market spurious securities, in many cases of companies the sole beneficiaries of which were mainstream participants in American organised crime. They were able to operate because of the laxity of the British regulatory requirements and because of the complete lack of interest in their activities expressed by the British regulatory authorities despite repeated warnings.

If you feel that this statement is a trifle harsh, consider this. Most of the information revealed in this chapter has been public knowledge for some years. It was reported, in the main, by a great personal friend of mine, the writer, Lorana Sullivan, whose work for the *Observer* newspaper has singled her out as a highly informed financial journalist. Over the previous three years, Miss Sullivan has published in excess of twenty-four articles in the *Observer*, warning the British public of the activities of Mr Bruckman, Mr Margolies and their associates. She has consistently warned the Department of Trade and Industry of the dangers involved in the marketing of various shares, including Derby Vision plc and others. She has attempted to provide evidence to the DTI to enable them to exercise their statutory powers to investigate the affairs of Trafalgar Capital (UK) Ltd and other, similar companies.

Throughout this period, her efforts have been ignored and she herself has been looked upon as nothing more than a nuisance. At the same time, her newspaper has been sued for libel by Abraham Margolies and by the Ravendale Group of Companies. Believing in the validity of her investigations Miss Sullivan and the *Observer* have defended these actions and at the time of writing have forced Margolies to withdraw his action. Latterly, the action by the Ravendale Group of companies has been discontinued, they having failed to pay into court the requisite security for costs. The whole affair has had all the hallmarks of the professional legal cynicism, previously identified by Melvyn Marckus and it is to the credit of the *Observer* and Lorana Sullivan that they stuck by their story and defended the action, with a resoundingly successful outcome.

The Department of Trade and Industry cannot claim to have been ignorant of the activities of Bruckman and his associates. On the contrary, they have been very well aware of the goings-on at Trafalgar Capital (UK) Ltd and associated companies for a long time. As in so many other cases, they have chosen to turn their face away from the truth and ignore palpable acts of wrong-doing, to the detriment of hundreds, perhaps thousands, of investors and of the good name of the City of London. At all times, they possessed the power to investigate Bruckman, to demand access to the books and records of his company and to prevent any further abuses of our laws. Why they failed to accept this responsibility will always remain a mystery.

Lest they should ever be tempted to claim a degree of ignorance of the facts as set out here, bear this in mind. The accountant who was threatened with grievous bodily harm by Quinn went to the police with his information. He told them that he believed that the company for which he worked was insolvent and that he had brought this fact to the attention of the managers. He produced documentary evidence to prove the vast amounts of money being invested in the shares marketed by the company and the losses being sustained by the clients. His evidence was dynamite and in compliance with instructions, he was immediately referred to the Department of Trade and Industry which, at that time was the only department with the necessary authority to conduct an examination of the company's affairs without delay. The accountant attended a meeting with officers of the DTI the same afternoon. He was ignored and no action was taken. A few weeks later, Bruckman had disappeared and the true state of affairs was revealed.

Since that time, the DPP has instructed that an investigation be conducted into the affairs of the company. Whatever the outcome, it is unlikely that Bruckman will ever be extradited to stand trial in this country for any alleged offences, even if he can ever be successfully apprehended.

In fairness to Bruckman, I wouldn't want you to think that no one made any profit from share dealings through Trafalgar Capital (UK) Ltd, because that would not be true. In March 1985 one woman alone made £22,000 dealing in the shares of AC Scotland plc.

Her name? Mrs Paula Bruckman. As a well-known satirical magazine has a tendency to say:

'I wonder if by any chance they are related?'

Trafalgar Capital (UK) Ltd was by no means the only company offering unusual and esoteric stocks for sale to potential customers in the UK and on the Continent, and Neil Bruckman was not the only market maker. Many British investors report having received a string of unsolicited telephone calls from companies operating from Amsterdam, with Canadian connections. Many of these companies are associated with Canadian fraudsmen and they offer shares in small, start-up situations, which have little or no chance of succeeding.

The most infamous company, which was closed down by the Dutch police early in 1986 was called Capital Venture Consultants, which was set up in 1980 under the name of Financial Planning Services. Another company which became the subject of police investigations, Tower Securities of Amsterdam, was closed after a raid in 1986.

The largest marketing operation recently active in Amsterdam was First Commerce Securities which marketed a newsletter called *Investors Alert*. Its owners were a matter of conjecture as the company refused to identify them. What is known however is that a regular visitor to First Commerce Securities offices was one Irving Kott, who so impressed a judge in Canada in 1976 with his entrepreneurial flair for managing other people's money, that he fined him $500,000 for a securities fraud. Mr Kott's regular visits to the company with information concerning its most prolifically traded share, Devoe-Holbein International, may simply have been nothing more than an excuse to see his son, Michael, who worked there as a telephone salesman, using a variety of different names, including Michael Evans.

The crackdown by police in Holland may have plugged a leak there but that doesn't mean that the salesmen will become discouraged. Take Bailey McMahon of Dublin, for instance, who have been pushing some exotic American offerings to investors in the UK by telephone.

An affiliate of J. B. Power Securities of Denver, Colorado, a company registered with the SEC, sounds reassuring enough but J. B. Power has been refused permission to trade in Iowa and its owner, Gene Olsen, has been dealt with by the National Association of Securities Dealers in America on a number of occasions, for breach of their trading regulations.

As a conclusion to this chapter, I want to examine another aspect of OTC trading which, I believe poses a problem for the regulators of the future. One of the big attractions for subscribers to OTC shares is the existence of the Business Expansion Scheme, which permits a subscriber to the shares of a newly floated company to claim relief at whatever rate the claimant pays tax for a maximum of £40,000 worth of investment.

The strings attached are not onerous. The main requirement, apart from the obvious need for UK tax status is that the subscriber must hold the shares for a minimum period of five years before he can dispose of them. This requirement exists for two reasons. Firstly, it means that the subscriber will be a bona-fide investor, and not merely a stock speculator. Any person who is prepared to tie up his capital for five years must, by definition, be a serious investor. Secondly, it means that the subscriber cannot simply use the scheme to obtain tax relief, which may be substantial, thereafter repossessing his capital by selling the shares.

The scheme works in this way.

The promoters of the shares in a new company will have ascertained from the Inland Revenue that the scheme is one for which BES relief will be available and the IR have granted the degree of recognition. A subscriber to the share will be allotted his quota and the call price of the shares paid up. When the price has been paid in full, the share registrar of the company informs the Commissioners of the Inland Revenue of the names of the subscribers and how much each person has paid for his shares. The Inland Revenue will then supply to the share registrar a series of certificates acknowledging the information, and the share registrar will, in turn, forward each certificate to each subscriber.

The subscriber may then make his claim for the relief allowed, by forwarding the certificate to the tax authorities when he submits his next tax form. Its effect is to reduce the investment income surcharge and can be very valuable in the hands of a wealthy investor. The receipt, by the tax authorities, of the certificate is the proof that the investor has paid up the sums upon which the relief is claimed, and the requisite amount of relief is usually granted.

If the subscriber should sell his shareholding within the next five years, the sale will be recorded by the share registrar, who will be required to note the change of ownership of the share and he will inform the Inland Revenue that the change of ownership has taken place. In any event, the person making the sale will have informed the Inland Revenue that he has sold the shares before the end of the five-year period, and will expect to be reassessed for tax, following his loss of BES relief.

That's the theory, anyway!

What happens, however, to a security which is marketed almost exclusively abroad, but for some reason enjoys BES status? A practice revealed by one of the accountants employed by Trafalgar Capital (UK) Ltd was that of allotting subscription rights to employees of the firm when the shares were brought to market. A number of the salesmen were shown as being allocated shares at par, or even below par. Bear in mind that many employees of companies like Trafalgar are employed on a 'consultancy' basis, which means, in effect, that they are responsible for managing their personal tax liabilities. These 'consultants' are, in many cases, paid very little by way of salary and are expected to earn their income from the commissions paid to them from the proceeds of their telephone sales. In many cases, their earnings from commission are quite substantial, which provides a great incentive for aggressive marketing.

Having been shown as a subscriber to the shares when they are first brought to market, the 'consultant' can then make his claim for BES relief should he so wish.

In the after-market, the sales of the shares are pursued vigorously and the price of the shares can rise steeply. The dramatic price rise of the shares represents a profitable opportunity for the salesman and the shares allocated to him are sold at an immense profit, in some cases representing a three or four hundred per cent increase. If the salesman has inadvertently failed to inform the Inland Revenue that he has sold the shares, and it is not hard to understand how a busy 'consultant' might easily overlook this task, how would the Inland Revenue know that the shares had been sold? The vast majority of foreign customers never received share certificates from Trafalgar Capital (UK) Ltd, so their shareholding would never have been recorded by the share registrar. The share registrar would not know that the 'consultant' had parted with his shares, because the shareholder owes no duty to the share registrar to inform him of his change of ownership. This is done when the registrar receives the original certificate after the sale, and issues a new one. If the transaction is never reported, how is he to know, and where is the independent source of corroboration for the Inland Revenue, without this information?

The practice of inviting salesmen to take up part of a new subscription is widespread in certain OTC stocks; one salesman told me that it was looked upon as a 'little perk', although he strenuously denied any attempt to cheat the tax man.

The Business Expansion Scheme has opened up a number of doors to investors, some of which, it must be said, represent a very valuable addition to their portfolio. It is well to bear in mind, however, that many of the schemes have undoubtedly been formed to take advantage of the atmosphere of de-regulation which is current in capital markets, and their proposals require very careful consideration by prospective investors. They are getting your money for five years, if you care to take advantage of BES relief, and there is no guarantee that they are going to be around at the end of that time. You will have picked up a degree of relief from the tax man, but you may well have lost your entire investment.

Another method of marketing BES schemes is to incorporate them into a fund whereby a group of companies are pooled together and new investors are invited to take up a percentage of the shares on offer, thus 'spreading' the risk factor of their investment. These BES funds are being considered for the growing market which it is contemplated will emerge after Big Bang. Representations have been made to the DTI by promoters of such schemes, to allow them to advertise their funds in future. At present such schemes cannot be advertised, although if they are considered suitable for authorisation, certain amendments will be necessary to the Financial Services Bill to allow their inclusion once the Act receives Royal assent.

BES schemes tend to come to the surface towards the end of the financial year, offering the investor a chance to grab some cheap tax relief, fairly quickly. Some of these offerings tend however to be of benefit only to the promoters, at the expense of the investor. One of the techniques is to permit extremely valuable re-purchase options to the company making the market in the share or to the founding directors. Issuing expenses can be very high, creating profit for the market makers. As many of these companies are being marketed by one market maker, the costs to the market maker can be whatever he wants them to be. The products on offer are new and in many cases represent an untried area of the market. Profit projections, which are illegal in America, can sometimes only claim to exist in the imagination of the person responsible for their creation.

The most revealing part of the prospectus for any company, but particularly start-up ventures, is the page which deals with the risk elements involved. These should be read and re-read with considerable care, because it's no good complaining later when the company collapses in just such a manner implied in its prospectus.

It is interesting to note that very few people who invested in Derby Vision plc ever saw a prospectus for the share. Had they done so and realised the implications of its risk factors, I doubt whether even the most gullible would have parted with their money. They went to great lengths to tell the reader that they were going to experience difficulties with this product, referring to the likelihood of 'unforeseen technical problems' and 'no guarantee of increased customer response'. They told them that other companies might build similar competing machines and referred to possible changes in the gaming laws of potential customer countries which would render the machine illegal. They even told the reader that the whole business depended on the prompt repayment of existing debts, but the crowning glory in double-speak and the most obvious 'rip-off' warning came in the last paragraph. It said:

'Trafalgar Capital (UK) Ltd will endeavour to make a market in the Ordinary shares of Derby Vision on an over-the-counter basis. There can be no guarantee that such a market will be developed or maintained. Investors may accordingly not be able to realise their investment.'

How right they were.

CHAPTER SEVEN
A Tiger By The Tail

Quinquireme of Nineveh from distant Ophir,
Rowing home to haven in sunny Palestine,
With a cargo of ivory, and apes and peacocks,
Sandalwood, cedarwood and sweet white wine.

Stately Spanish galleon coming from the Isthmus
Dipping through the Tropics by the palm green shores,
With a cargo of diamonds, emeralds, amethysts,
Topazes, and cinnamon and gold moidores.

Dirty British coaster with a salt-caked smoke stack,
Butting through the Channel in the mad March days,
With a cargo of Tyne coal, road rail, pig lead,
Firewood, iron-ware and cheap tin trays.

I trust John Masefield would forgive me for quoting in full his poem 'Cargoes' in a book which purports to deal with financial fraud. As an introduction to the study of commodities and commodity futures, the poem cannot be bettered, capturing, as it does so well, the diverse images of the transport of basic raw materials from country to country, a practice as old as time, but one on which so much of the quality of our life depends.

Since man first learned how to sail beyond the sight of his own coastline, returning home with strange and wonderful souvenirs of his travels, markets have developed to exploit the existence of natural products unavailable to the home market. Many of the early advances in world navigation were brought about by men, brave to the point of foolhardiness, who were sponsored by merchant princes to find the legendary Kingdom of Gold. Many did not make it and others returned home bringing items of a more mundane nature but which nevertheless became valuable commodities. Imagine the reaction of his backers when Sir Walter Raleigh introduced them to the potato.

Europe rapidly adapted its tastes to accommodate the steady influx of more and more foreign raw materials and up until the sixteenth century, Antwerp was the leading commodity port in Europe.

With the growing expansion of the British Empire however, the Pool of London began to play an ever more decisive role in the development of London as the leading international commodity centre. Ships from all over the known world would tie up alongside the wharves of the City of London to discharge their cargoes and they would be carried by mule and donkey cart into the City to the warehouses of the merchants and their customers. Early trading was done in the area which surrounded the Royal Exchange and the traditional route to the Exchange lay through the narrow streets and lanes that throng the banks of the Thames. Two of the most famous were Mark Lane and Mincing Lane, which run northwards, from Eastcheap, parallel to each other, and these two street names are synonymous today with the centre of the London commodity trading community.

In 1811, in an attempt to bring a greater degree of orderly dealing to the large quantities of Caribbean products such as sugar and molasses being traded, the London Commercial Sale Rooms were opened in Mincing Lane and from these early beginnings grew the highly complex marketing concept which today is housed in and around the building which lies between Mark Lane and Mincing Lane, called, appropriately, Plantation House.

The great problem in being a merchant with your raw materials needing to be transported thousands of miles is the general degree of uncertainty involved. In the days before modern methods of communication, the merchant had no means of knowing the condition of his commodity, prior to its arrival. It could be in prime condition and very plentiful, which would mean that his competitors would also be able to supply the same quality and volume and this would mean a reduction in the price at market. Conversely, it could be in very poor quality and in very short supply, which would mean a hike in the market price. His cargo might not even arrive at all because of the dangers inherent in the long sea voyage. All these factors contributed to the uncertainty of the merchant's ultimate profitability.

The same factors influenced the users of the raw materials whose businesses had developed from the exploitation of the newly available raw products. Shortness of supply would mean higher prices, which could affect the production costs, thus reducing profitability. Extreme shortage in the market could mean no raw material with which to work at all, thus putting the workers out on the streets and closing the business altogether.

Perhaps not surprisingly, these factors influenced the growers of the natural raw materials in exactly the same way and slowly the persons concerned at all stages of the contractual chain began to search for a way to minimise this degree of uncertainty, in order to bring stability to the price structures within the market and thus increase the efficiency of the markets themselves.

The basis for this stabilising effect is what has become known as the 'futures contract'. Simply stated, it is a contract to buy or sell a specific amount of a specific commodity of a specific quality at a specific price, for delivery at a specific date in the future. It can be seen immediately that the underlying principle of a futures contract is the very specific nature of its contents. The aim of the contract is to produce stability and harmony between natural market co-participants and therefore the contract is written in very carefully defined terms, in order to minimise the risk of misunderstanding or misinterpretation. It works in this way.

During a period of good harvests, the producers of raw materials will produce more than they can sell profitably. During a period of bad harvests, the converse will apply. The end price of raw materials will therefore behave in one of three ways. It will go up, it will go down or, rarely, it will stay the same. It is in the interests of market participants to be able to predict the price of their raw materials as far in advance as possible, as this will assist them to service their financial position, should they need to borrow funds to pay for future deliveries, or lend money against the certainty of payment at a prescribed date in the future.

One of the necessities of such an agreement therefore is a legally binding contract which is capable of enforcement anywhere in the world. Futures contracts are enforceable and are bound by the laws of a country which is agreed by both parties to the contract prior to its completion. Perhaps not surprisingly, many, if not most, futures contracts are bound by English law and as such enjoy a degree of certainty which they might not otherwise enjoy under other jurisdictions.

Let us assume that Mr X is a coffee grower in Brazil and Mr Y is a coffee roaster and grinder in England. (This example is going to be simplified in the extreme, using figures which bear no resemblance to reality, in an attempt to describe a complex concept in simple terms.)

X knows that in order to be profitable in the year ahead, he must be able to sell his crop at a minimum price of £100 per ton. His crop is due to be harvested in nine months' time, but at the moment, he has no means of knowing whether he can expect a good, bad or indifferent harvest. Y, on the other hand, knows that he must pay no more than £100 per ton for his coffee beans, if he is to maintain his profitability in the year ahead.

Both X and Y have cash-flow requirements and they have financial commitments to their backers. They need to be able to guarantee their respective sales and purchases for the coming year, without having recourse to any knowledge of the quality or quantity of the future crop.

Having done business together in the past, X and Y get together and discuss the forthcoming year and their individual requirements. Y agrees to buy 100 tons of coffee of a specific quality for delivery to his warehouse in England in twelve months' time, and he agrees to pay a price of £100 per ton.

X is now in the happy position of having sold his crop at the right price and Y is similarly pleased in having taken care of his annual requirements at a price which he can afford. Both men are now committed to a legally binding futures contract. A failure on X's part to deliver the coffee, or a failure on Y's part to take delivery will be settled in court.

However, this scenario contains a series of drawbacks which could produce onerous consequences. Suppose the harvest is bad and the coffee crop in short supply. X is committed to supply the coffee, and if he cannot grow sufficient to deliver his agreed amount, he will have to buy other coffee to make up the balance of the delivery. This will cost him more money than he anticipated and will eat up his profits.

In the event that the harvest is a record one, the price of coffee will drop and Y will find himself committed to take delivery of 100 tons of coffee for which he will be required to pay £100 per ton, when he could simply buy what he needs on the spot market at £50 per ton. Either market condition could have loss-making consequences for the participants, which would undo the primary purpose of the futures contract of providing price stability and market efficiency.

Both men will therefore enter into another form of contract, in order to hedge their exposure to unexpected or unforeseen price fluctuations which could reduce their profits. The aim of this procedure is not to speculate for profit, but to provide a hedge against loss, thus locking in the profit anticipated. I intend to separate the two contracts by referring to one as a physical contract and the other as a speculative contract. The system works in this way.

At the same time as X agrees to sell 100 tons of coffee at £100 a ton, which is his physical contract, he instructs his broker to purchase a speculative contract of the same coffee for delivery on the same date at £100 per ton. In other words he has balanced his physical contract with an equal and opposite spec. contract. Y will do the same, entering into an opposite contract from his physical contract, at the same price. Whatever happens from now on, both men are locked in to the anticipated profit they hope to make. If the price of coffee goes up, X, who will lose the increased profit on his physical contract, makes it up by realising the profit on his spec. contract. If the price of coffee goes down, Y will lose the increased profit on his physical contract but will balance himself by making it up on his spec. contract.

It is but a short step from the description of the hedging procedure for a speculator to realise that he could participate in the market, without the need to be a physical producer or user. The speculator simply enters into a speculative contract for future delivery, without ever intending to take delivery. His intention is to close his contract before the delivery date, hopefully at a profit. It is now generally accepted that approximately 70% of all participants in futures transactions on the markets of the world, are speculators. The markets still play a vital role in determining the world price structures of physical commodities, but in the main the bulk of the transactions take place between people selling that which they do not own to other people, who buy that which they do not want.

There is another type of contract which I want to describe, which will become the subject of much discussion later. This is the 'option' contract.

I described how the futures contract imposed upon the participants an obligation to deliver or take delivery of the relevant commodity, while the contract remained open. Another method which has been developed for market participants is the option contract, which, simply stated, confers the right to buy or sell a specific commodity at a future date. The system works like this.

Let us assume that I have formed the opinion that the price of coffee is going to rise dramatically in six months' time, when the news of a bad harvest becomes public. I wish to participate in this potentially profit-able price increase, but I have insufficient funds to be able to buy an immediate futures contract now or, alternatively, I do not want to expose myself financially to an immediate, outright futures contract. At the same time, I wish to be able to take advantage of the price rise should it occur.

The way for me to do this is to find someone in the market who will grant me the right to buy coffee at £100 per ton in six months' time. At this stage I haven't bought any coffee and I haven't got a futures contract, as such. What I have purchased is the right to be able to go to the man who sold me the option in six months' time and demand that he sell me coffee at £100 per ton, at which time I shall have to enter into the commensurate contract agreement. If coffee is trading at £150 per ton in six months' time, then it will be in my interests to exercise my option. If coffee is trading at £50 per ton, however, it will not.

In return for granting me the option, the grantor requires a small sum of money, known as a premium, to be deposited with a third party, which will be credited to his account, upon deposit, although he will not be able to claim it until the date and time agreed between us for the expiry of the option. If I decide to exercise my option then I shall be required to pay up the balance of the contract price, taking the deposited premium into account. If I decide to abandon my option, then the premium I have deposited becomes the property of the grantor.

Options can be granted to buy, known as call options, or to sell, known as put options. The premium is a considerably smaller sum than is normally required in other forms of trading and for this reason they are very attractive to small speculators, giving them access to the market in circumstances where they might otherwise be denied because of lack of funds.

Commodity futures are traded by a method known as 'open outcry'. To watch a futures market floor at work when the price is moving rapidly is an unforgettable experience. The traders will be shouting them-selves hoarse trying to get their bids for prices heard. They gesticulate wildly with their hands, each gesture carrying a different meaning to the initiated and indicating whether they are buying or selling. Deals are completed between traders in split seconds, either side knowing they have entered into a binding contract, the proof of that contract being a scrap of paper on which the terms of the deal agreed are written and lodged with the floor 'chairman' at the end of trading.

Let us assume that I have decided to become a prospective specu-lator in coffee, having read a lot about the enormous profits to be made in the coffee market. My first job is to find a broker who will operate my account.

This part of the job is not difficult. I simply go and buy any of the many investment magazines which throng the shelves of my news-agent. Having found a broker, he will agree to conduct such trading as I instruct, and for this service I will be charged a commission fee. Commission is charged on both sides of the contract, for buying and selling, and it is known as 'round-turn commission'. Commission rates are a matter for negotiation between client and broker, but generally the broker will have a standard commission rate for each type of commodity and he will expect me to be prepared to accept these rates.

Next, it will be necessary for me to deposit a sum of money with my broker, which will be sufficient for him to be able to commence buying my coffee contract. This sum of money is called 'margin deposit' and no broker will deal for a client without such a deposit first being made.

When the broker buys my coffee contract, he may be buying many other contracts at the same time. Commodity brokers traditionally act as principals in the transaction and are legally responsible for settling the contract price at the market themselves. If my broker is not satisfied that there are sufficient funds in my account to meet my financial commitments for my contract, he will not deal for me, because he will be laying himself open to the risk of having to settle the contract, should I default in payment.

Having deposited £2000 therefore with my broker, I instruct him to buy ten lots of coffee. Let us assume for the purposes of this illustration that coffee is trading at £400 per ton. Commodities are traded in lot sizes and one lot of coffee is five tons, so the contract price of one lot is £2000. Ten lots therefore will cost me £20,000, but I have only deposited £2000 with my broker.

This is the first lesson about commodity trading and the first great hurdle to be overcome in understanding its problems. Speculative commodity transactions are dealt with on 'margin', which means that only a small percentage of the total contract price is paid, usually about 10%, in fact. This means that relatively large numbers of lots can be purchased for relatively small sums of money, a practice known as 'gearing'.

Using this principle, my broker will purchase my ten lots of coffee, for which I shall be charged £2000. The brokers I have chosen are full members of the London Commodity Exchange, which means that they are permitted to trade directly on the floor of the exchange. In exchange parlance, they have a 'seat' on the floor.

The contract exists between the broker house which has bought the contract and the broker house which has sold the contract and it is their names which will appear on the contract note supplied to each other. My broker may, in the course of that day's trading, enter into many contracts to buy coffee for a large number of his clients. At the end of the trading day, the contract which is drawn up will identify my broker having purchased however many contracts of coffee he has bought, but it will be his responsibility to allocate the contracts back in his office to the accounts of his individual clients.

Unlike the Stock Exchange, commodity contracts are cleared daily and there is no account period within which to settle the amount owed. Back in the office, the broker will draw up a contract note which will exist between his company and me. On it will appear the details of my purchase, showing the amount of coffee bought, the price paid and the commission charged to me.

For the purposes of this illustration I have been debited £2000 in my account with the firm, and, in addition, the company have debited their commission to my account. This is the next hurdle of understanding to be overcome. Brokers deduct their commission from the sums available in the account of the client after every transaction. This can lead to great abuses.

The broker's next task is to watch the market price of coffee very carefully because in order to keep my account 'open' the broker will need to satisfy himself that the contract value, plus whatever sums remain deposited in my account, will be sufficient for him to settle the contract without loss to himself, should the need arise. My contract price was £400 per ton. At the end of trading on the following day, following an announcement of a possible coffee blight in Brazil, reacting to this rumour, coffee increases in price to £410 per ton. My contract is no longer worth £20,000 but £20,500 and I have already made £500 profit. Conversely however, instead of news of a blight, the next day another announcement of a possible record harvest is made, and the market goes down to £390 per ton. My contract is now worth £19,500 and if the contract were closed, my original deposit of £2000 would now be £500 down, leaving me with £1500. Let us assume that the rumours of the harvest are very strong and there is every likelihood that the crop is going to be a substantial one. The price plummets and by the next day coffee is trading at £360 per ton. My contract now is worth £18,000, which is a loss of £2000. If the broker were forced to close the contract now, my entire deposit would be wiped out and the broker would be out of pocket because there would not be sufficient funds to meet the contract price and pay his commission. In order therefore for my contract to remain 'open', the broker has a right to call me and demand that I deposit more money with him to make up the balance in my account. This is known as a 'margin call' and such calls will be made daily to keep the account open, all the time the price is falling. The amount of margin required will be that which, taken together with the contract value, plus the commission owed, will enable the broker to close the contract at no loss to himself.

Brokers reserve the right to close contracts at any time to protect themselves, if there is insufficient money in the account to keep the contract open. The degree of gearing can therefore radically affect the individual client's account and it explains why, in so many cases, private clients have found themselves being 'wiped out' of the market so quickly, without any suggestion of fraud or malpractice. Conversely, if the price is going the way in which the client predicted, then at the close of trading on each day, the amount of profit accruing to his account is credited to him. This notional profit can be used to purchase more contracts without any more money being deposited, and if the price keeps going the right way, can produce ever greater degrees of profitability. This practice is known as 'pyramiding' and in the wrong hands, it can be a very costly exercise if the price turns against the client. There can be no doubt however that to be a client trading on margin when the market is going steadily in the right direction, can be a very pleasant experience. So why is it that 80% of all speculators in commodities lose their money?

Up to now, I have described the markets in terms of their traditional, agricultural role. In many ways, the older commodity markets are a legacy of our Imperial past and have only been resorted to by speculators relatively recently, in historical terms. The speculator, it is said, brings a greater degree of liquidity to the market, taking a risk in the hope of profit and thus enabling the physical user to hedge his position. The old agricultural commodities however are being super-seded by new contracts, more in line with modern needs, and which bring a greater degree of flexibility to the market. Within the next few years, the new contracts will have taken over the lion's share of the spec. market, leaving the traditional commodity contracts to the physical producers and users.

From now on therefore I intend to cease talking about 'commodities' and refer instead to the rapidly developing market in 'futures', as it is in this area that by far the greatest degree of financial interest will be generated.

Financial markets can no longer consider themselves to be simply a 'home country' based facility. Without competition between market participants, monopolies have a tendency to be created. Markets wishing to attract new customers to their range of financial services must create new ways of providing efficient economic services in order to remain profitable. So what are these new facilities and how do they work?

Hedging is an efficient way to minimise risk in financial contracts. One of the biggest risks faced by businessmen who trade on international terms is the fluctuation of the value of foreign currencies compared with his own. A rapid depreciation of his home currency can occur very quickly, as we all know, and have catastrophic effects upon his exposure to foreign exchange requirements.

Imagine a businessman who imports heavy machinery from America. He will be required to settle his accounts with his US suppliers in dollars, as they are unlikely to want to be paid in sterling, but he has no means of knowing how much those dollars are going to cost him. He can now enter into a financial futures contract at a price which he can identify, for the delivery of dollars at a specified date in the future. He has hedged his exposure to unforeseen fluctuations in the value of the pound against the dollar.

These contracts in financial futures are merely one aspect of the developments in futures markets designed to bring a greater degree of efficiency to international financial dealings. Another factor which can have a marked effect on prices are interest rates. Fluctuations in the value of interest rates have an immediate knock-on effect in many other areas and these fluctuations can be caused by many different influences. Lenders and borrowers can be radically affected by a turn round in interest rates and will now make use of those contracts which are available in interest rate futures, to hedge their financial exposure.

One of the most dramatic new developments lies in stock index futures. A stock index is an analysis of the movement in price of a defined range of stocks, which cover a number of types of share. The index can be drawn so as to provide a series of indicators to establish a pattern of trading within a market. In simple terms, a stock index can act as a barometer with which to judge the state of a market at any one time. If the index is down, the general trend among the individual shares which make up the index will be down. If the index is up, the same is true of the general value of the stocks.

The sort of participant who might make most use of such a facility for hedging purposes could be a portfolio manager of a large invest-ment fund or unit trust whose portfolio contained a large quantity of shares represented in the stock index. During times of a depressed stock market, the value of the shares in the portfolio will be similarly depressed and the overall worth of the portfolio will be reduced. The manager can sell certain stocks which are not performing as well as he might expect and then reinvest the proceeds in other shares. This will be an expensive operation, incurring considerable costs in dealing fees. Alternatively, he can take a view that the market generally is going to decline and can enter into a stock index futures contract, predicting the degree of decline in the market, thus balancing his loss of value in his portfolio with a gain in profit from successfully hedging his exposure on the stock index.

To add an even greater degree of versatility to these new futures, which in all cases require the participant to enter into the contract, a number of exchanges in America offer a parallel range of options in the contracts described here, thus extending the facilities available to an almost limitless degree. These services can be extended to options on individual stocks themselves thus providing market participants with the widest possible range of alternatives.

I have constantly referred to market participants or practitioners when describing these new contracts and facilities. Make no mistake, these are highly complex concepts and while being the natural exten-sion of market activity for the professional, they are not the sort of arena into which the private speculator should consider wandering alone. The markets continue to attract speculators, which is hardly surprising considering the immense degree of flexibility which these new con-tracts offer, but they are areas of high risk for the uninitiated.

As the financial revolution gears itself up, the private client is about to become the target for a highly sophisticated sales promotion campaign, designed to interest him in the new futures, and it is in this area that the greatest degree of caution will need to be exercised. Traditionally, the private client, particularly the discretionary client, has been treated with a degree of cynical callousness by market professionals which, quite frankly, boggles the imagination. This sad state of affairs has resulted directly out of the dishonest and criminal methods which some market participants have adopted literally to fleece their uninformed private clients. What has made matters worse is that these activities have not simply been restricted to the actions of a few companies but have been common knowledge throughout the market and, in many cases, a conveniently blind eye has been turned by those responsible for ensuring an honest and orderly market.

The American companies have perceived that the private client market in the UK is ripe for development, following on from the integration of financial services, and they are taking steps to ensure that they will be in the forefront of those companies attempting to attract the private spec back.

Unlike the securities dealing, it is much more difficult to define a concept of insider dealing in futures trading. The markets are very susceptible however to outside influences and attempts to manipulate or 'corner' markets have been deemed unacceptable. Market manipulation is defined as being 'the creation of an artificial price by planned action, whether by one, or a group of men' and is a prohibited practice in America. Great efforts are made by the Exchange regulators and the Commodity Futures Trading Commission to ensure that the markets are seen to be a fair place in which to do business. Perhaps the most infamous example of an attempt at market manipulation in recent years was the attempt by the Hunt brothers of Texas, together with certain Arab co-partners, to corner the world market in silver and silver futures. Their aim was eventually to own the world's supply of silver in order that they could maintain the price on the world's markets and thus ensure that their own personal fortunes were removed from the pernicious influence of inflation. That they failed in their attempt can be of little comfort to the many thousands of people who lost their jobs in the cutlery and photographic industries during a period when the world and his wife seemed to be carried away on a tidal wave of speculation.

This whole story makes fascinating reading and no one has described it better than Stephen Fay in his remarkable book *The Great Silver Bubble*. His description of the Hunts' attempt to corner the world market in silver is a classic piece of understatement which best describes the dangers inherent in market manipulation. He said:

'To attempt to corner the silver market means, I suppose, that you are greedy enough to be quite unconcerned by the disruption of a world-wide market. To wish to corner silver itself suggests a new dimension to our concept of greed.'

Market manipulation does not rely solely on the actions of the mega-rich, however. Other practices of a more mundane description are defined as manipulative. Futures markets are very finely tuned instruments and will react to heavy buying or selling orders by adjusting the price of a contract accordingly. Take the activities of a floor trader who is instructed to place a heavy series of orders for a large institutional client. Knowing that once his orders start to be filled the price will begin to climb the trader places a series of orders on the floor which he intends to mark down to himself. Having satisfactorily obtained a number of contracts at the early price, he then proceeds to buy for his client. The volume of trading forces the price up on the floor and the trader then fills the remaining contracts for his client from the contracts he bought for his own account at the commencement of trading. This practice is called 'trading in front of the client' and is prohibited in America, where it is perceived it to be an unacceptable activity.

The futures markets have been used in a similar way to securities markets to launder the dishonest assets of a number of criminal groups, using methods that are not, in themselves illegal, but which bring no credit to the operation of the market. One of the most common methods which has been widespread has been the practice of providing American tax payers with documentary evidence of futures transactions showing their having made a loss in the dealings. The system worked in the following way.

In America, a higher percentage of allowances is permitted to tax payers when computing their tax liabilities. One of the allowances that can be claimed is for losses sustained in certain financial transactions. In order to create a satisfactory proof of loss on an investment, the customer would instruct his broker to enter into a 'straddle' contract. Straddle trading is a legitimate form of strategy which has been used by market professionals to make profits from unusual price differentials in the same commodity in different forward months. The straddles entered into by the tax avoiders however were used to create a fictitious short-term loss which could be used to offset profits created elsewhere. Under the existing tax laws prior to 1981, American citizens were charged tax at 70% for short-term capital gains, long-term gains being taxed at 28%.

The technique was quite simple and could be conducted with

literally no risk to the client. The client would instruct the broker to buy and sell simultaneously the same contract in the same market for different forwards months. The loss on one leg of the contract would be balanced by the profit on the other leg. The loss-making contract enabled a wealthy speculator or a criminal with money to launder to turn a short-term loss into a tax deduction. Prior to the change in the tax laws, straddle trading was legal in America for the purposes of avoiding tax. Stephen Fay has calculated the loss to the Internal Revenue service as being in the region of $1.7 billion annually. Once the technique was outlawed in America, those concerned in conducting such trades turned their faces towards their British cousins, who had no such qualms. The British brokers with their complete lack of American-style regulatory requirements were only too pleased to be able to supply their clients with straddle contracts and the practice continued.

The clients deposited their monies with the broker of their choice and he entered into the contracts, charging the clients commission for his services. But wait, contract notes between broker and broker do not identify the name of the client when the deals are made on the market floor, and we know that the broker may conduct any number of deals in one day. At the end of the day he simply identifies those trades which he has allotted to his clients, and draws up the contract notes between himself and his client accordingly. How would any inquisitive investigator ascertain whether the trade shown on the client contract note had ever been conducted on the market at all, without being able to identify all the clients for whom the broker had dealt on the day in question? The broker would have no duty to identify his other clients, and if the contract note showed a trade having taken place, well presumably that is what would have happened.

It was all as simple and as silly as that.

The next step would be for the broker simply to make up such trading records as the client required and to send back the client's deposit, minus a generous commission deduction, in a new cheque, and the client could then claim to have come by this sum or sustained this tax-deductible loss from trading commodities on the London markets.

Now, I know that you're probably thinking, 'That's not right, you can't just go around making up paper transactions and try and pretend that they are genuine trades which took place on the market.' You would of course be right and any suspicions that such activities took place on a regular basis would have been totally unfounded.

A similarly totally unfounded suspicion would have been aroused if the existence of client records for a group of unidentifiable Arab clients from Bahrain had been discovered, in the offices of London brokers during the existence, prior to 1979, of Exchange Control Regulations. Exchange Control was perceived as being a peculiarly pernicious aspect of financial policy, which operated to prevent wealthy Britons from exporting their capital abroad. Regulations were created which disallowed any person from taking any more than a certain amount of capital out of the country and thus out of the reach of rapacious Chancellors. If however an Arab client in an oil-rich region such as Bahrain were to open a trading account with a London broker, he would be required to make margin deposits with the broker which would be placed in the company bank account to be held to the use of the client's trading account. Proof, if proof were needed, of the existence of the Bahrain client, could be supplied by a telex from Bahrain to the broker's offices in London giving the client's name and address together with details of his bank in Switzerland and the amount of money he wished to deposit by way of margin. This deposit could be seen later in the broker's bank account.

After a period of trading in certain commodities the Arab client's trade accounts and contract notes would show him to have made a profit or a loss or indeed, to have broken remarkably even, after commission deductions were made and the balance of his account would then have been returned to his numbered Swiss bank account in Zug.

If any investigator had come to the conclusion that these Arabs could have been merely fictitious identities, designed to provide a convenient smokescreen to disguise the activities of rich Britons, laundering the contents of their deposit accounts out of the reach of the Revenue, it is to be hoped that such an unworthy conclusion would have been discarded as being too fantastic to be true.

The techniques described above are but a small example of the many ways in which the futures markets can be used for disguising capital sources. One of the problems lies in the fact that futures brokers act as principals in all their contracts and had no requirement previously to identify the individual client for whom they traded. Another great problem is the fact that British markets have never insisted upon a mandatory record of price changes in the market, nor have private client contracts been the subject of time stamping.

Suffice it to say at this stage that the Americans have long recognised the need for greater protections for the private client within the speculative area of futures trading. Some commentators would say that the US regulatory controls go too far and indeed stifle speculative activity. What is clear is that the Americans have gone to great lengths to provide protections for the private client, protections which have not existed in Britain.

I have not attempted to touch upon some of the many techniques which are used by the floor traders themselves for attempting to obtain an individual benefit at the expense of their fellow traders, because these activities, by and large, are conducted at the expense of the physical traders and brokers who are shrewd enough to take care of themselves. They know what goes on and if they are prepared to put up with these practices in the market within which they deal, then they have only themselves to blame. Professionals stealing from one another on the market floor is not a new phenomenon. Stephen Fay reported a conversation with a Wall Street broker:

'On the floor, eighty per cent of the traders steal in one way or another. The temptation is so great; it's just like taking an apple from a barrel.'

The development of markets in futures has radically altered the face of the world's commodity dealings. What is still vital to the liquidity of these markets is their continued attraction to the speculator, whose cash is necessary if their efficiency is to be assured. What is interesting is the degree to which speculators in London can trade on American markets with the same ease that they can gain access to those in London. A failure by the British authorities to provide the same degree of investor protection in London will simply mean that more and more speculators will be encouraged to trade on US exchanges. A wider degree of international co-operation between market regulators may lead towards a degree of unification of inter-market dealings but a failure to provide these understandings could prove to be expensive for Britain. Michael Prest, writing in *The Times* said:

'Internationalization of these markets and of futures trading particularly could become a colossal spiv's charter. Commodity markets should not and cannot ignore their wider responsibilities.'

CHAPTER EIGHT
That Ain't Working

The truth as I see it is that the world of commodity dealing is a jungle, suitable perhaps for hunting by large and experienced animals, but one in which the small animal is at very serious risk; even though with a degree of luck he may survive. The dangers to the small investor now, it seems, for the first time entering this jungle, even in the absence of any fraud at all, are frightening. These dangers arise, at least to the small investor, from the whole state of commodity dealing in this country.

These words were spoken by His Honour, Judge Rodney Bax QC, in his speech at the end of what became known as the Miller Carneigie trial in January 1983. At the end of the case for the prosecution, the judge dismissed the charges, giving his reasons in a lengthy speech which was widely reported in the world's press.

His words have been subsequently derided by many professionals in the market place saying that the judge was wrong and that his beliefs were misguided and that the speech did great harm to the futures business, etc., etc. In only one area, I believe, was His Honour mistaken in his judgement and that was when he referred to private clients in the markets as 'investors'.

Whatever else futures trading might or might not be, one thing is abundantly clear, investment it 'ain't' and anyone who tries to describe futures as having the slightest degree of resemblance to investment is possibly kidding himself but is far more likely to be attempting to deceive his listener. The use of futures by market professionals as a means of providing an added dimension to their investment hedging strategies is one thing. The speculative purchase or sale of futures contracts for non-hedging purposes is nothing more elevating than gambling, and most of the private losers I have seen would have been far better off going to the betting shop on the corner of the street, if they wanted a punt. Bookmakers give you better odds, they don't charge commission and you pay less in tax if you win. What's more, if you lose, they don't come after you for more cash to square their books.

Why then do otherwise normally sensible people part with considerable sums of money, in many cases to nothing more than a voice on the end of a telephone, to be used to buy futures contracts for huge amounts of aluminium or coffee beans or Japanese yen, which they don't want and for which they are charged exorbitant sums of money in commission?

The first and possibly most insidious way has been, until recently, the use of the unsolicited cold call. A group of (usually) young people are employed, together with a very carefully prepared script, to make unsolicited telephone calls to subscribers, offering them an opportunity to invest in futures trading. The scripts they use assume every possible objection by the recipient of the call and allow the salesperson to follow the relevant line of chat as soon as the receiver makes one of the listed objections. The scripts even presuppose that there will be recipients who will be totally resistant to the sales pitch and they are identified early in the script in order to enable the salesperson to finish those calls quickly, and move on to the next call. Few of these salespersons have any real practical knowledge of the conduct of the future markets, but they will rattle off the carefully prepared sales 'spiel' in an attempt to sound as knowledgeable as possible.

Once a potential punter has been identified, the salesperson will then move into the next phase which is to ask him how much he wants to invest. The figure stated by the potential client is then used to form the basis of a bargaining platform. The client who says that he might consider parting with £5000 is hardly worth the effort, while the customer who says he has been thinking of investing £100,000 really gets the treatment. He will be subjected to an extremely hard sell and the salesman dealing with him will be the subject of intense pressure to get him to part with his money. The salesman will then ring off, promising to come back to the 'client' if a suitable investment opportunity presents itself.

In most cases, the salesman is back on the phone within a couple of hours. He has, perhaps not surprisingly, identified an 'interesting' movement in orange juice futures or frozen pork bellies, which his company's financial analysis department has interpreted as being a 'positive buy signal' or some other such meaningless gibberish. Is the punter, sorry, client interested? If the client is resistant, the salesman will tell him that he is putting him on to the head of the analysis department who will explain the opportunity to him. The phone is then handed across the desk to another salesman who assumes whatever identity is needed for that call. Another outpouring of futures jargon and financial doublespeak then follows in many cases using quite an aggressive and condescending manner, followed by a demand to know whether client intends to send in a cheque.

Closing the agreement can be quite a difficult prospect. An ex-salesman of one of the most notorious companies who specialised in this type of selling described how, when he was talking to a customer whom it was known had a large amount of disposable cash to spare, he would be under a constant barrage of instructions from a senior manager, standing at his elbow, hissing: 'Close him, close him, just get his dosh and close him.' The phrase 'close him' meaning, 'get him to agree to enter a contract.' It did not matter which contract, as long as the firm got the client's signature on an agreement form.

If the client demurs, the salesman presses harder. 'The opportunity may be missed if the client doesn't make up his mind quickly'. The client wants time to think. 'All right, the salesman will ring back later.'

Within a couple of hours, the salesman is back. 'The opportunity has gone, too bad! If the client had agreed to send his money, his contract would have increased by 15% in value in the last hour. The market in orange juice has gone wild.' The client is disappointed. 'Never mind, it just so happens that there has just been another buy signal identified in Soyabean meal, is the client interested? Just give us your agreement and we'll close the deal now. By the way, the price of Soyabean meal looks like it is going to take off. Look, I'm going to send a despatch rider, he can be with you in fifteen minutes, if you have the cheque ready, then we'll do the deal. I'll tell you what, I'll open the contract anyway, it's a pity to let this opportunity get away, and then when the despatch rider picks up the cheque you'll be in the money.'

Once the client has parted with his cheque, he might as well write it off. What usually happened was for the client agreement form to be forwarded by return of post with a request that it be completed. This form would contain a number of unusual terms, exonerating the broker from just about every conceivable occurrence and act of negligence on his part and pointing out that futures trading was very risky and that the client could lose all his money.

The next stage is easy. The client has parted with £5000 for his

Soyabean contract. This figure will have been used in toto to purchase the contract, using the leverage principle, buying £50,000 of futures. The next stage is for the client to receive another telephone call, telling him what has happened to his contract. If it has gone up in price, so far, so good. The salesman, who has now mysteriously been elevated to the position of account executive, tells him that he feels that the contract should be closed and the whole amount rolled over into some other high-yielding futures contract. The client, pleased, and not a little relieved, agrees.

The other scenario is for the client to receive a telephone call telling him that the Soyabean contract has unexpectedly taken a down turn and will require further sums of margin deposit to keep the contract open. It is believed that this is simply a temporary movement but the client has signed the contract form and the AE has to require more funds to keep the contract open. Inevitably, the client sends more money. Bear in mind that these salespersons, some of whom were not much older than twenty, were earning phenomenal commission payments which fuelled a lifestyle out of all proportion to their age and experience. Any failure on their part to obtain further payments of money from their clients resulted in threats of dismissal from the company or a removal from their list of a particularly profitable client who would be 'given' to a more successful salesman.

Whichever way the market turns is irrelevant from the brokers' point of view. They are earning their money from the huge amounts of commission they are charging the client and that commission will be deducted whichever way the market goes.

Another method of attracting clients is by the use of mail shots. This method is nothing more than a ruse to get round the new provisions regarding cold calling. A person who returns a mail shot to a company requesting further details of their services is no longer looked upon as an unsolicited client but a person who has requested information on his own volition, and once such a return has been made, the company can then feel free to telephone him as much as they like. The real danger in such sales techniques lies in the fact that the salesman is unidentifiable. He is a name and a voice at the end of a phone. He can make what promises he likes, he can distort, deceive, cheat and lie, and in the vast majority of cases, the client will never be able to identify him. The managers of the company can always claim to have no knowledge of such activities. Trying to prove that the company and its managers have committed any criminal act would be virtually impossible in an English court, yet these companies continue to generate phenomenal profits and the complaints from dissatisfied clients flood in.

So, having parted with the money, or having been induced to deposit money with a broker, what delights await the private client? Like the licensed dealer, the commodity broker has not been required to maintain any form of segregated client account. This state of affairs has now changed, but it is too early to say how well the new provisions are working. The client's monies were inextricably linked with those of the company but, unlike his counterpart who might be induced to trade securities, the futures client has been unable to identify his individual contracts for two reasons. Firstly, there has been no requirement to provide a time stamp upon the contract and, secondly, the original contract was between principal and principal, thus depriving the private client of any proof of purchase. The system works in this way.

Futures prices fluctuate throughout the trading day. The contract may open the day trading at £100 per lot and may close the day trading at £103 per lot. During the course of the day the price may have dipped to £94 per lot and gone as high as £108 per lot, so although the reported high and low prices of the day will show a £14 price range, the opening and closing prices will simply show a £3 differential. As long as the contract which the client receives is within the range on the day, he is unlikely to be able to claim that he has not been 'filled' at the correct price.

The opening and closing average differential is £101.50. The average price of the range on the day is £101. Even assuming that the broker trades only 1000 lots per day, and it must be remembered that these figures are hypothetical, then by buying at the range and settling at the differential, the broker will make an average of £500 per day for himself at the expense of his clients. This is in addition to the commission rate the broker charges.

There is another way, however, that the broker can make even more money for himself, again at the expense of his clients. Using the figure shown above, and assuming the the broker purchases all his discretionary contracts at an average of £101.00 per lot, he will pay a total of £101,000 for his total contracts. He then passes them on to his discretionary clients at the 'high' of the day, being £108 per lot, realising a total of £108,000, or a daily profit of £7000 for himself, in addition to any commission charges.

The principle works the other way as well, when the broker comes to close his contracts. Assume that the range and the opening and closing prices remain the same on the following day. If this is so, then the broker will close the 1000 contracts at the same average price of £101.00 per lot. He will, however, inform his clients that he sold them at the low of the day, being £94 per lot. The broker will realise another £101,000, but will pay his clients £94,000, realising a profit of £7000 for himself, in addition to his closing commission rates. In the space of two days, the broker has managed to 'clip' off for himself a hidden profit of £14,000 from such dealings. The major irony of such activities is that they are considered to be legal, bearing in mind that the futures broker acts as a principal in his contracts and can therefore charge the client what price he likes. Caveat emptor indeed.

We have already talked about 'churning' when we discussed the discretionary activities of certain licensed dealers. Churning is just as widespread in futures trading and just as damaging to the interests of the client. Every time the broker opens and closes a client's contract, he will charge him whatever rate of commission has been agreed between them. 'Churning' has been defined as 'deliberately overtrading the client's account for the purposes of generating commission'. Every time a contract is opened and every time it is closed, his account will be debited by the amount of the broker's commission. Add to this the fact that the broker will charge the client commission per lot and he may trade many numbers of lots per day, and you can begin to see why churning became a major problem.

By way of example, consider a client for whom the broker decides to trade coffee. At the time of trading, coffee is averaging out at £400 per ton. Coffee is traded in five-ton lots, so the average price is £2000 per lot and the agreement between broker and client is to pay £25 each way, or £50 per round-turn commission per lot.

The broker enters into a contract for his client, purchasing ten lots of coffee at an average price of £2000 per lot. This will cost the broker £20,000, for which he will have to account. The range on the day showed coffee trading at a high of £404 per ton and the client is subsequently charged £20,200. In addition he is also charged £250 commission for the transaction, making a total contract price of £20,450. Within a couple of days, the price of coffee has gone up across the range and is now trading at an average price of £408 per ton. The broker closes the contract at the average price, realising £20,400, but marks the contract to the client at the daily low of £405, thus realising for him a figure of £20,500. However, for this service he charges another £250 commission, which, with the clip-off at the selling end of the contract, means that the broker has made an additional £400.

All in all, the broker has made £850 for himself out of this one contract and the client has made a profit of £50 on the deal. Unfortunately, it has cost him £500 in commission, so he has ended up £450 down on the overall transaction. It would be very hard, however, to prove to the satisfaction of a British jury that the broker didn't do everything he could for the benefit of his client. He sold the contract at a profit, even though it cost the client ten times what his profit was worth to do it. On a deposit of £5000, the client has already lost £450 in one round trading transaction, even though, in theory, he made a trading profit. At that rate, he will be wiped out in twenty days and yet the broker will still be able to claim that every trade conducted for his client made a profit.

In the illustrations used above, the commission rates have been pre-defined. The client has been paying commission at an agreed sum. There are some companies, however, who charge commission on a percentage basis. Most metal trades are conducted on a percentage basis. One example is a company which charges 4% commission on trades. What they don't tell the unsuspecting client, or, at least, what few of the clients understand, is that the commission is charged on what is called total contract value (TCV), and this can make a considerable difference. The method works in this way.

Returning to our example of the client with the coffee contract, it was established that the broker bought ten lots of coffee at an average of £400 per ton, which resulted in a theoretical TCV of £20,000. The broker marked the client up to £20,000, using the prevailing range rates and thus the broker using the percentage method of computing commission rates would, at 4% per completed trade, charge the client £808 commission on the contract, instead of £250. Not bad, eh! Then, when the broker came to close the contract he would still make £20,400 but would continue to clip the client on the trade, paying him £20,250. This time, the broker would make £1158 on one trade, nevertheless still having made the client a paper trading profit.

'That ain't working, that's the way you do it, money for nothing.' (With considerable apologies to Mark Knopfler.)

Ah! but if that were all. How about the existence of the dreaded house account? This little gem was a common feature of discretionary trading a few years ago and was used by a number of brokers with a monotonous degree of profitable regularity. Some enterprising opera-tives soon realised that, as their accounts were all computerised, there was no immediate identification of individuals on the computer records and that the company, broker or account executive could operate his own account on the computer at the same time as the discretionary clients.

Imagine that you are a discretionary client of X Commodities Ltd and I am your broker. I maintain an account within the company, within which I trade for my own account. You are but one of 100 discretionary clients for whom I trade. Using our earlier example of coffee trading at £400 per ton, I decide to enter into a series of day trades, which means opening and closing the relevant contracts in the same day. I buy 100 contracts of coffee at £2000 per contract when the market opens, for which my company will be charged £200,000. At exactly the same time, I sell 100 contracts of coffee for the same delivery month, at the same price, for which my company will be credited with £200,000. On paper, therefore, my company's books are squared.

Remember that the range on the day is between £94 and £108 per ton.

Later the same day, having watched the movement of coffee, I decide that the price is going to close up, and I sell the 100 contracts for £105 per ton and buy, or close out, my short contracts at the same price.

I now hold 100 contracts of coffee on which I have made a profit of £5 per ton, which is a total of £2500, and I have an equal number of contracts on which I have made a loss of £5 per ton, which is an additional £2500. On paper, I have made no profit at all. But watch this!

At the end of the day's trading, I allot all the loss-making contracts to each of my discretionary clients, showing them as having gone short one contract of coffee each. Each of them is required to pay commission on this trade, however, which amounts to £25 each. Day trades are generously charged at only half commission, making a total of £2500. The remaining 100 lots I allot to my own house account, making a profit of £2500 for myself. I have not incurred any expenses on behalf of my company, and I have charged my clients £2500 for the privilege of making £2500 at their expense. It wouldn't matter which way the market moved, as I would be in a position to take advantage of the movement at either end of the scale. The customer would always be the loser. I know that the purists will say that I have ignored the market fees and the administration charges and they are right. Quite frankly, I don't think you need to be worried with these minor additional charges.

The fact is that these and other practices were widespread in the private client market. One case stands out vividly in my mind. A London-based company introduced the idea of trading discretionary accounts to a group of putative investors in Northern Ireland. These people were introduced to the idea of futures trading by local 'investment advisors' who were little more than small-time insurance salesmen. One of these salesmen was responsible for introducing a considerable number of his clients to the brokerage, yet his own account had quickly been extinguished, by clipping and churning. Had he realised the unpalatable fact that he was broke, it is unlikely that he would have been prepared to continue introducing wealthy clients, so, when he asked the company if he could realise £1000 from what he thought was a profitable account, to take his wife on holiday, the brokerage transferred to him £1000 which he did not possess. They were ripping off so much money from his other introductions, it was worth it to them to give him £1000, to keep him sweet.

Another company which was the subject of an earlier investigation, trading under the name of Highfield Commodities, was compulsorily wound up in 1985, having defrauded clients of approximately $12 million. Of the monies received, about 89.5% was split between the company and its sales agents in the form of commissions, fees and expenses. At the winding up, the company was described as 'a simple conduit of fraud'. The company was described as having used 'boiler room tactics, bombarding people with telephone calls to invest in strategic metals. In almost no cases was metal bought and at the end of the investment period, the conspirators engaged in wholly fictitious transactions purporting to show a sale of the investors' metal.'

Now, if you think that the figures referred to here could possibly be exaggerated, when we come to talk about the rip-offs that have gone on in options trading you will begin to see that so far, we haven't even touched the tip of the proverbial iceberg.

Remember Hans, to whom I introduced you in the introduction? This was his particular speciality and he was extremely good at it. Financial investment in Germany is conducted mostly through the banks, and many German citizens do not like to identify their trading activities too closely to their bank managers, believing, rightly or wrongly, that the banks will be required to report their dealings to the German tax man. Futures trading has been denied to German citizens for years. There are, to my knowledge, no practicable futures markets in the FDR, partly because futures trading is looked upon as nothing more than gambling.

Hans had decided to pander to the oft-expressed desire of his countrymen to indulge in futures trading, and accordingly, he had obtained a post with a London-based futures trading company. He found that his peculiar talents were well rewarded.

Hans explained how the London company enabled German sales groups to make considerable profits at the expense of their clients. He told of the enormous amount of 'black money' held by successful German businessmen, about which they were less than anxious to inform the tax man. Hans and his friends had decided to relieve these gentlemen of their worries and they had come to London to set up companies which would assist them in their aim.

They found that one of the methods which was very attractive to the German investors was options trading. When a client purchases an option, he is buying a right to buy or sell the specific commodity in the future, for which he pays a premium. The grantor of the option, the person who is in effect taking the risk that the purchaser is going to want to come back and exercise the option in the future, will calculate the premium to be paid for the option very carefully. The greater the likelihood that the option will be exercised, the more expensive the premium is going to be; the less likely, the cheaper. Calculating premiums is a carefully controlled science and in reality is undertaken by very experienced market professionals. Options trading can be a valuable tool in the hands of these professionals, if used correctly, the profitable use of the specific option strategy being determined by an exact computation of the premium to be paid.

Premium cost is related to the degree of potential fluctuation in the futures price. Charge too much for the premium, and it will become useless as a hedging strategy for the professional client's purposes and he will go elsewhere. Charge too little, and the grantor stands a good chance of losing a lot of money.

These finer considerations did not apply, however, to the private client market as Hans and his friends soon discovered. What the clients did not realise was that every step of the contract chain represented an ever-increasing degree of loss to them and their capital. The method worked in the following way.

A salesman in Germany would find a client anxious to trade London commodity options and futures and would then contact Hans in London who would open an account for the client. He would only use a computer code number for the client in the company's records as names meant little or nothing to Hans. The salesman would have forwarded his client's margin deposit and, upon receipt of the money, Hans would proceed to rip the client off.

Hans explained how he would purchase, as an example, one copper call option. Copper is traded on the London Metal Exchange in lots of 25 tonnes and, using a strike price of £750 per tonne, merely as an illustration, an option would be purchased for a premium of £30 per tonne. The premium price to the client therefore would be 30 times 25 tonnes or £750. In addition to the premium, the client would be charged commission on the transaction, which in the case of the foreign clients was as high as 1%. This commission was charged on TCV, which would amount to an additional £187.50. The total cost to the client would be £937.50 for one call option in London copper.

Hans would then create the necessary paperwork to pass on the transaction to the German sales company. Having paid £30 per tonne for the premium, Hans would mark up the premium to £34 per tonne, the additional £4 per tonne being retained by Hans for his company. Hans would charge the German sales company £40 per tonne and send them the relevant paperwork to show the premium cost at that price. He would retain the additional £6 per tonne to be repaid to the sales company by way of a 'kick-back', or a 'refund' at a later date. Having received the paperwork, the German sales company would mark up the premium by 100%, charging the client £80 per tonne. Throughout the entire chain, commission at 1% of TCV would have been charged, and passed on, so the final cost to the German client would look like this. 25 tonnes of copper times £80 premium per tonne equals £2000, plus £187.50 commission, and the client has paid £2187.50 for a call option which cost £937.50 to purchase originally.

Having paid £87.50 per tonne premium, the price of copper would have to rise in price from £750 per tonne to £837.50 per tonne in three months for the client simply to break even, and without making one penny profit. An upturn in the copper market of 87.5 points over a three-month period, without any downward movement is, I suppose, possible. Hans and his friends made sure that the likelihood of the client being able to exercise the option at a profit was not very likely.

Hans would have made £287.50 for his company on that one option transaction. He told me that during the period he was with them, at a time when options trading was very much the rage among German speculators, he was trading an average of 300 such options a day, which meant that his company were earning in the region of £86,240 per day, simply by marking up the premiums and adding their commission.

Hans soon decided it would be more advantageous to operate his own companies and he proceeded to create a network of interlinking operations, which, together with his friends from Germany and elsewhere, he soon developed into a fraudulent empire which was responsible for milking literally millions of pounds from the pockets of unsophisticated foreign investors, using the reputation of the City of London as the bait with which to attract them.

Hans had discovered that it was possible to set up a London-based company without the need for any great degree of available capital; indeed, he could buy one, ready made, 'off the shelf' from one of the large number of company formation agents which abound in London. No checks were apparently made on the background of the person setting up the company and there were few restrictions as to the business premises which they needed to occupy. In addition, it was only necessary to pay up £2 of the share capital of the company, and you were in business.

Hans had found that there were a large number of companies in London which offered 'prestige' addresses, from which businesses could be conducted. These premises had been converted by the companies which owned them into small, self-contained offices, sharing the use of international telex facilities with the other users. A switchboard was provided which could be used to screen calls, and above all, they were very discreet. They provided an enterprising con-man with everything he could wish for.

Hans had discovered something else. British banks were discreet and offered a considerable degree of client protection from nosy enquiries. In addition, they maintained branches in the Channel Islands and the Isle of Man. Hans liked the Isle of Man, he liked it so much that he became a regular visitor to Douglas, the capital, where he set up a number of off-shore companies for the use of himself and his friends. Eventually, Hans became a one man off-shore company broker, but at the time of this particular story, he was busy running a series of rip-offs, using the services of a company called Eastearn Brokers Inc.

Hans knew that, in order to disguise his activities completely, it was necessary to go off-shore. He was using the services of a Panamanian company formation agent, which operated out of one of the many lawyers' offices in Panama, and together with some other friends, he had created Eastearn Brokers Inc. (Panama) which he used as a dummy broking operation.

Towards the end of 1981, a Swiss broker named Manfred Muller arrived in London with instructions to set up a commodity broking company. Muller bought a company off-the-shelf and renamed it Boston Financial Services Ltd. The company obtained premises from an office accommodation company in Mortimer Street, in London's West End. Muller had instructions to meet a Mr Johnson who, he was told, would be in a position to provide him with specialist broking services. In due course, Muller met Mr Johnson, an expatriate German con-man whose real name was Karl Leimbach. Leimbach was expecting Muller and together they discussed the technique which they intended to use to fleece a large number of German clients.

Muller explained that German sales groups were actively canvassing interested German clients who would be encouraged to place considerable sums of money with the company which he was operating from London, Boston Financial Services Ltd. The clients would be told that the company was the British subsidiary of a major American finance house which would be able to conduct commodity trades on American exchanges. The clients would be expected to sign contracts which would tie up their invested capital for a minimum period of six months, at the end of which time the clients would be given the opportunity to take their profits, and a further opportunity to re-invest for another six months.

Leimbach, in turn, explained how he could provide the necessary paperwork to create the impression that the clients' funds were being invested in America. He told Muller that it would be necessary for him to obtain a daily copy of the *Wall Street Journal*, in which all opening and closing commodity prices for the previous day's trading on the American commodity exchanges were reported. Muller and his staff would then make up individual trade accounts for each client. These 'trades' would be given to Leimbach, who possessed a computerised word processor, which could be used to create totally fictitious broker statements, using American-style trade documents. Leimbach had access to a printer in London who could reproduce the exact documents. The computer was programmed to complete the documents which were exact copies of similar ones produced in America. The top of the document would purport to show the American broking concern as being that well-known futures house, 'Eastearn Brokers Inc. (Panama)' and all trades would be shown to have been placed on American exchanges.

The documents which would be sent to the client would be

prepared, quite legitimately, in London, using the services of one of the companies which provide computerised business records. The client 'account statements' would be sent in longhand to the company, who would, in turn, using their highly complex computer system, produce neatly printed, and extremely official-looking documents, which could be sent to the clients in Germany, showing their investments increasing in value.

Towards the end of the six-month investment period, the clients would receive contract notes, showing a series of drastic and unfortunate investments which had virtually, if not completely, extinguished their invested capital. The contracts would be accompanied by a letter containing a suitable degree of concern and sympathy, pointing out the volatility of the market and expressing regret at the unforeseen losses and the hope that future business would be more profitable.

Using this technique, Boston Financial Services Ltd attracted a figure of approximately £500,000 in six months. Not one brass farthing of this cash was placed on or near a futures market and the clients lost the lot.

The method used by those responsible for the operation of Boston Financial Services was fairly unsophisticated by modern techniques. It was, nevertheless, extremely successful. When the clients' funds arrived in London, they were placed into two bank accounts, one with the Midland Bank and the other with a small licensed deposit taker, the Cavendish Guarantee Trust Ltd. The Midland Bank was used because they offered a highly efficient clearing system for funds transferred by telex transfer. As soon as the funds were cleared, they would be removed from the bank in the form of cash and divided among the various parties to the fraud, money being handed around in registered envelopes, brown paper bags and any other means which came to hand.

The matter came to light when Guenther Bury, an unhappy German investor, flew to London to find out what had happened to his investment of $100,000. Finding that he could get no satisfactory response from the manager of the company, Manfred Muller, and becoming very concerned for the security of his capital, Bury went to Marylebone Police Station and in his broken English, persuaded a Detective Sergeant that he believed that he had lost a lot of money through BFS.

Marylebone Police Station covers an area in the heart of the West

End of London and it is one of the busiest police stations in the metropolis. The pace of life for its officers never flags and they are kept busy twenty-four hours a day; it is therefore to the eternal credit of a very over-worked Detective Sergeant that he took the time to listen carefully to the story which Bury unfolded. Even with a German interpreter, the story was highly complicated, using the almost incomprehensible jargon of the commodity world. The DS decided that the matter needed further investigation and with a couple of other detectives, he went to the offices where he found Manfred Muller about to decamp. Muller was arrested, the company documents seized and everything taken back to the station.

Muller was later interviewed by officers from the Fraud Squad, and to their utter amazement, he unfolded the tale as told here. He made a complete confession of his part in the fraud and named his co-conspirators as Karl Leimbach and Marcel Kaiser, another Swiss petty con-man. Within forty-eight hours, these men had been identified and arrested, Leimbach being found cowering naked in the bottom of a wardrobe. When interviewed, they too made a full confession, identifying the bank accounts where the money was deposited and identifying the address where the word processor had been taken.

Such complete frankness was unusual to say the least and the officers, in passing, asked the three accused men why they were prepared to be so forthcoming in their answers, professional fraudsmen not normally being so co-operative. All three men were of the same opinion that they would not be prosecuted. It was a well-known fact, they said, among their friends and fellow con-men, that the Director of Public Prosecutions had consistently refused to prosecute other fraudsmen for similar offences and they honestly believed that he would not prosecute them.

The three men were invited to return to the Fraud Squad offices in forty-eight hours' time, to be told the outcome of the DPP's decision. In ordinary circumstances, a foreign fraudsman, finding himself released from custody and invited to return in forty-eight hours, would have spent the intervening time putting as much distance between himself and the police as possible. In this case, however, their confidence that they would not be prosecuted was so strong that the three men agreed to return voluntarily, believing that they would be treated in the same way as other similar German fraudsmen.

They were mistaken and in this instance the DPP did prosecute them. Their conviction and imprisonment should have served as a lesson to the DPP's office that successful prosecutions could be mounted against foreign fraudsmen operating in London, and the intelligence gained from the case could have been used to mount a major campaign against the hordes of other foreign fraudsmen who were then currently active in London. Unfortunately, the opportunity was lost, which resulted in even more criminals coming to London to set up their bogus companies. More and more off-shore companies were developed, more and more spurious trading funds created.

The bare-faced cheek which accompanied some of these company creations was quite breath-taking. One company trading under the name of Nettleville Investments Ltd, had as its directors a certain Dr Johannes Wiesmuller and a Dr Phillipe Marlowe. The unlikelihood of the most famous actor to play Tarzan together with the most famous American detective of fiction running a London investment brokerage seemed to escape most people. Nettleville even continued their policy of sarcasm by showing in their brochure a picture of Piccadilly Circus, complete with a number of red London buses. On the side of one of the buses, an advertisement showed the name Nettleville. This company was run by one Volker Scharmann, to whose house in Kent the word processor from Boston Financial Services was taken, when Muller was arrested. This company used the services of that well-known broking concern, Rothschild Rubenstein Grain Dealers Inc., Chicago, a completely fictitious broking company created for Scharmann by an off-shore company formation agent in the Isle of Man. Exhilarated by the financial success of the grain dealing company, Scharmann later formed Rothschild Rubenstein into a bank, which he intended to use for a bond dealing scam, utilising a fictitious Luxembourg-based company.

Perhaps the high spot of the ambitions expressed by the German con-men was their attempt to take control of the New Orleans Commodity Exchange. They had, by now, spent a small fortune in creating an army of companies with which to trade American markets through London. What they could not do was to find an American company who would trade their accounts in the same way that Hans had traded through London. In America, while not impossible, it is much more difficult to make up paper trades because of the severe regulations imposed by the Commodity Futures Trading Commission and the Compliance Departments, which are employed by every exchange to oversee all floor activity.

Hans had given the matter a lot of thought and he realised that the only thing to do was to find a market on which he and his friends could obtain floor membership. If this could be achieved, they would then 'close the vicious circle of fraud', being able theoretically to create documentary proof of trading between themselves across the floor of an exchange, of which they would be legitimate members. With such memberships, the persons concerned would have been enabled literally to 'steal the world', because no investigative authority would have been in a position to gainsay the truth of their documentary records.

Looking around, Hans found the New Orleans Commodity Exchange (NOCE), a small, insignificant trading operation in the Deep South which still retained recognised trading status offering a small number of contracts in cotton and rough rice. It was an exchange which had fallen into disuse, particularly after most of the major agricultural contracts had transferred to Chicago, but it still possessed the one criterion for which Hans and his friends so desperately sought. It was a recognised exchange, with available floor memberships, trading a Federally recognised contract.

Hans flew to New Orleans and entered into negotiations with the administrators of the exchange. I imagine that they were somewhat bemused by the sudden interest from a group of German businessmen in purchasing the seats on their exchange, but the unforeseen offer of large portions of hard cash proved irresistible. Hans purchased, or arranged to purchase a number of seats, and set about marketing these seats to his friends in the fraudulent futures business.

Thankfully, the American authorities are not stupid and they conducted a series of enquiries into the backgrounds of the applicants for membership of the NOCE. They were informed that all the applicants without exception were involved, either directly or indirectly, with companies and methods of trading which had been investigated for allegations of criminal wrong-doing. With this knowledge, the CFTC refused to recognise the membership applications, and subsequently, the NOCE was amalgamated into membership with the Mid American Commodity Exchange, in Chicago, this time without Hans and his friends as members. It had however, been a close-run thing.

The lessons from this series of activities taught the Fraud Squad a great deal. They learned that the ease with which a company can be created in the UK, and the derisory amount of paid-up capital required, mean that literally anyone can start a business in London, using prestige address facilities and attracting millions of pounds without any check being made on the *bona fide* nature of the directors or the managers of the organisation. They learned that British banks maintain a blinkered attitude towards a high turn-over of cash within an account. They learned that the existence of off-shore companies with their secrecy rules, nominee director facilities and an 'ask no questions' policy mean that they will obtain no co-operation from the judicial authorities in those jurisdictions. They learned that off-shore banks will not co-operate with mainland enquiries, even though they have the same name and logo as the familiar bank in every High Street. They learned that when dealing with futures transactions, nothing can be gleaned from a broker's records as long as futures brokers are viewed as principals, and thus able to charge what prices they like to their clients. They learned that there is virtually no method of proving the truth or otherwise of a broker's statements, because the records of the broker and the market records bear no resemblance to one another; that a broker can make up any document he likes, as long as it looks realistic, and no court in the land will be able satisfactorily to say that the trading record contained within the document did not take place; they learned that until futures brokers in this country are required by law to identify each client when they conduct a transaction, and time each trading record, which is backed up by an equally timed floor record, for corroborative purposes, maintained by an independent company, then the private, discretionary client is going to continue to be subjected to all the various methods of being parted from his money which I have described here. They also learned that if a company was operated to the detriment, predominantly, of foreign nationals, despite the incredible damage to the reputation of British investment markets, the DPP was unlikely to sanction any prosecution of the perpetrators, even when caught red-handed. London was a safe haven for con-men—and they flocked there in their hundreds.

There are other methods which have been commonly used, but which have become merely variations upon the central theme of general wrong-doing. Having learned these lessons, it is instructive to turn to another fraudulent technique which may still enjoy some popularity in the future and examine the trading methods employed during the operation of what came to be called the Vegas Trust.

Profitable futures trading rests upon a considerable degree of gearing, rather like making an odds-on bet, and few individuals can afford the large sums of money to be used for margin deposits. The logical end result, surely, would be to pool a number of different contributions to create one large pool of money to invest in a series of commodity futures transactions, and then to share out the profits equally among the contributors, to each according to the size of his original deposit. This method has a certain degree of similarity with a unit trust, and it is for this reason that the Department of Trade has consistently denied recognition to such investment trusts which depend upon futures transactions for the source of their earnings.

The DTI has adopted this view for very simple reasons. Futures trading has always been considered by them too risky to recognise as an authorised investment trust. Nevertheless, such an investment concept has always proved to be attractive to those persons who are likely to be attracted to the idea of futures trading, but who possess insufficient funds to finance the original margin deposit. Recognising that fact, the DTI has maintained a careful watch on the activities of investment trusts and required them to conform to stringent regulations. In fairness, it says quite a lot for the DTI that, in recent years, there have been very few allegations of wrong-doing in relation to the management of unit trusts. The activities of the salesmen are another matter and are not covered here, but the central investment management of the main units has generally been well regulated.

No such rules operate off-shore, however, and a large number of futures-based investment funds, pools, trusts, schemes and plans are maintained in all the sterling off-shore areas. There is no restriction on a British citizen placing money in such a scheme, subject, of course, to his declaring any profits!

The Vegas Trust was just such a scheme and was conducted in a manner likely to cause the maximum prejudice to the invested funds of the clients. The scheme was originally created as a means of re-imbursing a group of investors who had lost in excess of £100,000 in an earlier fund trading under the name of Chartech Trading Trust. They were solicited by the promoter of the fund and invited to consider re-investing in another off-shore fund, set up to trade commodity futures, in an attempt to recover their original losses and to create more profits.

The trust was based in Guernsey, bought off-the-shelf from an accountant who specialised in the creation of such creatures. The trustees were employees of a Panamanian law firm, who, having been appointed as trustees for administrative ease, conveyed their duties to a group of managers who were the beneficial owners of a company based in the Turks and Caicos Islands. These managers were, just by chance, also the beneficial owners of a Panamanian company which was designated to be the management arm of the Guernsey Trust, the nominee Panamanian directors of the management company being some of the same people who were the original trustees of the trust and who had so recently conveyed their responsibilities to the managers. Are you confused yet? It gets worse!

In accordance with their responsibilities, the managers of the trust then appointed a London-based commodity trading company to trade the funds of the trust, the director of the commodity broking firm being one of the managers of the trust. What they ended up with was a trust and a management service company, with totally secret beneficial ownership, disguised behind a façade of Panamanian secrecy, operating through a similarly secret facility in Guernsey, trading the funds of the investors through the very commodity company owned by one of the beneficial owners. As a recipe for financial disaster it had no equal. Nor, indeed, was it intended to have.

Clients' funds were paid into a Guernsey bank, which was itself an off-shore subsidiary of an international banking group, albeit one which few people would recognise in their High Street. The particular facility offered by this bank was that the cheque book could be mandated in any name by use of a rubber stamp. Once the funds were cleared, they remained in the account until the time came for them to be transferred to the trading account of the commodity futures trading operation. These funds could be used for any other purpose, as long as the cheque concerned contained the right rubber stamp.

So far, nothing illegal had occurred. The commodity broking concern was trading accounts for a number of clients, including another company, the beneficial owner of which was one of the managers of the trust. When the time came, the clients' funds were transferred to the account of the commodity broking concern and were used by them for futures trading. The only problem was that the funds were used to pay the bills of the trading company and to settle margin calls for other clients' affairs, including their own. They created a set of paper trading records which purported to record real transactions having taken place, when, in reality, they had made these trades up, using extant prices to create the illusion of accurate trading figures.

They were faced with a major problem, however. They had agreed to have the fund audited every six months, and a record of trading performance provided by an auditor for the inspection of clients. When the first six-month period came to an end, they had already extinguished the available client deposits and were unable to show any real profits from trading, which would enable client confidence to be maintained in the efficacy of the fund managers. In order to provide a sufficiently profitable set of records, they created a paper chase which might never have been discovered but for the most incredible stroke of luck.

In this particular instance, the traders of the account had already entered into a silver futures purchasing contract with an established metals broker. The contract was closed at a considerable loss to the trader some time after it was opened, the price of silver having decided to drop like a stone. The traders had in their possession two contract notes, one showing the opening purchase and the other showing the closing sale. The point about contract notes is that they do not require the brokers to state whether the transaction is an opening or a closing one. The principals allowed a few days to pass and while the price of silver was still falling, they gave instructions to their brokers, and entered into what was known as a cross transaction which took place only in the books of their brokers. The contract was never placed on the floor of the exchange. This meant that they purchased and sold the same number of silver contracts on paper as in their original bargain. The point however is that the purchase and the sale were simultaneous, the traders being required to account to their floor brokers for nothing more than their commission for having undertaken a seemingly meaningless paper transaction which appeared to possess no obvious commercial value.

What the transaction did provide were two more genuine broker statements which could be added to the first two original documents. Having discarded the first purchasing contract note and the last sale contract note, the principals were able to create the impression of having entered into a short contract for the sale of silver, subsequently closing the contract at a profit. These contract notes were to be made available for the auditors to examine and report on the seemingly profitable exercises.

Any client whose suspicions might have been aroused by this seemingly profitable transaction and who had made enquiry of the broking company, would have ascertained that both contracts were correctly placed on the market by the brokers and had gone through their books. Having ascertained that both contracts had been properly dealt with by an established broker, we shall never know what prompted the officer dealing with the case to ask whether the two contract notes referred to the same transaction. By considerable fortune he did, and ascertained that they didn't. This in turn meant that all the figures so carefully identified to the clients as their profits were untrue. From that moment on, all the other assertions made by the parties to the fraud became obviously deceitful and the rest of the immediate enquiry became a matter of routine.

In many ways, the Vegas Trust smelt like a rip-off from the start. It had just the right combination of fantastic proposals, coupled with cast-iron guarantees of profit, backed up by the usual parade of characters, doubling as investment advisers, some demanding fantastic salaries for their valuable business acumen, a titled gentleman, who genuinely knew nothing about the business but who would accept an honorary consultancy in return for an annual fee. A trust, bought off-the-shelf, whose original objects included the provision of funds for the Guernsey Wild Life Fund, a Panamanian service company with an improbable name and an interchangeable series of nominee trustees and directors, the identities of whom were all protected by Guernsey or Panamanian law.

Quite how any of the original investors believed that they would ever see a penny of their money back is completely beyond me. Ironically, due almost entirely to a timely warning by the *Observer* and the action taken by the police, the affairs of the Vegas Trust were brought to a shuddering halt. The promoters of the scam, in a desperate attempt to evade being prosecuted, brought a cynical High Court action against the Commissioner of Police in an attempt to recover the records of the Trust, in order, so they said, to repay the original investors, the company's affairs having been irrevocably damaged by the police. In the end, all the investors were repaid their original deposits. Not one of them even had the courtesy to say 'thank you'.

As a last thought, it is perhaps a useful illustration of how low the regulatory reputation of the London market had sunk that the promoters of the Vegas Trust could peddle this sort of junk and believe that they could get away with it.

CHAPTER NINE
All The Queen's Men

The public no longer believes that the legal system in England and Wales is capable of bringing the perpetrators of serious frauds expeditiously and effectively to book. The overwhelming weight of the evidence laid before us suggests that the public is right. In relation to such crimes, and to the skilful and determined criminals who commit them, the present legal system is archaic, cumbersome and unreliable.

This unequivocal statement was made, not as might be thought by some sensationalist television presenter, anxious to boost his ratings, nor by some cynical, hard-bitten Fleet Street journalist, but by the Fraud Trials Committee, chaired by The Right Honourable The Lord Roskill, PC, one of Her Majesty's senior Law Lords. These words were not tucked away in some obscure sub-paragraph, in an appendix to the work, but comprised the first three sentences of the opening statement of the report. The composition of the committee, their terms of reference and their findings should make the Roskill Report one of the most important influences on Criminal Law revision in the twentieth century. Whether its proposals will be implemented can, at this point, only be guessed at.

Fraud as a general criminal problem involves the investigative resources of a number of agencies, including the Customs and Excise, the Inland Revenue and the Department of Health and Social Security. Investment fraud almost exclusively is dealt with in the first instance by the police or the Department of Trade and Industry and it is on the role of these two agencies that I intend to concentrate. Both organisations conduct investigations into related fraudulent activities, and in many cases their jurisdictions and operations may overlap.

Both departments are required, under the Prosecution of Offences

Regulations 1978, to report certain types of criminal allegations to the Director of Public Prosecutions at some stage during an investigation, and it is on the role and function of the DPP that I intend to concentrate first.

The Director of Public Prosecutions is a public official, answerable to the Attorney General, and is required to 'institute, undertake or carry on criminal proceedings in any case which appears to him to be of importance or difficulty or which for any other reason requires his intervention'.

In addition, there are a number of offences which chief officers of police are required to report to the DPP and this list includes offences where proceedings may not be commenced without the authority of the Director. There has long been a requirement for chief officers of police to seek advice from the DPP at an early stage in an investigation of fraud, particularly where the subject was likely to be heavy or complex or both, and the tendency within police forces had been for the 'early report' to the DPP to become shorter and shorter in terms of elapsed time from initial receipt of the allegation to the submission of the first report.

Until very recently, the staffing of the Fraud and Bankruptcy Division of the DPP's office comprised about twenty-four people, which included clerical and ancillary support staff and which handled approximately 150 cases annually. The senior representatives are all qualified barristers or solicitors.

The DPP's role is similar in some ways to that of a filter and he is required to consider the advisability of prosecution in those cases which are presented to him, and to screen out those which he feels are unlikely to succeed. Criminal trials are highly expensive affairs and a number of techniques are adopted which can make them even more costly, so the DPP is unlikely to proceed, nor should he prosecute, in a case where the totality of the evidence is unlikely to result in a conviction. For him to prosecute in such circumstances would be wasteful of the public purse and oppressive to the accused person.

Over the years, the policy has been laid down of what is somewhat euphemistically called 'the 51% rule'. This is embodied in the *Attorney General's Guidelines*, which make it clear that there should be a better than 50% chance of conviction if a prosecution is to proceed. This policy, however, is subject to a highly subjective degree of interpretation and it is in this area that the first hurdle for fraud investigators is encountered.

It is hardly surprising that many critics of the DPP's office regard him as a political servant first and a legal administrator second. The widespread publicity surrounding the decisions to prosecute Clive Ponting over the *Belgrano* papers or the so-called Cyprus spy case trial have tended to reinforce that belief in a number of circles. In other circumstances, the existence of the 51% rule enables the Director to refuse to sanction any prosecution, on the basis that he believes that a conviction cannot be sustained. This perception is highly damaging to the reputation of the Director's supposed impartiality and attracts criticism from Parliament and country. In a House of Commons report of oral answers to Parliamentary questions on 2 December 1985, Mr Nicholas Brown MP reported that in 1983 324 serious frauds were reported to the DPP, of which 37 prosecutions were sanctioned. While talking about the proposed Crown Prosecution Service Mr Brown made the point that the provisions were 'totally inadequate and will give the general public the impression that the only Act under which fraud will be prosecuted is the old pals' Act'.

Dennis Skinner, MP for Bolsover and one of the Conservative Government's fiercest critics over their handling of allegations of City fraud, is quite unrepentant in his belief that the DPP brings a political dimension to his prosecution decisions. He has been highly outspoken in the House of Commons about the apparent failure of the Director to bring prosecutions against Peter Cameron-Webb and Peter Dixon relating to the allegations that they have dishonestly missappropriated immense sums of money belonging to their clients at Lloyds, and has said that there seems to be one law in relation to the prosecution of bankers and City financiers and another relating to working people. During the preparation of this book I interviewed Mr Skinner and I asked him why he believed that the DPP was politically motivated in some of his decisions. He said:

'People are products of their own environment and the DPP is not somebody who has derived his experience from the Wapping picket line . . . the DPP comes out of the belly of the Establishment and it would be incredible if anybody that took on that mantle of responsibility could act in a manner other than favouring his own class.'

The important factor is not so much whether one necessarily agrees with Mr Skinner's highly class structured view of the DPP's role, but whether the public could be led to that view by the continuing failure to prosecute certain cases which demand a public airing. Another labour MP, Bryan Gould, believed that a greater willingness to prosecute would have a salutory effect upon those wrong-doers who believed that they could get away with fraud, simply because the allegations against them were highly complicated. Support for this contention came in a report by the highly influential all-party association of lawyers, Justice, in their evidence to the Roskill Committee. They said:

'A more forceful policy in regard to the prosecution of fraud cases is required . . . Major commercial frauds often go unprosecuted, partly because of the lesser likelihood of a successful result, but mainly because the resources in manpower and money, as well as techniques, are not available to ensure successful prosecutions. There ought to be a greater readiness to prosecute important and more complicated frauds, despite the expense and the many difficulties known to exist in the conduct of the trials.'

One of the groups of cases which the DPP consistently refused to prosecute was where the allegation involved foreign fraudsmen who were using British facilities to defraud other foreigners, but where no British losers could be identified. The public awareness of the policy spread like wildfire and it is no exaggeration to say that foreign fraudsmen came to look upon London as the safest place in Europe from which to conduct enterprises of a criminal nature. The BBC *Panorama* programme recorded one such 'businessman' estimating that in excess of £400 million was ripped off by such frauds in the space of a few years. The American advance-fee fraudsmen flocked to our top-class hotels. Latterly, the OTC con-men have arrived with their offers of worthless US shares which they have proceeded to sell in Europe to the financial detriment of their clients.

Another criticism of the DPP's attitude by experienced detectives is that the senior officers within his department appear to adopt a defence counsel mentality when considering the probative value of the evidence presented to them, which leads to a belief in the existence of a less than positive attitude towards the question of prosecution, a sort of 'we don't want to prosecute if it can be avoided' feeling. This question of attitude can make all the difference between deciding that there is more than a 51% chance of success and deciding that there isn't. The value of the evidence remains the same.

Bryan Gould had this to say:

'There seems to be just a lack of competence, a lack of zeal in the DPP's office. Now, I don't know why that should be, whether it's a lack of resources or what it is but I think that the evidence over the past couple of years is pretty considerable that the DPP's office is not doing its job as thoroughly as it ought to be . . . I don't think that the public are aware of this lack of competence, although I'll tell you one thing that I think did lift the lid off it a bit and that was the fiasco over the extradition of Evelyn Glenholmes. I think the public, the people who are interested in these matters, suddenly thought: "My God, if they could make a hash of that relatively straightforward thing, what chance have they got of getting together a case that'll stand up against very sophisticated criminals in this difficult area?" and I think that was perhaps the first indication. Certainly when I've been pursuing these matters over the last couple of years I've written on occasion to the Attorney General and others and also to the DPP saying, "Why are there no prosecutions?" because my own belief is that a couple of really good prosecutions in this area would do wonders. There's no doubt that the Attorney General, when he's replied to me, you don't even need to read between the lines, it's pretty overt what he has to say, he himself from eighteen months or two years ago, has been pretty critical of lack of action from the DPP's office. Now, you don't find a Government Minister allowing that impression to be gained unless he intends it to be and he's very worried himself.'

Sir Michael Havers, the Attorney General, (the DPP's direct superior in Parliament) has stated that he finds the level of reported fraud 'unacceptable'. John Wood has said that his belief in the explosion of white collar crime stems partly from the derisory sentences handed out to convicted fraudsmen. Stung by criticism of his department's record of prosecution, Dorain Williams, the Principal Assistant Director of Public Prosecutions and head of the fraud investigation group wrote to *The Times* on 30 November 1985, defending the record of his office and making a strong statement of support for his staff. He made a number of points, some of which are worth reiterating here. He made a sideways swipe at the degree of resource allocated to the prosecution of fraud and provided a heartfelt insight into his attitude towards fraud when he said:

'We clearly recognise fraud as a significant destructive factor in our national life. It gives birth to a deep and corrosive cynicism.' And later: 'It is divisive in terms of class because where the law enforcement agencies fail—for whatever compelling reason—to prosecute those whose conduct has been demonstrably and grossly dishonest, the cry goes up that "there is one law for them and another for us".'

I believe his most telling point was when he said:

'Failure to prosecute is due neither to lack of will nor lack of determination, but to lack of evidence.'

I thought that I would try and test the correctness of that statement and I examined the figures of fraud cases reported to the Metropolitan and City Police Fraud Squads for the years 1979 to 1985, to discover how many of them were dealt with by the DPP and how many were prosecuted. The City of London Commissioner had no difficulty in providing the answers. During the years 1979 to 1985, 465 substanti- ated cases of fraud were reported to the City of London Police Fraud Squad. These figures do not reflect the total case load of the City Fraud Squad, as many of their investigations would have revealed less than adequate evidence to justify describing the allegations as 'sub- stantiated', and for this reason the figures I am quoting here will differ from those reported in Appendix K of the Roskill Report.

Of those 465 substantiated cases, 133 of them were reported to the DPP for advice, counsel or guidance, or approximately 28.5%. The remainder would have been dealt with by the police themselves through their own solicitors' department. Of those reported to the DPP, prosecutions conducted by him were sanctioned in 42 cases, or approximately 31.5%, or less than a third.

For some reason, the Commissioner for the Metropolitan Police was unable to supply a similar set of statistics, although the reasons are not exactly clear why his colleague in the City could provide them and he could not. The figures were obtained by Dr Oonagh McDonald MP by way of a series of Parliamentary questions and the results reported here are as the answers were given to her. Dr McDonald tabled a series of questions relating to fraud statistics and in each case she was told that the figures for the Metropolitan Police could only be provided at disproportionate cost, and she was referred to the statistics as reported in the Roskill Report. My suspicion that Dr McDonald was being fobbed off by the Home Office increased however upon receipt of one of the replies provided for her by the civil servants.

MPs, journalists, writers and other interested parties have, in recent years, come to refer generally to large, institutional financial fraud as 'City fraud'. As such, the description differentiates such activities from Social Security fraud, cheque and credit card fraud and small acts of crim- inal deception. As such, City fraud is the sort of activity investigated by specialist departments such as the Fraud Squad. In tabling one of her Parliamentary questions, Dr McDonald asked the Home Office to supply the figures for the number of new investigations into City fraud started by the Metropolitan Police since 1979. How many had led to prosecutions, how many were referred to the DPP and of those, how many led to prosecutions? It was a serious question, tabled by a Member of Parliament and an Opposition Front Bench spokesman for financial affairs, acting in the proper exercise of her elected office, and as such she deserved a more considered and less flippant answer.

The answer, provided by the Home Office on 2 December 1985, read as follows:

'I understand from the Commissioner of Police of the Metropolis that it is most unlikely, because of the geographical boundaries of his force, that any new investigations into City fraud were started by his force during the period specified. Such frauds are normally investigated by the City of London Police.'

There can have been no doubt in the mind of the civil servant presented with this question what Dr McDonald meant. The reply was trite and, frankly, insulting. One can just imagine the hilarious laughter in the office of the civil servant or mandarin concerned at their exquisite use of semantics, which had enabled them to avoid answering a question that might have had embarrassing results. The follow-up questions, tabled some weeks later, were answered on 27 March 1986 with the 'disproportionate' argument. The overwhelming feeling one is left with is wondering what the Home Office had to hide.

Returning to the point made by Dorain Williams, the major stumbling block to any criminal prosecution is the availability of admissable evidence to prove the case. If such evidence is not available in an acceptable form, then no prosecution can be sanctioned, no matter how strong the suspicion or how bad the reputation of the suspect. The responsibility for collating the evidence rests upon the shoulders of the police, primarily, and, to a lesser degree, on the DTI. If the public do not have a high regard for the ability of the investigators to obtain the evidence necessary, they are less likely to report matters to the police or to co-operate with any investigation, making the provision of necessary evidence harder to supply.

Dr Michael Levi, in his report on the 'Incidence, Reporting and Prevention of Commercial Fraud' makes the following observation regarding the decision whether to report an allegation of fraud to the police. He says:

'The general view seemed to be that it was worthwhile reporting suspected fraud to the police provided (a) it was not very complicated and (b) you had done a very thorough internal investigation first, so that you could present the police with a clear picture of what had happened. Where these conditions did not apply, there was less satisfaction with and confidence in the police.'

In his survey, Dr Levi found that less than half the business executives he interviewed were positive in their attitudes towards the competence of the police in handling a major fraud.

What therefore is the composition of the London police squad which is available to deal with allegations of major fraud? The Department is a joint one, under the title of the Metropolitan and City Police Company Fraud Department. It is a department of the Metropolitan Police, using the abbreviation C.6. for identification. It was formed, in its present state, in 1946 and is staffed by officers from both the Metropolitan and City Police forces. It is under the overall control of a Metropolitan Police Commander, who liaises with his colleague in the City, but in practice, both departments go their separate ways, joining together only for certain, specialist operations.

Fraud squads and commercial branches are maintained in all other police forces, although some smaller forces will have less than a dozen men in the department. In the statistics produced in the Roskill Report, the Metropolitan Police fraud section contained 147 officers, the City section containing 62. Despite a radical increase in percentage terms of reported allegations of fraud, the Metropolitan branch was reduced by 10% in 1983.

In the 'Met', officers are posted to the Fraud Squad usually for a three-year posting, although this can be extended in certain circumstances. Their colleagues in the City of London receive a considerably longer posting. All officers receive a four-week course of training in general fraud techniques and practices, but in no particular instance could the course be considered to be definitive, consisting as it does of a series of talks from visiting lecturers and academics coupled with a basic introduction to book keeping and the briefest incursion into the realms of company law. Once completed, no further specialist training is contemplated, the officer being expected to pick up expertise through practical experience. The course can take place at any time after the officer's first arrival in the department. In some cases offices have waited as much as a year to attend such training.

During my time in the Squad, there appeared to be no specific policy of appointing solely those officers who had indicated a wish to be considered for such work, or who showed a special aptitude for fraud investigation. In some cases, men were appointed to the department

ALL THE QUEEN'S MEN

who very obviously did not want to be there. A man with no incentive to excel in his duties, master his responsibilities or find enjoyment in his workload, makes an unhappy colleague and, eventually, becomes a departmental burden. The discipline code means that he can be ordered to conduct his investigations. It doesn't mean that he will bring the same degree of flair or commitment to the work. You can lead a horse to water, and so on!

Such a factor was not true of many officers, it must be said. Indeed, many of my colleagues between the years 1981 and 1985 were men of the highest motivation, who loved their work and were able to turn their hand to any new problem, using that old-fashioned mentality which was 'let's do the best with what we've got'. It was surprising how often that attitude was able to overcome considerable difficulties and resulted in a man's value to his department being determined by his investigative ability, regardless of his rank. Such an attitude however has become increasingly rare. More and more officers, attracted by the promise of accelerated promotion to senior rank, coupled with the force policy of not leaving detective officers in any one post for more than a few years, for fear of a perceived propensity towards corrupt practice, found themselves, as another rung on their career plan, being posted to the Fraud Squad at middle management level, some for the first time in their careers. This had a tendency to concentrate administrative decision-making in the hands of men who in some cases had little or no experience of major fraud investigation and who were, perhaps understandably, more concerned with protecting their future career prospects than they were with taking decisions which could conceivably attract criticisms at a later time.

The responsibility for the day-to-day management of the Criminal Investigation Department has passed from senior detectives to the hands of their uniform colleagues. This policy was formulated by Sir Robert Mark at a time when drastic measures had proved themselves necessary and has been implemented by his successors. Where, before, an officer who succeeded in being appointed to the CID would look upon such an appointment as almost an end in itself, and would sacrifice promotional opportunities to become specialist in his particular role, the new breed of officer, possibly entering the service with a degree or certainly evidence of higher education and attracted by the possibility of senior admininstrative rank at an early age, would use the CID as merely a stepping stone towards a career goal. The end result was that where before an experienced officer would have made an administrative decision regarding the conduct of an investigation, his modern counterpart, anxious to avoid making any perceived error of judgement which might count against him in the promotion race, might seek ways in which to have the decision-making process adopted by another agency, usually the DPP's office. This was done in the hope that if in retrospect the decision proved to be politically unpopular or, worse, misguided, the responsibility would be passed on to another. I can recall a number of instances where reports were made to the DPP, whose representative would query their purpose, such queries tending to deal merely with administrative matters, normally the province of the police.

Another area of difficulty was in the degree of importance attached by the senior management of the police to the investigation of fraud.

Michael Levi: 'Fraud has traditionally commanded a low priority within the police service, partly because it is outside the action-orientated culture of police work and partly because there has been, at least until very recently (and then only in London), little political pressure for fraud work from the media and the police authorities.'

The investigation of major fraud, while appearing to possess all the same characteristics as any other criminal investigation, differs from every other kind of case by its sheer size and the volume of investigation necessary to prove the allegations. Our legal system demands a high degree of proof of allegations concerning acts of dishonesty—and the basis of all fraud is dishonesty. Proving a sophisticated, deliberate financial fraud can involve a large number of witnesses from all over the world. It can require the production of literally thousands of documentary exhibits. Fraudsmen love paper. It is a fundamental rule of our legal system that, if I seek to produce a document in support of a contention, then I should produce the original, if possible, and in addition produce a witness who can testify to the validity of the document.

The skills required of fraud detectives have been developed over a long period of time and are not acquired overnight. In a fraud trial it is imperative that the officer producing an exhibit is able to state with absolute certainty where he found the document, how he found it and be able to identify that exhibit among many hundreds of other documents, many months later. For this reason, the Fraud Squad has perfected a searching and recording technique which is second to none. The contents of an entire office can be seized, logged, identified and subsequently referred to with pin-point accuracy. Such a technique is vital to the success of an investigation. Without it, the defence will be able to claim at the trial that there is a degree of doubt concerning the existence of the document or its possession by the defendant.

Other skills are demanded, which are not normally found within 'the action-orientated culture' of the police: the ability to be able to examine financial records and documents, maintaining an 'exact to the last penny' account, reconciling and cross-balancing at every stage. This is a time-consuming and brain-numbing exercise with none of the accompanying heroics more usually associated with the popular picture of detective activity. Many Fraud Squad officers have become minor experts in the workings of the more esoteric aspects of international maritime law, bankruptcy and corporate liquidation procedures, futures and securities transactions, foreign property ownership law, such knowledge being acquired in their own time, simply to enhance their investigative skills. Yet these are the men and women who are referred to by certain senior officers as nothing more than 'paper cowboys'.

In many cases, the evidence to support an allegation of investment fraud has to be obtained from abroad. Even the simplest request for assistance addressed to a foreign police agency is subject to elaborate bureaucratic procedures and must be transmitted via Interpol or the Foreign Office through a foreign embassy. This process can take weeks or even months. It is not easy to persuade a foreign national to co-operate with a police enquiry, unless he wishes to do so voluntarily, and he cannot be compelled to come to this country to give his evidence. Foreign banks cannot be compelled to provide evidence and foreign broker houses are resistant to providing details of their dealings with suspects, on the basis that while the person may be under suspicion in the UK, he or she has committed no offence under their jurisdiction. Foreign courts have difficulty in establishing a degree of reciprocity with our jurisprudential methods. Considerable efforts have been made to obtain mutual assistance treaties between European countries for such enquiries, but they are tenuous agreements and exist in many cases more in popular belief than in practical reality.

Attempts to obtain any assistance from off-shore areas are next to useless. Our own off-shore areas, the Channel Islands and the Isle of Man, will provide a limited degree of assistance, commensurate with their legal status but even they are constrained by their laws. Trying to get help from such areas as Panama, Liberia or some of the Caribbean tax havens is a complete waste of time. They will not provide any assistance at all. Is it any wonder then, that fraud investigation is considered to be one of those jobs which so many detectives prefer to avoid at all costs?

A shortage of investigative resources (due partly to a low perception of its importance in the criminal scale and partly to its less than glamorous image) reduced man-power, despite increasing work loads, time-consuming investigations and overly bureaucratic work procedures (conducted in the main by individual officers, working alone and under extreme pressure) complex jurisdictional opposition, reduced facilities for training and the development of better skills, in a post and at a time when an officer may be confronted with legal and commercial concepts he has never dealt with before, coupled with a limited period of posting, all combine to reduce investigative efficiency and thus make the provision of the requisite degree of evidence to the DPP harder and harder to obtain, which brings us full circle, because if the DPP cannot get the evidence, he cannot prosecute.

A not dissimilar series of problems affects the DTI in their investigative role. Dr Levi, in his recent survey, canvassed public opinion of the efficiency of the DTI as compared with the police and his findings prompted him to make the following statement:

'Considerably less confidence was expressed in the competence of the Department of Trade to deal with a fraud of the same size. In the interviews, one executive stated that the DTI's resources and attitude to deal with fraud were "pitiful and disgraceful", and cited his experience in reporting fraud. He believed that there was a lack of will in the Department of Trade to engage with the problem of fraud.'

The DTI has a number of powers which it can exercise to conduct investigations into the conduct and management of companies, some more efficient than others. The most immediately practicable weapon in the investigation of investment fraud is given to the department by virtue of Section 447 of the Companies Act 1985 which enables it to require a company to produce its books and papers for examination. This provision requires past or present officers of a company to explain entries in such books or records, and a failure to comply with this requirement is a criminal offence. The findings arising out of such examinations can be disclosed to the DPP and to the police, although the latter have only recently been defined as being 'authorised persons', entitled to receive such information. Subsequently, criminal charges can be brought.

The DTI have jealously guarded their responsibility for exercising the powers of inspection under Section 447 and have been unwilling to share the facilities, even in those instances where the police and DTI might have worked more efficiently together. One memory I vividly retain is of putting the question to a DTI examiner as to the viability of conducting a search of some office premises together, the police to conduct their search and seizure role and the DTI to commence an immediate examination of the books and papers found in the premises. It could have been an efficient if somewhat unorthodox technique. A look of horror passed over his face and he quickly shook his head.

'Oh dear me, no!' he said. 'Our masters would not want us to be publicly associated with the police.'

An amusing sideline came out of a similar meeting. The DTI had been considering conducting an investigation under Section 447 into the affairs of a particularly blatant firm of German commodity fraudsmen who had opened a series of offices from which they were really coining it in. The problem had just about reached epidemic proportions and even the DTI were beginning to sit up and take notice. One of their investigators had been granted an order under Section 447 and he was intending to visit the premises to order the handing over of the books and records. He had popped in to the Fraud Squad to gather any latest information which might help him. Having been told what was known of the conduct of the operation, he left, with the best wishes of the detectives ringing in his ears. A couple of weeks later, he returned. Naturally the detectives were anxious for some news. How had he got on?

'It's a funny thing,' he said, 'I rang them up to make an appointment to go down to see them so they could hand over their records, and they were extremely helpful. They said I could go down at any time, and we made an appointment for a few days later. When I got there, the offices were empty, and there was a big pile of shredded paper in a sack. Everything else had disappeared.'

Oh really!

The DTI conducted 247 enquiries under Section 447 or its predecessor in title between 1980 and May 1984. Of those enquiries, 73 had been passed to other agencies for further consideration, 59 had found no evidence of misconduct, 98 had found evidence of mis-conduct but no further action was taken, and 9 prosecutions had been undertaken of which 7 had resulted in convictions for offences mainly involving dishonesty. These figures were taken from the Roskill Report and I imagine they are accurate. Not all these enquiries will have related to investment fraud allegations. Even ignoring those cases passed to other agencies such as the police and the DPP, it becomes hard to understand how with 98 cases showing evidence of misconduct, only 9 prosecutions were undertaken in 4 years.

Assuming however that a successful investigation has been completed and the police are now in a position to commence arresting the suspects, I intend to describe just a few of the techniques used by successful lawyers in the defence of their clients, after arrest, before and at trial, to show how many pitfalls still await the investigator and the legal process.

The initial stages of an investigation of an allegation of fraud of any kind are the most delicate. Police will wish to test the truth of an allegation before making any irrevocable move, to ascertain whether the allegation is capable of substantiation. If the police suspect that an investment company is a sham but they go in too soon, they may find insufficient evidence of criminal activity to justify a subsequent prosecution and will then face considerable criticism from those representing the company that they have acted beyond their powers, and damages will be sought. If they wait too long to garner sufficient evidence, and innocent persons are induced to part with money in the interim period, the police will face criticism from the losers for failing to act with sufficient speed to protect the public. A sort of 'Heads I win, tails you lose' situation.

Evidence to support mere suspicion is not necessarily sufficient to support direct police action. Once that evidence is established, the primary requirement is to discover the whereabouts of any illegally obtained assets, in order that they can be 'frozen', followed by the need to secure all the available evidence. Fraudsters' victims are primarily concerned with recovering their investment funds, in whole or in part. If these funds can be located and identified, it is possible to freeze their movement using civil process in the High Court. In the event of consequent conviction of the parties to the fraud, particularly where a limited company is involved, the assets become the responsibility of the liquidator or receiver who will need to be appointed to decide their disposal to the creditors.

A search of an accused person's business premises is the starting point for the securing of evidence and this is usually done under the authority of a search warrant, granted by a magistrate or a judge. This procedure removes from the possession of the accused person all the documents and records of his business. The practice has grown in recent years for professional fraudsmen to 'fight back' by immediately protesting their innocence, and issuing interlocutory proceedings against police, demanding the return of all papers and documents, injunctions against supposed defamatory statements and damages for the disruption of the business. This procedure is a highly effective way of putting immense pressure on the investigating officer and distracts his mind from the immediate aim of the primary investigation. He is required to spend a considerable amount of time in preparing affidavits which will be used in the civil proceedings, defending his actions and stating his reasons for seizing the documents. He must justify his enquiries to defend himself against the allegations of slander and must outline his future actions in order to justify the retention of the documents. It immediately gives the accused person an idea of the nature of the investigation, the degree of knowledge possessed by police and the direction their enquiries will take. This knowledge in turn can be used by the accused to circumvent the enquiries proposed by the officer, to interfere with witnesses, or to attempt, where relevant, to buy them off.

Even if the action fails at the civil court, and in most cases they do fail, in whole or in part, the accused has usually managed to obtain some form of concession from the police as to the disposition of their documents, plus undertakings as to regular access by the accused man to his papers, 'for the purposes of his business'. This is usually all poppycock, but I know of no other procedure which is capable of disrupting a complex fraud enquiry at its initial stages as effectively as the civil interlocutory writ. Another facet of its effectiveness is that it places the investigating officer under great personal strain. Civil proceedings are fairly complex and are usually outside the experience of most police officers. Loud protestations of innocence are made coupled with threats of action for punitive damages against the relevant chief constable or commissioner for the totally unjustified disruption of the plaintiff's business. Unless the investigating officer is completely sure of his ground and has the confidence of his supervising officers, the High Court can be a very lonely place indeed. At a time when he should be concentrating upon the preliminary marshalling of his evidence, he is spending most of his time defending his actions in court proceedings.

I was the subject of just such a procedure during the investigation into the affairs of the Vegas Trust, the matter being fully reported in

The Times of 1 August 1984, the case having gone to the Court of Appeal. It was reported under the name of Arias and Others *v.* Commissioner for the Metropolitan Police and Another. This case involved a bogus investment trust formed off-shore in Panama and Guernsey, the director of the Panamanian company formation service and titular plaintiff being one Roberto Arias. The action was brought in his name, although he, poor man, knew little or nothing about the matter. During the course of the proceedings it was established that the case was being brought by and paid for by the very men who were under suspicion for the way in which the company was run. The point of the case was to recover copies of the documents which were held by police as part of their investigation, the plaintiffs claiming that they wished to repay all the investors, the police having destroyed their business.

They had been supplied with the names and addresses of all the investors, but this was apparently insufficient and they needed all the papers. After a long and sometimes bitter argument, the court decided that they were entitled to copies of the papers, despite strong arguments against this decision being put forward by Counsel for the Commissioner, Mr Michael Hyam (now His Honour Judge Michael Hyam).

The court granted the police three weeks in which to supply photocopies of all relevant documents. Their solicitor attended Scotland Yard and requested copies of everything found in the premises, a Herculean task. This job had to be undertaken by the civilian photocopier employed for the task, in between her duties in providing photocopies of work for all the other officers at the Fraud Squad, and it took the full twenty-one days allowed by the court. On the last day, we were still copying telephone directories, computer print-outs and all the other detritus of a busy office when at 6.00pm the telephone rang. It was the plaintiff's solicitor informing me that his patience was exhausted and that he intended to apply in the High Court the next day for an order committing me to prison for contempt for failing to have complied with the order. It was at times like those that one wondered whether there were not easier ways of earning a living.

I mentioned the confidence of supervising officers as being of importance. There are very few such officers who, faced with the prospect of being required to justify their supervisory ability over the actions of subordinates in the event of the relevant police force being required to pay the costs of such an action, will not begin to doubt the wisdom of continuing such a case and who will instead seek a means of compromise rather than confrontation. Experienced civil solicitors know this to be the case and will use the technique outlined above to bring indirect pressure upon the investigating officer from within his own force.

Once a suspect is charged and brought before a magistrates' court, then the professional defence techniques really begin. It may be necessary to charge a defendant in order to obtain certain conditions imposed by a magistrate regarding the defendant's movements or future business activities and to extract an undertaking concerning his future attendance at court, fraudsmen not being known for their willingness to wait around pending the outcome of a case. Hampering an officer's enquiries can easily be achieved by a number of methods. Consider for example a request to the court by a defence solicitor for access to the defendant's papers in the possession of the police, which will be granted. The officer must then arrange for unfettered access to be granted to the defence solicitor or his nominee to examine and take copies of such papers as they wish. The officer or a colleague must be present throughout the examination, a procedure which has been known to take days, and he must arrange for the relevant copies to be made available as described above. It is also not unknown for witnesses suddenly to become unavailable for interview, despite prior appointments, particularly if they were on friendly terms with the defendant before the investigation and if they have suddenly found that their original investment has been repaid.

The next stage is that of committal for trial. These proceedings are a way of finding out whether a case is a suitable one to be tried before a judge and jury, ie whether there is what lawyers call a *prima facie* case. If the evidence does not disclose a *prima facie* case, then it is open to the magistrate to discharge the defendant, which happens very rarely. What does happen however is that the defence lawyers will attempt to use the committal proceedings to conduct a 'dress rehearsal' for the trial. Another method is to require the attendance of witnesses from abroad to see firstly, if they are willing to attend this country to give evidence and secondly, if they do appear, they are subjected to such a rigorous and hostile cross examination that they find themselves unwilling to come back again for the main trial. A failure on the part of the prosecution to produce a live witness at the subsequent trial will be used by the defence to suggest that the case against their client is not capable of substantiation, the relevant witness having failed to attend the court.

Magistrates' courts' diaries are full up many months in advance and court space is always at a premium. Trying to find sufficient available space and time to conduct a 'live' committal for even five days' duration can be next to impossible at short notice. It is necessary that the whole proceedings be heard by the same magistrate and this can mean booking a court nine months, even a year ahead. One example where the committal proceedings were used as such a dress rehearsal was in the Miller Carneigie case, where the committal proceedings took thirty working days to complete. During these delays, the fraudster is able to continue his operations under other guises. As time passes, witnesses' memories become confused, events become hazy, some elderly witnesses may even die. Some witnesses become impatient at the delays and, realising that they are never likely to see their money back, which after all is the only thing they are really interested in, become less willing to attend court voluntarily.

A few days before any major trial is due to begin, it is customary for defence and prosecution counsel to telephone each other to discuss the case, in an attempt to see whether there are areas of the case on which both sides are agreed and which need not form the subject of strict proof in court. Such an agreement is valuable as it shortens the proceedings and saves precious time. The witnesses concerned can be informed that their attendance will not be necessary, thus making an additional saving in their fares and expenses, not to mention saving their time.

Fraud cases rarely ever resulted in a list of formally agreed facts being presented to the court, particularly where the evidence was to be given by a person from abroad. On the contrary, it was not unknown for defence counsel to be unable to discuss the case in the week preceding the trial due to the fact that they had not received the final instructions from their instructing solicitors concerning their client's case. The reason for this might have something to do with the customary requirement that the prosecution must serve any last-minute evidence upon the defence seven clear working days before the date of trial. Any suspicion however that the defendant and his solicitor could be waiting to see if any further evidence might be forthcoming prior to finally committing themselves to a defence strategy, should be treated as being unworthy and totally unjustified!!

The basis of all fraud cases is the element of dishonesty on the part of the accused person, and the jury will be asked to infer from his behaviour and his activities that he was dishonest. The requirement is to differentiate between the man whose failure was due to bad luck and the man who was simply incompetent. There is no legal definition of dishonesty, the courts having traditionally left juries to determine the definition for themselves on the basis that dishonesty is an ordinary English word capable of being understood. A number of cases have been considered by the Court of Appeal in an attempt to regularise the problems relating to an acceptable definition of dishonesty, the law being admitted to be in a 'complicated state' (R v. Ghosh. 1982 QB 1053). In that case the court stated that dishonesty should be defined as follows:

'In determining whether the prosecution has proved that the defendant was acting dishonestly, a jury must first of all decide whether according to the ordinary standards of reasonable and honest people what was done was dishonest. If it was not dishonest by those standards, that is the end of the matter and the prosecution fails. If it was dishonest by those standards, then the jury must consider whether the defendant himself must have realised that what he was doing was by those standards dishonest.'

As you might expect, this definition has been welcomed by some and criticised by others and has generated a considerable amount of academic argument. No doubt this and other definitions will continue to be argued about for years but this will not help those men and women who will be called on to perform jury service in the future. They are constantly told by the judge in his summing up that they are the sole judges of fact, and on the facts as presented to them they must establish whether or not they find that the defendant has been dishonest.

The first major difficulty which faces any man or woman called up for jury service and finding that he or she is being required to sit on a fraud trial is the amount of time which the case is likely to take. Technically speaking, jury service lasts two weeks, but fraud trials can last many weeks, indeed some last months. The vast majority of people summoned to perform jury service want to take part and fulfil their social duty. The greatest criticism by far made by those people who have performed such a duty is that little thought is given to their comfort, their needs or their understanding of what is happening. I have seen jurors being herded from court room to court room by an usher, or sitting around in shabby rooms, with few amenities for their comfort, waiting to be called to sit on a jury.

Even if they are called, some of them may be challenged by the defence on totally arbitrary grounds and told to stand down. Few attempts are made to explain to them why they have been challenged; indeed, the defence is not required to show cause at the present time, although this may be subject to change in the future. This aspect can be deeply hurtful and can cause great resentment. Jurors are not reimbursed in realistic financial terms. While this may not necessarily cause hardship to the man or woman whose employer is sufficiently understanding to continue paying their basic wages while they are absent, there is no requirement for the employer to do this and some refuse. For the self-employed man or woman, such a lack of payment can represent a real drawback and provide a powerful disincentive to their agreement to sit in judgement on their fellows.

Before most potentially lengthy trials, the judge will inform the jury that the case is one which may last for some time, and he will hear representations from those jurors who may have good reasons for wishing to be excused from such duties. Judges try to be accommodating as far as is humanly possible and will excuse those whose business or employment could suffer. Inevitably, however, juries may tend to be comprised, at least in part, of people who may begin to find that their civic duty is fast becoming a civic burden.

Defence counsel are not unaware of this and one of the popular techniques is to attempt to bore the jury into submission, hoping that if the case drags on and on, the jury will eventually become so confused and bamboozled with conflicting arguments, cross allegations and legal rhetoric that they will vote for an acquittal as being the line of least resistence. In fairness to those juries which I have observed, it is my experience that they have conducted their duties with considerable fairness and a high degree of responsibility. It always surprised me however that we treat these people with such little regard for their needs and their understanding.

Another important group of people in such trials are the witnesses. In fraud cases, such people may be those with considerable demands upon their time such as businessmen, bankers, brokers and accountants. Again, little concern or consideration appears to be shown for their requirements. Many witnesses are kept hanging around for hours, if not days, on end, waiting to be called to give their evidence. Witnesses can only be paid a daily maximum fee for attending court, except in the very rare instances where they are defined as being 'expert'. In the event, most of them find themselves out of pocket as a result. One businessman who came to give evidence in such a fraud case told me that he would never again report a fraud to the police after his humiliating experiences at court. He was kept waiting for days to be called, and was then subjected to a scathing attack upon his character by the defence counsel. It was, he said, as if he were the person on trial and in future he said that he would prefer to 'arrange matters in his own way'. Faced with these experiences, is it any wonder that members of the public are loath to become witnesses in a criminal trial?

Another technique is to produce documents and evidence at the trial which it is claimed have only just come to light and, in fairness to the accused person, should be admitted even though the prosecution has not had a chance to examine the contents. In the trial of those responsible for operating Boston Financial Services Ltd, during the defence case and after the prosecution case had closed, one of the defence lawyers produced a set of photocopied trade documents which, it was claimed, provided his client with a complete explanation for the existence of large sums of money about which he had been questioned by the police. His answer originally to the police had been that the money had been obtained by fraudulent means from unsuspecting clients, but here, suddenly, were documents, albeit copies, which purported to show that he could explain these sums of money as being trade profits from his dealings on American futures markets. Bearing in mind that the trial was all about the provision of forged trade and broker statements, it seemed incredible that the lawyers could suddenly claim that these documents should be admitted into evidence, as proof of their client's truthfulness.

Having come this far it is not difficult to appreciate the truth of the solicitor's statement about the unwillingness of fraudsmen to 'do a deal' before trial. In the event of a conviction being recorded, what sentence can such a defendant expect? Invariably, sentences imposed by judges for such frauds are light, in terms of immediate imprisonment. This point was remarked upon by John Wood in his speech to the American Bar Association. Armed robbery attracts draconian penalties, fraud doesn't. Perhaps society is really expressing its fear of violence in such long sentences rather than its concern for the sums of money involved. Yet, it is really only the likelihood of an immediate custodial sentence on conviction that can be said to provide any degree of deterrence to someone determined to commit crime. Professional criminals take the probability of imprisonment into their calculations when determining the profitability of carrying out their scheme. I am not talking here about opportunist crime, anti-social acts of vandalism, alcohol-related acts of violence, minor drug pushers or petty shoplifters. I am talking about people who deliberately set out upon a concerted scheme of criminal activity for profit. As one fraudsman put it to me:

'It's only the porridge that might put me off, and then it depends how much. Anything else is a result. Benders [suspended prison sentences] are f... all, and fines are nothing more than a Hire Purchase commitment.'

It is as if judges share a similar view to the rest of society that fraud, or white-collar crime, is somehow different from all other acts of criminal activity, and therefore deserving of different treatment. Michael Levi attempted to explain this phenomenon in his study of another kind of fraudulent activity in his book *The Phantom Capitalists*. He said:

'Despite the fact that the long-firm fraudster is one of the types of business criminal most prone to be regarded as an "anti-capitalist" outsider, judges find it easier to empathise with such men than they do with other types of criminal.'

Dr Levi also expressed his concern in another way. He said:

'The reader may be surprised at the relatively short sentences imposed upon the principals of conspiracies to defraud, for they undermine the trust between those who transact business on credit, on which the capitalist system depends, and one might have expected that the threat they pose to the interests of commerce would attract the wrath of the judiciary.'

Having seen how easy it is for the determined professional to conduct his criminal activities, how difficult it is to apprehend him, bring him before a court, and convict him, is it any wonder that those people charged with the responsibility for dealing with such men find themselves believing that their efforts were in vain? Particularly when they watch the subjects of their investigations walking away from court, having received in some cases little more than a stern ticking off and a fine. Yet these operators pose a far greater threat to the economic wellbeing of society. It was this element of dishonesty to which Dorain Williams referred in his letter to *The Times* when he said:

'As it flourishes, honesty is less and less practised because less and less expected. Confidence is undermined, not only in our great financial institutions, but in the probity of all who have something to purvey, whether it be goods or services or news or even a political point of view.'

CHAPTER TEN
Roskill—A Blueprint For The Future

The first thing we do, let's kill all the lawyers.
Shakespeare, *Henry VI*, Part 2, Act IV, scene 2.

The terms of reference applied to the Roskill Committee were:

'To consider in what ways the conduct of criminal proceedings in England and Wales arising from fraud can be improved and to consider what changes in existing law and procedure would be desirable to secure the just, expeditious and economical disposal of such proceedings.'

In view of the far-reaching brief given to the Roskill Committee, it is perhaps a pity that the media tended to concentrate on one specific aspect of the subjects for study, namely the vexed question of the continued retention of jury trial in major fraud cases. I suppose that such a report would attract that kind of sensationalist interest from reporters, concentrating as most of them do on stories that can be written in words which rarely use more than one syllable and managing to trivialise even the most important issues.

The major importance of the Roskill Committee's deliberations lay in the realisation that the increasing degree of de-regulation which would inevitably come in the City would mean that fraud would become an ever more dangerous financial probability. In the Committee's own words:

'There was also a general feeling at the time of our appointment that since much serious fraud appeared to escape deception or successful prosecution this served only to encourage its growth, with potentially harmful consequences not only for the unfortunate victims of fraud, but also for the reputation of the nation, and in particular the City of London, as one of the world's great financial centres.'

One of the fundamental stumbling blocks, in the path of efficient fraud investigation, identified by the Roskill Committee at an early stage, was the singular lack of a unified approach by the various agencies responsible for conducting such investigations. In their introduction to the report, the Committee made this observation:

'We welcome the closer collaboration between the prosecuting authorities which the establishment of the permanent Fraud Investigation Group arrangements has initiated. However, we think that the need for a new unified organisation responsible for all the functions of detection, investigation and prosecution of serious fraud should be examined forthwith.'

Much has been made in the press and media of the existence of the new Fraud Investigation Group or FIG and, in common with so many reorganised departments developed at a time of political expediency, much is expected of it and great success is predicted for it. In his speech to the Bow Group on 3 July 1984, the Chancellor of the Exchequer, Nigel Lawson, said:

'This [the FIG] will be a multidisciplinary team of prosecuting lawyers and accountants headed by a Controller reporting directly to the DPP and the Attorney General. The Group will be able to request investigations of company books using the DTI's statutory powers, and will work in close liaison with police fraud squads. It will replace the existing ad hoc groups which investigate particular cases, and the DPP's staff and other resources will be strengthened accordingly. This is an important new initiative which I believe will greatly improve the effectiveness with which these cases are dealt.'

Its pedigree goes back as far as 1978, when a working party was established by the Attorney General, 'to review the arrangements for the investigation and prosecution of fraud, particularly company fraud, and examine the role and co-ordination between each of the authorities with responsibilities in this field.'

One of the functions of the working party was to examine the possibility for greater co-operation between the various investigatory agencies. The outcome of this report was the setting up, in 1979, of a working group to examine the proposals and to consider what was needed to 'improve the speed and efficiency in detecting, investigating and prosecuting commercial fraud.'

This working group then continued its deliberations for approximately two years until in 1981 an informal trial run was made in two cases involving the DPP, the DTI and the Metropolitan Police Fraud

Squad. The Roskill Report does not identify which two cases were investigated, although one would expect if the method had produced a resounding success in terms of the prosecution of a major fraud, the report would have mentioned the fact, which it doesn't. In July 1984, it was announced that the ad hoc arrangements would be placed on a permanent basis and, from 1 January 1985, the FIG arrangements were brought into being.

The primary objectives of the FIG are threefold and they are intended to bring together the various statutory powers available to the various investigatory agencies, to ensure that all disciplines work closely together and to ensure that investigations concentrate upon major issues and major offenders in order to facilitate a speedy investigation.

The sort of cases envisaged as being suitable for the FIG are those involving frauds upon Government departments or local authorities, large-scale corruption, shipping and currency offences, frauds discovered during the course of DTI investigations, frauds committed by persons connected with Lloyds, the Stock Exchange and other Commercial Exchanges and frauds with an international dimension. It can be seen immediately that most, if not all, allegations of investment fraud will come under the FIG aegis.

The aim of the FIG is to establish as quickly as possible the investigative parameters of any allegation, to identify the main aspects of the investigation and to concentrate resources upon a speedy investigation of those important elements, thus reducing the perceived tendency of police to concentrate on seemingly unnecessary and time-wasting enquiries. The guidelines anticipate that allegations suitable for a FIG will be reported to the DPP as soon as possible, following receipt by police. An early conference will be held to decide whether the case is a suitable one and an investigation strategy will be defined. Regular meetings will be held thereafter between police and FIG officers who will be responsible for co-ordinating the relevant specialist departments if their expertise is considered necessary.

In theory, the FIG concept is a good one and with the right degree of resource allocation plus the right quality of specialist staff it could represent a major step forward in the investigation of complex fraud. There are however a number of fundamental flaws in its concept which should be examined to place the FIG in its proper perspective.

The structure of the FIG envisages an investigation being conducted along the lines of a committee, with the legal officer in charge of an individual case, guiding the investigators towards those aspects of a case which he feels should attract the greatest concentration of resources. This immediately removes the discretion from the investigating police officer to conduct his investigation in the way in which his experience might dictate to be necessary. There is a tendency among certain commentators to overlook the importance of practical experience in criminal investigation and this is not possessed by academic lawyers employed in Government departments. This experience is possessed however by detectives who have spent a career developing skills necessary for the successful investigation of the affairs of professional criminals. Hitherto, the DPP's staff have always been reluctant to interfere with the day-to-day decision-making processes normally the province of the police but inevitably the tendency will develop for the case-controller to take over the mantle of directing the course of the investigation and the detectives will act on his directions. This procedure is very common on the Continent, where most major criminal investigations are directed by a prosecutor who is a lawyer, not a trained investigator, the police conducting their investigations at his command.

Such a proposal is not possible under our law as it currently stands. It is for this reason that police are not directly involved in the structure of FIG. Police officers in the UK hold the ancient role of constable and as such exercise their powers under the Crown. In law they cannot be subject to direction as to the exercise of those powers.

The Roskill Committee identified this problem, albeit indirectly, when they came to consider the structure of the FIG. They reported: 'the fact that even now only two departments (DPP and DTI) are directly involved in these arrangements, that the police retain their independence and that the Inland Revenue and Customs and Excise remain outside the arrangements are all matters of concern.'

It is for this reason that Roskill recommended the creation of an organisation responsible for all the functions of detection, investigation and prosecution of serious fraud. It would be staffed by lawyers, accountants and investigation officers, trained in all the skills appropriate to the complexity of the work involved. The Committee went on to identify its reasons for making this proposal. They said:

'Such an organisation with unified control and direction would have a number of distinct advantages. In particular, fewer serious frauds would be allowed to escape prosecution by slipping through the net of a series of independent organisations working in this field; overlapping of resources could be avoided; it would enable the investigation process to lead to more effective prosecution; there would be scope for greater efficiency and the reduction of delays; unhelpful restrictions on the disclosure of information from one organisation to another would be avoided and a unified organisation would have full powers of investigation.'

Why did the Committee make this recommendation?

'We recognise that bringing about changes of this kind would not be easy, because it would involve bringing together under one roof organisations which have for historical reasons worked apart. There is, we believe, a degree of institutional reluctance among the organisations concerned to work fully and effectively together.'

It is interesting to note that the Roskill Committee made this proposal right at the start of their report in the first chapter. Everything that follows in the lengthy and carefully constructed document must be seen as taking second place to the overwhelming importance of the creation of an independent body, properly trained, and provided with adequate staff and resources to enable them to conduct realistic investigations into the activities of professional criminals.

The other aspect of fundamental importance identified by Roskill and reported in the first chapter of the report was the provision of adequate resources, in general to deal with fraud. They said:

'The evidence we have received has left us with the firm impression that the resources, both in terms of manpower and ability, are in many cases barely adequate and in some cases totally inadequate to cope with the volume of work generated by the increasing number of reported cases of fraud . . . It is essential, however, that the overall shortage of resources which clearly exists must be remedied as a matter of priority. The Government and others responsible for the provision of manpower must therefore ensure that adequate resources are provided to deal with this area of criminality.'

Within twelve months of its official creation, the Committee noted that a report in Hansard of 2 December 1985 admitted that the resources of the FIG were 'seriously stretched'.

There can be no doubt that the Roskill Report threw the gauntlet down to the Government and challenged it to provide the resources necessary for the efficient investigation and prosecution of fraud. In addition, it not only identified the need for the Government to review its policies but indirectly invited chief officers of police to reconsider their attitudes towards the provision of resources to be applied to fraud investigation. They said:

'Another question which concerns us is whether the policy of short-term three-year postings to the Fraud Squads is conducive to the efficient handling of investigations of serious fraud cases . . . a long stay in the Fraud Squad is the exception and is often regarded as damaging to an officer's career prospects, but short stays give no opportunity for extensive training and acquisition of expertise . . . We acknowledge that senior officers both in the Metropolitan Police and in other forces must have regard to the operational requirements of their force as a whole. However, we take the view that the provision of a career structure within Fraud Squads is essential, particularly having regard to the increasing levels of sophistication of fraud.'

Having looked at the new method for the co-ordination of investigations, let us now turn to the Committee's recommendations for reforming the criminal justice system in order to make fraud trials more effective. Again, the Committee's own words illustrate far better than I could hope to do their attitude towards the changes which they deem to be necessary. In the summary to the report at paragraph 15 they said:

'Some of our proposals may shock traditionalists. The same was probably true of the proposal to abolish the mediaeval practice of trial by combat . . . We intend that the true aggregate effect of our recommendations should be to tip the balance in favour of justice, economy and expedition and against injustice, waste and delay.'

In a way the conduct and efficiency of fraud trials mirrors the fundamental problems of fraud investigation generally. Fraudsmen are not, by nature, violent criminals, so they rarely spend much time in custody before trial. Court time is at a premium and the courts are under great pressure from the Lord Chancellor's Department to give priority to those cases where the defendants are held in custody. Inevitably, fraud cases tend to take a considerable time to come to trial. During this time, the defendant can be creating another business, organising another fraud, or manufacturing evidence.

All the time an alleged fraudsman remains on bail, little or nothing can be done about arranging reimbursement for the losers, even if access can be gained to their funds. The question of restitution or compensation cannot be made until the criminal case has been completed and the defendant convicted. If he is acquitted, there is nothing the criminal courts can do. The primary consideration in the minds of the victims of fraudsmen is the likelihood of recovering their money. For many such victims, recovery is the utmost priority, giving evidence against the perpetrator of a fraud is very much a secondary consideration.

It is right and proper in a civilised society that a man should not be convicted on evidence which does not reach a sufficiently high standard. On the other hand, it become inequitable when the standard of proof required and the procedures for introducing such proof become so onerous that maintaining a realistic degree of efficiency becomes impossible. When this happens, the loser or victim is discriminated against in favour of the rights of an accused man. It is a fundamental duty of all free societies to maintain the fine balance between both parties, thus ensuring that belief in the efficiency of the rule of law is ensured. If such a belief is eroded, victims will tend to take matters into their own hands, in an attempt to adjust the balance. This inexorably leads to a cynical disregard for the operation of the law, which in itself poses an additional threat to the continued stability of society.

There already exists an attitude among a number of large institutions that reporting certain types of fraud to the police or the DTI is a waste of time, effort and energy. Instead, many senior executives will instruct the growing number of so-called 'security consultants' whose activities are rapidly becoming a second-tier operation in the business of fraud investigation and asset tracing. These companies exist without the least form of regulatory control or supervision and anyone can set up such an organisation, staff it with unqualified personnel and go into business offering security services. The dangers inherent in the use of such organisations are many because they operate, in part, with the tacit encouragement of solicitors anxious to provide the most efficient service for their clients. There are examples of companies which operate very efficiently, within the law, and which provide a very good service. There are others whose activities are quite frankly nothing more than criminal.

Such organisations operate in one of two ways. They will offer to provide a service for fees, either a single fee or on a daily rate. There are others who will operate for a percentage of whatever funds are recovered. Whichever way you look at it, the service being offered is going to cost money and the original loser is going to want to minimise any further financial exposure as much as possible. The inevitable result is that many of these 'consultants' cease to become investigators and simply cut corners in an attempt to get the required result in the shortest possible time. A number of their activities must provide a considerable cause for concern because they act outside the law and in a way which the law specifically prohibits to its authorised law enforcers such as the police and the other enforcement agencies.

One example is the access which can be obtained to the information concerning the contents of a private bank account. Should a police officer in the course of his investigations wish to ascertain the existence or contents of a bank account owned or operated by a person whom he suspects, the banks will not give him this information voluntarily. The officer must first seek an order under the Bankers Books Evidence Act 1879, which is granted to him by a magistrate or a judge. Before such an order will be granted, the officer must satisfy the magistrate that proceedings have commenced against the suspect, ie, that he has been charged or a summons has been issued, and that he has sufficient grounds for believing that this search will provide him with evidence. The order, once granted, will apply only to the records contained within the 'books' of the bank, even though they may be contained on computer tape or microfilm. The order does not apply to the recovery of paid cheques, or correspondence between the bank and the customer, such records being required to form the subject of yet another legal device to secure their production before a court.

In addition, there are certain powers contained within the Police and Criminal Evidence Act 1984 which may assist police officers in applying for orders to examine banking evidence prior to the commencement of proceedings. These are limited in scope and carefully monitored.

There are perfectly good reasons why Parliament felt it necessary to provide such safeguards when the question of the confidentiality of bank accounts was considered. In a free society it is right that people should be permitted to conduct their legitimate business dealings privately and without hindrance. One such privilege is everyone's right to own a bank account, which they can operate secure in the knowledge that it will not be pried into by any unauthorised person and that such authority should only be granted to a supervised person who has genuine and legitimate reasons for making such an enquiry. The only forum which has the means of assessing the worth of such a request is a court. It is also right that a series of checks and balances should exist to ensure that the privilege is not abused. It is only in these and other ways that a civilised society can prevent too great an incursion into the liberty of its subjects while providing the necessary degree of facility to conduct efficient criminal investigations.

At no time did Parliament ever envisage that private agencies should have access to the contents of bank accounts without the necessity for court orders, yet access to such information can be obtained through a number of agencies on the payment of a small fee, and without the necessity for any kind of court order. I am not going to speculate on the methods which such agencies adopt to obtain this information but the likelihood exists that, in performing such a task, they could find themselves in conflict with the laws which exist to prevent bank employees from breaching their employers' trust and the terms of their employment, in return for money or payment in kind.

Another technique which must cause concern to anyone with a degree of regard for the concept of the rule of law is the ease with which some 'consultants' can supply the means to provide unauthorised telephone taps. Again, should such a facility be required by the police, in the course of an official investigation, they must first satisfy the Home Secretary of the need for such a facility and he must personally grant the authority permitting the use of such equipment. Again, it is unlikely that Parliament contemplated the likelihood of unauthorised private persons being able to supply such services, yet they exist and are widely resorted to by the cowboy element.

Other techniques resorted to by the plethora of security consultants include the unauthorised interception and examination of mail, burglary of home and office premises to steal information or to plant electronic listening devices, and bribery or attempts to corrupt public officials in return for access to privileged records.

For these services, most consultants charge fees which are astronomical in their scope, and which, when coupled with the kind of expenses which are always included, represent little more than an additional exploitation of the victim of fraud. These organisations flourish for the simple reason that the official agencies are impotent to deal with the concerted efforts of professional criminals and their advisors, and the consultancies know that many losers will be prepared to pay to get at least some of their losses back and will not want to ask too many questions. Despite the many claims of the efficiency and success of their methods, the dubious results achieved by many of these 'consultants' do not arise out of anything more than burglary, coercion, or blackmail. Hardly an elevating example for a society which claims to be governed by the rule of law. If these 'consultants' wish to spend their time grubbing around in dustbins to find discarded notepaper or trying to dig up dirt to blacken the reputation of company directors or newspaper magnates, that is, I suppose a matter for them. We live after all in an age when some people will do anything for money, no matter how shabby or dishonourable. Such persons should not be permitted however to meddle in matters which should properly be the responsibility of the regulatory authorities, provided for and supervised by Parliament.

The Roskill Committee reported that the present legal arrangements for the conduct of fraud investigations and trials 'may even encourage the defence to conduct its case like a prolonged and orderly retreat from the truth. This we find unacceptable.' It is to be hoped that their proposals will provide the degree of assistance necessary to reverse that process, which will, in turn, put so many of the cowboy outfits currently masquerading under the guise of 'security consultants' out of business, as their esoteric services will no longer be required.

During the period of press speculation which preceded the publication of the Roskill Report, much was made of the suggestion that the Committee would recommend the abolition of jury trials in certain cases of fraud. It is a topic which is most likely to exercise the minds of the vast majority of public commentators and is an ideal theme for the editors of newspapers and periodicals because it is capable of being seen in terms of black and white, right and wrong, for and against. I am against the idea of the removal of the right of trial by jury for any criminal case which involves the element of dishonesty. In this instance, I am forced to declare an interest in my belief in the continued retention of the jury in fraud trials and I believe that much could be done to make fraud trials less onerous to those required to perform jury service without removing any of the necessary protections from the accused man, a constitutional move which would be utterly reprehensible.

It is an undeniable fact that fraudsters can usually afford to pay very hefty sums of money in preparing their defence. This is hardly surprising as in many cases they are paying with money which belongs to their unfortunate clients. It would be asking too much of human nature to expect many solicitors to turn down the opportunity to earn a considerable amount of money in fees from such a client, knowing that they can charge virtually what they like, and it will be paid. It is a sad fact, but widely perceived to be true by experienced fraud detectives that the amount of work provided by a solicitor specialising in defending fraudsmen is directly proportional to the regularity with which his client deposits money for his fees. Another factor which must be considered in the equation is the ease with which many people charged with fraud are granted legal aid. This is a guarantee of payment to the solicitor from the public purse and as such will provide a degree of legal assistance for the person who is genuinely without sufficient means to pay for his own defence. It is an old saying among certain members of the legal profession that 'a legal aid fee gets a legal aid job'. Another way of defining it is 'you only get what you pay for'. The practice of 'toppers' is therefore widely practised.

'Toppers' is a word given to the practice of 'topping up' a legal aid bill by private means, using the State funds to pay for the basics, and then providing the solicitor concerned with the balance of his fees from out of the client's private resources. I can hear solicitors all round the country screaming in outrage at such a scurrilous assertion, but let me assure you and them that among a small minority of practitioners, the practice is rife and goes on all the time. These activities are not condoned by the vast majority of the profession who conduct their dealings honourably, but the practice has been described too often by defendants to doubt its existence.

The aim of the professional solicitor is to ensure that his client secures an acquittal. They will tell you that their purpose is to provide their client with the best professional advice possible and to act in his best interests, and there is no doubt that they do perform this service. Again, it is a fact of life that the solicitor who gets a name for ensuring a high rate of acquittals will attract an ever larger clientele. It is the methods employed by such lawyers to secure acquittals which have represented a series of damaging inroads into the good practices of the law and led the Roskill Committee to refer to their behaviour as a 'prolonged and orderly retreat from the truth'. It is these practices which the Committee has sought in part to reform.

The question of the method of transferring fraud cases to the crown court and the other technical matters which surround the choosing of a venue and the appointment of a trial judge, the appointment of counsel to supervise the case from an early stage and the other recommendations, are merely reforms of an administrative nature. These provisions, while going a long way to assisting in the removal of technical anomalies and providing for a more efficient transfer to the jurisdiction of the crown court, do not make for very interesting study for the non-lawyer and I do not intend to include them.

The first reform I wish to discuss is that which deals with the provision of documentary evidence, particularly that which comes from abroad. This is directly relevant to the question of the understanding of the jury, as it is from documents and evidence such as this that they will be required to decide guilt or innocence.

In a fraud trial if I want to put a document into evidence, I must also be able to produce someone who can testify to the accuracy of the document. Such a document may be very important or it may simply be one of a long series of documents which make up a single transaction. In cases where such evidence has to be produced from abroad and the witness subsequently proves to be reluctant to attend the court in this country, the documentary evidence cannot be admitted and the jury cannot see it. It is hardly surprising therefore that many defence lawyers have used the preliminary committal hearings to subject foreign witnesses to such hostile cross-examination that they are unwilling to return again to repeat the experience. These rules of evidence provide a major stumbling block to the efficient conduct of fraud trials and Roskill recognised this fact. The Committee said:

'If society wishes to see the successful prosecution of those who are believed to have swindled large numbers of people, whether large investors or small investors, out of their assets, it must be prepared to stop the use of these ancient rules of evidence. They were devised as a protection for the innocent against the risk of wrongful conviction, not as a shield for those who, at least in the eyes of many, have been guilty of exceedingly serious and ingeniously devised frauds upon their victims, the concealment of which has often been as ingenious as the mode of their perpetration.'

The Committee further argued that the removal of such ancient forms of procedure would not remove any degree of protection from defendants who genuinely had a good defence. The only person they assisted was 'the skilled fraudster with no real defence to obstruct the administration of justice in the hope of gaining some advantage'. Roskill finally said what so many professional policemen had known for years:

'We have been informed of a sufficient number of instances where defendants have not been prepared to "agree" documents, where the only possible motive for their being unwilling to do so was a desire to prolong the trial, to confuse the jury and to take advantage of every conceivable opportunity to play the system.'

In their recommendations concerning documentary evidence, the

Committee sought to bring a degree of modern relevance to what had become a procedural and jurisdictional nightmare for prosecutors. A summary of their findings in this regard means that documents should be admissable as evidence of proof without formal proof of their contents, and that evidence taken abroad should become admissable, subject to certain guidance to the jury that it has not been tested by cross-examination. These recommendations do not alter in any way the fundamental role of the jury to decide upon the defendant's honesty or otherwise. They will remove a whole range of time-wasting techniques and pitfalls which have prevented evidence of a totally non-contentious but valuable nature being admitted in the past and which have been resorted to by professional criminals to further the likelihood of their acquittal.

The only function of the jury in any criminal trial is to decide upon the honesty or dishonesty of the accused. They will be continually told that they are the sole judges of fact. The facts of any case are, surprisingly, usually very simple and do not need a great deal of explanation. To this end, the Committee made a number of recommendations regarding the use of pre-trial procedures intended to identify those aspects of a case which would form the basis of contention in order that the areas of direct dispute could be simplified. Again, many of their recommendations are of an administrative nature, the most radical reform requiring the defence to outline the nature of their defence during the preparatory stages of the pre-trial procedures. A failure to comply with this requirement being the subject of comment by the prosecution and the judge at the trial and in the case of an unnecessarily prolonged trial, the sanction of costs against the defendant being available, the defendant being warned in advance of the trial of the possible consequences of his failure to disclose his case. In addition, the Committee recommended that pre-trial admissions of agreed facts and agreed documents should be prepared by both sides, and all obviously contentious points of law should be determined before the trial commences. A failure to comply with any of these points would be reflected in the costs sanction in appropriate cases.

The vast bulk of evidence in all fraud cases is usually non-objectionable and one must presume that a defendant who is dealt with for an allegation of fraud knows at a very early stage, having sought legal advice, whether his conduct is lawful or unlawful. If he intends to contest the nature of a prosecution case against him, what possible harm to his civil liberties can be posed by requiring him to state the nature of his defence, before the case comes to be heard in the final form? The basis for the present requirement of proof of every aspect of a prosecution case dates back to the days when the death penalty was very common for even relatively minor offences, and when defendants were not permitted to give evidence on their own behalf. The reason for this draconian rule, according to some historians, was that it was commonly believed that no man, faced with the prospect of the hangman if convicted, would tell the truth when speaking in his own defence, and if allowed to give evidence, having taken an oath on the Bible, would be in jeopardy of damning his immortal soul by telling lies to defend himself.

Since 1898, criminal defendants have been allowed to give evidence on their own behalf but the rules of evidence have not been altered very greatly to accommodate the change in advantage which has become firmly placed in favour of the defendant. It is not uncommon, particularly in fraud cases, for the defence to decide upon their final strategy in the week prior to the crown court hearing.

It never ceased to amaze me, however, how often a defendant would arrive at his trial, armed with a complete explanation for all the allegations put to him during his interview with the police. The regularity with which this practice occurred, particularly where certain solicitors were engaged in the client's defence, led me to ponder on solicitors' uncanny ability to find clients who were so obviously innocent and who, if their stories were true, should never have been standing in the dock.

The proposed changes outlined here will do much to render a number of defence techniques obsolete and will lead to a greater degree of clarity of the salient issues placed before the jury. The purpose of the Roskill Committee was to consider all aspects of the fraud trials procedure and, inevitably, the question of the retention of the jury in certain trials was raised as a matter of importance, and became an issue which has tended to overshadow the more vital aspects of the Roskill Committee's findings. In the report the Committee stated:

'Society appears to have an attachment to jury trial which is emotional or sentimental rather than logical.'

This may well be true but it may be thought to be an attachment well worth retaining. The most penetrating conclusion reached by the Committee, one member, Mr Walter Merricks, dissenting, was that the traditional jury, chosen at random with little requirement for specialist qualification, was an anomaly when considered against accepted standards in every other area of the law. The Committee said:

'The most important conclusion to draw from these considerations however is that in almost every area of the law, society has accepted that just verdicts are best delivered by persons qualified by training, knowledge, experience, integrity or by a combination of these four qualifications. Only in a minority of cases is the delivery of a verdict left in the hands of jurors deliberately selected at random without any regard for their qualifications. Thus those who advocate that complex fraud trials should be conducted before a select, as opposed to a random, tribunal are arguing not that such cases should be treated in any special or unique fashion, but that they should be treated in a manner more akin to the way the vast majority of all other legal cases are treated today.'

The Committee had discussed the large number of cases which were tried before single judges, lay magistrates and specialist tribunals, which, they said, proved that literally millions of cases could be satisfactorily handled without the suggestion that a defendant had been denied the fairest form of trial, ie trial by jury.

The fundamental error in the logic of the Committee's finding lay not so much in the proposal to deny jury trial to yet another, albeit a very small, area of criminal activity, but in the creation of a specialist class of offence, described as 'complex fraud'. By defining complex fraud, the Committee created the concept of a crime which it was felt was beyond the comprehension of ordinary men and women because the methods and techniques used were so specialised, and it should therefore be removed from the responsibility of the jury.

It is true that many more defendants are dealt with in this country by single stipendiary magistrates or lay benches and indeed there are a large number of offences for which a defendant does not have a right of trial by jury. In fairness, no great injustice is done if a man is denied a jury trial for breaking a milk bottle or for blackening his neighbour's eye. These are the sort of acts which will inevitably take place in any robust society and no man's reputation would suffer unduly upon conviction for such an offence. Many fine men and women have served prison sentences without anyone thinking any the less of them. Consider the example of the late Emmanuel Shinwell. As far as I am aware however no man or woman in this country can be charged with an offence, the definition of which includes the concept of deliberate dishonesty as opposed to omission, for which he or she does not have

198 TOO GOOD TO BE TRUE

the right to be tried by a jury. This does not mean that the person concerned must be tried by a jury, indeed the vast majority of people still consent to be dealt with by magistrates, but it is, I believe, a fundamental right of any person in a free society to be tried by a jury if conviction for an offence will fundamentally alter that person's reputation for good character.

Indeed, the only factor which a jury is required to decide is whether what the defendant is alleged to have done, was dishonest by the ordinary standards of the time. There is no tribunal which could provide a more independent assessment of dishonesty than the jury system, as there can be no independent definition of dishonesty. It is for this reason, among others, that the law has never attempted to produce one.

A man can be a boozer and a brawler and his friends will smile and wink and say what a fine fellow he is. His employers will turn a blind eye as long as his work doesn't suffer. His conviction for such an offence will be put down to fate and forgotten. Prove the same man to be a thief and the attitude of society changes radically. From a sample examined by him, Dr Michael Levi has produced some remarkable figures of the attitudes of businessmen towards persons convicted of an offence of fraud. Over 90% of those questioned said they would avoid such a convicted person socially. It is this aspect that makes the proposal to remove the right of trial by jury for 'complex fraud' so controversial. Once a man's reputation can be altered by a tribunal, it seems to me to have created a very dangerous precedent. Once that precedent is established, what other inroads could not be made into our civil liberties by a Government of a different political persuasion? I believe that it was Lord Devlin who said: 'The right of trial by jury shows that the lamp of freedom still shines.' We should not underestimate the influence of juries in resisting the encroachments of an ever more powerful State machine which would seek to use the criminal process to silence its critics or to punish its servants. The acquittal of Clive Ponting and the defendants in the Cyprus spy case are very pertinent examples. Once we establish the precedent, Governments will always find reasons to justify their actions in extending their scope.

It cannot be beyond the wit of Parliament to reform the criminal trial system so that juries can represent a true cross-section of the community and not simply a 'group of housewives and unemployed men'. There are a number of proposals made by the Committee which would go a long way to providing for those reforms. There can be little argument for example with the requirement that potential jurors should be able to read, write, speak and understand English without difficulty.

If the Roskill proposals in other areas of the report are adopted, they will make a fundamental difference to the way in which evidence is admitted and presented to the jury. The use of pre-trial reviews to establish areas of contention, the agreement of aspects of non-contentious evidence, the requirement for the defence to outline their case at an early stage and the use of modern methods of presentation to describe evidence, using projectors, screens, schedules and diagrams can only assist in the simplification of the process. This is particularly the case where these procedures have been agreed before trial and the jury are not constantly being required to leave the court and wait in an ante-room while counsel argue about minutiae, a technique adopted on a number of occasions and used for no other reason than to confuse, irritate and discomfort the jury.

There are a large number of methods identified by Lord Roskill's Committee which could be adopted to facilitate jury comprehension, even in the most complex circumstances. These would sustain public confidence in the system and avoid the temptation to create a new and dangerous precedent which could have far-reaching and unforeseen constitutional consequences. Public confidence in the fairness and efficiency of the legal system is one of the biggest safeguards of a free and democratic society. The biggest stumbling block which stands in the way of the introduction of most, if not virtually all, the recommendations is the degree of public spending which will be required to provide the necessary facilities identified by the Committee. It is to be hoped that the Government will not leave the introduction of the reforms for another seven years, in the way they did over the introduction of the Fraud Investigation Group concept, although I am dubious of their willingness to indulge in spending on such a scale, despite their public protestations of concern. I am not alone however in believing that they will prefer to duck the issue. When I discussed the Committee's report with Professor Gower, he said:

'I'm afraid that I take a rather cynical view and I have thought it likely that their report will not be implemented to the same extent as mine has.'

CHAPTER ELEVEN
Still, Small Voices

Our regulatory framework must command the confidence of users, both here and abroad. It does not take many scandals to sully the reputation of a multitude of decent traders. There can be no conflict of interests in this matter between producer or provider on the one hand and the customer on the other. Unless the markets command the confidence of potential customers, here and abroad, they will not attract the business they need to prosper and develop.

The Secretary of State for Trade and Industry, Norman Tebbit, 16 July 1984.

In his speech to the House of Commons in opening the debate on the Gower Report, Norman Tebbit identified a series of important elements in the maintenance of confidence in the reputation of the City of London. The Gower Report on Investor Protection had concentrated the collective mind of the City and its practitioners on the structure of the investment facilities available and created a lengthy debate on the need for a radical change in regulatory procedures. The need for such a review was brought about partly by a general awareness of the approaching revolution in international financial dealings and partly by the scandalous collapse of a number of large City financial investment firms and stock brokers such as Hedderwick, Sterling Gumbar, Norton Warberg and Halliday Simpson, with the loss of considerable sums of client monies. With the failure of certain speculative commodity broking operations, such as Michael Doxford, plus the perceived criminal allegations made against Miller Carneigie Securities, coupled with the growing perception of scandals brewing within the Lloyds Insurance market, it is not difficult to see how urgently such a review of existing procedures was needed, if Britain was not to be excluded from the international investment market, having been 'blackballed' by investors and institutions not anxious to become the latest victims of bad faith, incompetence and downright fraud.

Professor Gower recognised the importance of his role when in his discussion paper he said:

'. . . recent failures of firms involved in investment management with loss of funds entrusted to them by their clients clearly show the need for some action without waiting for a thoroughgoing review and the availability of Parliamentary time.'

Professor Gower had been commissioned in July 1981 to undertake a review of Investor Protection with the following terms of reference:

a) to consider the statutory protection now required by (1) private and (2) business investors in securities and other property, including investors through unit trusts and open-ended investment companies operated in the United Kingdom;

b) to consider the need for statutory control of dealers in securities, investment consultants and investment managers; and

c) to advise on the need for new legislation.

Professor Gower's report has largely been overtaken by events, which have a greater degree of relevance and interest. It is instructive however to review his terms of operation and to consider a few of his findings as they will provide a useful comparison to the model proposed by the Government, which will ultimately form the new investor protection provisions for the future.

The first problem encountered by Professor Gower was that, taking all the existing statutes into consideration, he found that investment theory and practice had moved ahead of legislation and that most existing laws did not provide for a sufficient degree of protection for certain kinds of people who were encouraged to use new forms of investment. This led him to observe: 'It is not possible to restrict this review to dealings in securities in the strict sense.' Later in the review he said:

'Not only has there been a proliferation of investment media; there has been a similar proliferation of those who deal or advise. Today, someone who consults a bank manager, stock broker, insurance broker, investment manager or investment consultant on how he should invest to protect his future may end up with stocks and shares, options, an endowment policy (linked or unlinked), units of a trust, (authorised or unauthorised), ground rents, diamonds, kruger rands, shares in a commodity pool, commodity futures, financial futures, money on deposit etc. etc. or a combination of them.'

Having reviewed all the methods of investment open to the private

and business client and having considered all the various regulatory
methods then current, Professor Gower made some general conclusions concerning the situation at the time he was conducting his review.
His findings were that no overall system of regulation of the investment
media and securities industry existed and such unrelated elements of
regulation which did exist consisted of a hotch-potch of undetermined
controls exercised in part by Government directly, as through the DTI,
through quasi-Governmental agencies, such as the Bank of England or
the Registrar of Friendly Societies, or through a form of lax self-
regulation. In assessing these various methods, Professor Gower made
one very telling comment when he said:

'It is not easy to detect any rationale for the choice of one method of
regulation rather than another. All one can perhaps say is that the
practice has been to avoid any form of regulation until some scandal
has shown it cannot be avoided and then to choose statutory Governmental regulation unless there is a traditional self-regulatory agency in
existence to which the task may be left.'

It is perhaps inevitable that Professor Gower should have been led to
consider the advisability of the setting up of a Securities Commission,
along the lines of the American Securities and Exchange Commission.
He said:

'Logically a single Commission is the obvious way of producing
cohesion out of diversity and of focusing Governmental regulation
through a body that might prove more expert and efficient.'

The professor recognised however that such a recommendation
would not be 'practical politics'. In examining the City's attitude
towards such a body he was led to observe:

'I have been left in no doubt of the City's rooted objection to a
Commission and it cannot be ignored even if it may be thought
somewhat irrational in the light of the fact that a Commission need not
(and should not) rule out at least as much self-regulation as we have at
present.'

He was also able to observe, in addition to the institutional objections to such a Commission, that historically the time was not right for
the creation of a Securities Commission. He said:

'The early success of the American SEC was to a large extent due to
the desperate circumstances which led to its creation and to the fact
that it was seen as part of the Roosevelt New Deal and attracted some
of the most able and idealistic products of the universities and Law
Schools. Under present circumstances here, I cannot envisage a UK

Securities Commission exercising a comparable appeal.'

The professor's final proposals were a carefully constructed mixture of legislation, self-regulation and Government supervision encompassing the industry as a whole. He recommended the passing of a Securities Act which would replace the Prevention of Fraud (Investments) Act, and thereby make it an offence to carry on business in securities unless registered with one of a number of Self-Regulatory Agencies which would be recognised by the Department of Trade, plus containing various general anti-fraud provisions. Professor Gower made a recommendation that the co-ordination of the affairs of the SROs should be undertaken by the Council for the Securities Industry, despite the criticisms made of the Council's apparent difficulties in maintaining an harmonious relationship with the DTI, 'each having displayed a tendency to blame the other for not taking effective remedial action when something goes wrong'. In making this preliminary suggestion, Professor Gower was trying to make the best use of existing City bodies in an attempt to utilise immediately available skills and expertise, despite the fact that 'there are many in the City and elsewhere who regard it [CSI] as a fifth wheel on the coach with little prospect of ever becoming anything more useful.'

Regarding self-regulation, Professor Gower did not shrink from acknowledging the difficulties which he felt existed and he believed that such SROs would need to be supervised by a Government body with the power to alter the rules or constitutions of such organisations if it was considered necessary in the best interests of the consumer. Some of the dangers inherent in uncontrolled self-regulation observed by Gower were practices which seemed patently objectionable to outside observers because they gave rise to possible conflicts of interest, but which did not seem objectionable to those whose interests were affected. Another area which Gower identified as being a valuable service offered by potential SROs in supervising the activities of their members was in the establishment of certain minimal standards of professional competence. He said:

'A test of competence seems to me to be particularly needed in the field in which, at present, it is most conspicuously lacking—investment management and advice. More investors, I suspect, have suffered from the incompetence of their advisors than from their dishonesty. When there has been dishonesty, more often than not in recent years it has been to conceal, or to seek to get round, difficulties caused originally by incompetence.'

All in all, you may feel, a fairly unremarkable set of recommendations, designed to make the best use of existing facilities without the requirement of too great a degree of additional public spending, coupled with a recognition that either side of the industry, practitioners and regulatory alike, owed a duty to ensure the honest and efficient running of the British financial market. Gower offered an opportunity to the City literally to 'put its money where its mouth was', and prove that it was able to regulate its own affairs. At the same time, the professor placed a spotlight in the hands of the electorate because any failure of either side of the industry in the future would be the subject of immediate identification and public scrutiny. Had Gower's proposals been adopted there can be little doubt that they would have led to the most gentle of revolutions. They were not so much a series of new and revolutionary ideas as a means of tightening up a framework that already existed in part, a clarification of areas of authority plus a general acceptance of a greater degree of individual responsibility by practitioners within the industry to supervise the activities of their members, thus proving that they were best placed to spot the wrong-doer and to root him out.

In his report, Professor Gower identified the major difficulty which lay in defining the nature of the body which should have the primary responsibility for supervising the activities of the SROs. In his discussion paper, the professor had suggested, almost as a practical compromise, that a controlling role should be played by the Council for the Securities Industry. In the subsequent report, he had been bolder in making the suggestion which, I believe, was closer to his heart, that of a choice between the Department of Trade and Industry or a self-standing commission, which was his first choice in his discussion paper. Even then, he proffered the DTI as the more acceptable of the two alternatives, 'for practical and political considerations'.

The Gower Report was published in January 1984 and was subsequently debated in the House of Commons on 16 July 1984. In the interim period between publication and debate, it was obvious to the Government that the major issue would be the question of the composition of the relevant supervisory body the establishment of which would undoubtedly be recommended. Invitations were extended via the Governor of the Bank of England to ten leading City practitioners, to advise on the potential structure of a practitioner-based system which could advise on the institutional structure for regulation.

The debate on the Gower Report is an enlightening illustration of the polarisation of political attitudes towards the question of investor protection. From this debate, independent observers will be able to draw conclusions which will enable them to judge the willingness of the Government to introduce practicable regulations for the protection of investors. Fundamentally, the debate identified the difference of philosophies between those whose financial interests lie in the continuation of a self-regulated City, believing that market forces should be permitted to be the primary arbiter of efficiency, and those whose tastes are more towards creating an atmosphere of control, provided by a statutory body and reporting to Parliament.

The debate was opened by the then Secretary of State for Trade and Industry, Norman Tebbit, who indulged in a number of generalised statements, without really committing himself to a defined line of thinking. His approach was a mainstream monetarist line, seeing the needs of the future as providing 'the maximum freedom for market forces to stimulate competition and encourage innovation'. He made an oblique reference to the expected efficiency of the Fraud Investigation Group, noted that he was still awaiting the findings of the Roskill Committee and finished by making a clear preference for self-regulation, 'responsive to the needs of investors', coupled with some form of as then undefined intermediate body, upon which he was still waiting to be advised.

His speech was criticised by Peter Shore from the Labour front bench for failing to provide a sufficient lead in the direction of his thinking but he tended to ramble in the early part of his speech. He criticised the Government for their methods of approach, saying that investor protection was placed second to financial efficiency and he quoted various police reports which claimed that one of the main problems of combating fraud lay in the inadequacy of clear legislation. He identified the need for self-regulation as being inevitable and necessary but he came down clearly in favour of the creation of a self-standing securities commission. He made a very good point right at the end of his speech in which he declared that, if there were to be a statutory role, then it would not be an appropriate responsibility for the 'near-spectral Council for the Securities Industry' and he quoted from the Gower Report on this point:

'. . . there is a limit beyond which the relationship between Governmental regulation and self-regulation ceases to be a partnership and becomes a take-over. For the CSI to undertake the statutory role envisaged for a commission would exceed that limit—in effect, would be a takeover of the CSI by the Government.'

The next speech, by the then Mr Peter Tapsell, was a traditionalist rearguard Tory pronouncement which hardly addressed itself to the nature of the Gower Report at all. It became an 'I told you so' type of speech, in which he spent a considerable amount of time identifying the problems which would arise in the City of the future because of the nature of the changes being introduced. Mr Tapsell could well be criticised for speaking off the point, but as his speech developed it became clear that he was making a masterful argument for the introduction of a 'full-blooded securities commission'. His argument was, 'I don't agree with the changes which are coming, because I believe they are bad for the City of London. They will provide us with problems which we have not encountered in the past, which will have a direct bearing on investor confidence. However, if this is the way we are going, let us go the whole way and be done with it.' I am persuaded that his view was an inherently political one as opposed to a financial one and he made it perfectly clear that he was speaking as a politician and not as one of the country's leading stock brokers.

His contribution marked the end of the presentation of the major themes in the debate, much of what followed being a series of reiterations of the same arguments with the predictable political slant being applied to the points made. Speakers from both sides of the House and from all shades of opinion, for a number of reasons both financial and political, came down on the side of an independent commission being created to supervise the activities of the Self-Regulatory Organisations. In addition, virtually none of those who spoke believed that the role was suitable for the Department of Trade and Industry. It was fascinating to see the degree of unanimity which existed in favour of an independent, free-standing commission, or statutory body, despite the almost universal fear expressed in the media and in the City of a body similar to the Securities and Exchange Commission. One interesting speech in the debate was made by Stuart Bell, the member for Middlesbrough. Among the points made by him was one which deserves a greater degree of attention than most because it neatly describes an aspect of the City debate which many have perceived but few have commented on.

Many commentators have identified the disparity which exists between the interests of those who are in favour of unbridled competition and market forces, believing that such forces will inevitably apply a natural law to the activities of those who populate the City jungle; and those who come to the City uninitiated in its mysteries and who become the natural targets for the exponents of free market operations. Stuart Bell said:

'The real dilemma for the Government is whether they go the whole hog with a securities commission or let the City get on with it by way of self-regulating bodies. It is a genuine dilemma, well recognised by the City, which acts in some ways as though it were a race against both time and the Government.'

After reviewing the proposals to allow the group of City practitioners to make recommendations regarding an overall regulatory structure he said:

'All of that suggests to me that it is being done to show the Government that the City is prepared to have some kind of self-regulation, but that it should be what it says and does not require outside interference. That reminds me of the Council for the Securities Industry, which was set up in 1978 as part of the City's defensive response to the Labour proposals of 1974 for greater statutory regulation. The City is now seeking, through its institutions, to pre-empt Government action by its own measures.'

Mr Bell went on to challenge the Government that its present proposals would not assist in its policy of creating a share-owning democracy because, he said, the theme expressed by the present attitude towards investor protection, and he quoted Mr Tebbit, was that 'in "a speculative high-risk venture, which fails for straightforward commercial reasons, an investor cannot look to any recovery of losses arising from his own misjudgements." In short, if the private investor is fool enough to buy when the market value is high and sell when it is low, so be it . . . It hardly augurs well for those who believe in a share-owning democracy to let it be too widely known that such a democracy is built on the premise that a fool and his money are soon parted, but that amateur investors are welcome and, indeed, invited so long as they leave their money behind when they go.' He ended his speech with an uncompromising request to the Government:

'I wish that I could believe that the Secretary of State will pay more than lip service to the Gower Report and not leave the City of London to regulate itself. I hope that he will grasp the nettle of a thorough, tough-minded securities commission; that he will not leave the City of London in the hands of the professionals—the old boys on the same old-boy network, where scandals when they arise can be hushed up;

where losses can be swept under the carpet or into a Bank of England lifeboat; where money will continue to make money at the ultimate expense of the nation in increased bank rates, mortgage rates, reduced investment in manufacturing industry, losing rather than creating jobs, a world of money not a world of industry; and where, if there are fingers to be burnt, they will be those of the investing public.'

After the debate the Minister received representations from certain City practitioners who advised him on the nature of two bodies, drawn in part from practitioners themselves, which could advise on the institutional structure for regulation and for practitioner-based regulation for the marketing of life assurance and unit trusts. These two bodies came to be known as the Securities and Investments Board and the Marketing of Investments Board (SIB/MIB).

The White Paper, entitled *Financial Services in the United Kingdom, a new framework for investor protection*, was presented to Parliament in January 1985. It acknowledged that the existing investor protection laws were out-dated and incomplete and identified the need for them to 'be made more straightforward, more consistent, more comprehensive and more suited to the present and future challenges facing the financial services industry'. However, early in the introduction, the Government spelt out quite clearly their primary intention. Everything else that follows should be read in the light of this statement:

'This does not mean excessive regulation. That would impose unnecessary monitoring and enforcement costs, and would stop or delay new services and products being developed in response to market opportunities. The Government therefore intend that the regulation of the financial services industry should be no more than the minimum necessary to protect the investor.'

So, despite Professor Gower's best efforts and the many sensible regulatory proposals put forward by him, plus a lengthy and almost unanimous debate in the House of Commons on the need to provide a form of securities commission, the Government was prepared to provide only the minimum protection, based upon the concept of self-regulation. The White Paper represented a major step forward in the recognition of a need for a new framework for regulatory control. How successful it will ultimately prove to be is a question to which nobody at the moment has the answer. By the time this book is published, the nation will have had only a short time to observe the new system in operation and it will take a few years before anyone is able to say with any degree of certainty whether or not Britain has an efficient system of investor protection. If you have read this far, you yourself will be one of those best placed to make that judgement.

The major reforms proposed by the White Paper were:

Investments were to be defined, which would include financial and commodity futures and option contracts. There was no provision to include property passing into the physical control of the purchaser. Investment business was to be defined and a new offence created of carrying on an investment business without proper authorisation; and provisions created to allow the Secretary of State a suitable regulatory body to delegate his authority—to supervise the activities of authorised persons, subject to certain criteria. This latter point defined the necessity for a test of qualification for a potential SRO.

Two practitioner-based bodies would be created, SIB and MIB, whose duties would be to recognise SROs as providing the necessary authorisation required for an investment business. These boards would be under the supervision of the Secretary of State for Trade and Industry, to whom they would be required to report annually, and their reports would be placed before Parliament.

The rules relating to the authorisation of unit trusts would be relaxed and new criminal provisions would be introduced to tighten up the law relating to the making of false, deceptive or misleading statements in the course of marketing investments, which would include acts likely to defraud or deceive investors.

Other provisions were put forward regarding the supervision of pension funds. Investment advertisements were to be permitted, but only by those authorised businesses. New provisions with regard to Insider Dealing were contemplated in the hope that the enforcement of the criminal provisions could be strengthened. Finally, the new regulatory board and its SROs would be responsible for enforcing their respective rules, all other elements of the criminal law being left in the hands of the DTI and the prosecution authorities.

The publication of the long-awaited White Paper aroused a considerable amount of comment in the press and media, which have traditionally tended to follow certain well-defined political lines. The most important element to come out of the report was the announcement of the creation of the Securities and Investment Board and the Marketing of Investments Board, because it is these bodies, now both amalgamated simply into the Securities and Investments Board, which took the lead in the public's mind in the creation of the new controls. The City reacted cautiously to the concepts contained within the White

Paper and waited to see how the new structures would be hammered out once the Bill introducing them to the House of Commons was presented. Naturally, there were a number of dissenters to certain points raised by the new proposals. The Chairman of the Stock Exchange, Sir Nicholas Goodison, wrote to *The Sunday Times* stating that there was no question of the Stock Exchange passing to the SIB any incriminating evidence its own investigators might obtain against one of its members, as anticipated by the authors of the White Paper. 'This will never happen,' said Sir Nicholas, 'because the Stock Exchange has adequate and refined disciplinary procedures of its own.' Be that as it may, the stage had been set for the detailed debate on the Bill, once it was published.

After the publication of the White Paper but before the presentation of the Financial Services Bill to Parliament on 19 December 1985, a number of extremely damaging allegations of financial irregularity were reported, which had a tendency to 'concentrate the mind wonderfully' of the Secretary of State for Trade and Industry. Firstly there was new and startling evidence in what was loosely called the Johnson Matthey affair, which had been dragging on for some time. Evidence emerged late in 1985 of gigantic swindles involving the bank and certain foreign dealings in Nigeria, and a FIG had been formed to investigate the affair, which one report suggested could involve figures in excess of £1 billion. MPs of all parties were alarmed at the number of fraud allegations, which appeared to be growing daily. Another scandal of titanic proportions was threatening to blow the lid off Lloyds and certain public figures were doing their best to play down the scale of the known losses from dishonest dealings in a number of syndicates. Figures involving hundreds of millions of pounds were quoted as the reported losses continued to grow. Dennis Skinner MP was demanding to know why Peter Cameron-Webb and Peter Dixon, who were involved in certain allegations at Lloyds and who were living 'a life of luxury' in America, could not be extradited to Britain to stand trial. The ripples over the inordinate profits made by certain City financiers over the floatation of British Telecom had only just died down when Andrew Alexander, writing in the *Daily Mail* on 4 December 1985, put the point very neatly. He said:

'The plain fact is that the issue of City fraud and inadequate City regulation—what one might call collectively the unacceptable face of capitalism—has reached the point where the Government could be confronting a major electoral liability.'

Melvin Marckus writing in the *Observer* put it another way:

'What the City now realises is that the Financial Services Bill represents the last chance for self-regulation. If this fails and City scandals continue to erupt, then both the City and the Government must come to terms with what the US authorities realised fifty years ago. Too often, self-regulation means no regulation.'

Faced with a growing clamour from Parliament, press and public, the Government introduced the Financial Services Bill, containing its aims for practitioner-based regulation within a statutory framework. Leon Brittan outlined his and the Government's thinking by saying:

'The reason for adopting this approach, rather than a direct one, totally incorporated in statute and administered by bureaucrats, is not a reluctance to take a tough line, but rather a recognition that regulation will be more effective if it is administered by people of unquestionable integrity who are close to the market and are allowed to respond in a flexible way to fast moving developments in the market.'

Press comment quickly moved from cautious congratulation to critical evaluation, the attitudes expressed following the predictable philosophical lines. All concerned however realised that the battle lines had only just been drawn. The real in-fighting was to take place in the committee stage of the Bill. The one comment which came out of the early reporting of the publication of the Bill, and which contained a note of confidence for the future, was that made by Sir Kenneth Berrill, the Chairman of SIB, when he said, in answer to a reporter, 'We are much nearer an SEC than people think.'

The committee stage of the Financial Services Bill lasted for nearly three months but I have chosen to examine only a selection of topics, in an attempt to clarify the willingness or otherwise of the Government to prove that the proposed legislation did represent a serious attempt to provide an adequate degree of protection for the investor of the future. It is not sufficient, I suggest, to take Government pronouncements of intention at face value, particularly in a Bill which had aroused so much concerted opposition from the City, without testing some of the more important proposals debated in the committee proceedings of the Bill.

The essential difference between the Government and the Opposition parties in the whole vexed question of City regulation can be boiled down to the basic conflict between the concept of self-regulation as opposed to statutory regulation. Self-regulation, say the Government, within a statutory framework, is the best form of supervision for the City, because it provides the degree of minimum protection necessary for the investor, as identified by Norman Tebbit, but does not inhibit the unfettered activity of market forces, which the monetarist believes provides the most natural form of market efficiency. Leon Brittan defined the requirements for such a system's administrators as being 'persons of unquestionable integrity who were close to the market'.

Those opposed to this argument adopt the view that such a system allows too great a degree of latitude in which conflicts of interest can arise and these will always take precedence over responsibilities towards investors. The tendency will always exist, if those front-line regulators are drawn from the ranks of the practitioners, for the old-boy network to close ranks and protect its friends, in the event of a major scandal involving a highly placed member. They argue that such a dilemma can be avoided only by providing a watchdog with statutory powers, supervised by Parliament, and staffed by persons who are unlikely to experience any conflict of interests. Indeed, they go further and say that, if the new regulations are introduced by persons who themselves could be said to have a conflict of interest, then there is something inherently unsatisfactory about the very nature of the proposed legislation.

Within the parameters of these conflicting ideologies, the Financial Services Bill was debated in committee. The membership of the committee was drawn from all sections of the political spectrum, the Government team being led by Michael Howard and the Opposition being led by Bryan Gould. Included among the Opposition team were Brian Sedgemore and Austin Mitchell, both of whom provided injections of irreverence into the proceedings which assisted in lightening for me some very turgid pages of reading.

The debate got off to a controversial start when, within the first half-hour, the fundamental question of the Government's attitude towards conflicts of interest was questioned by Bryan Gould. The problem identified by Mr Gould revolved around Mr Howard's membership of Lloyds. At the time of this debate, he was a member of Lloyds in a non-underwriting capacity. The point raised by Bryan Gould was whether the Minister should be able to be part of the committee, bearing in mind his financial interests in Lloyds. Membership of Lloyds in an underwriting capacity carries with it a number of financial benefits and obligations. Liability at Lloyds is unlimited and the syndicates can call upon a member for his share in the liabilities for three years after he has ceased to be a member. At the same time, he will also be able to collect any profits which might arise from the successful dealings of those

syndicates for the following three years. It is a Parliamentary requirement that persons holding certain ministerial posts should not be a
name at Lloyds, and the list of disqualified persons includes the
Secretary of State for Trade and Industry. The disqualification
distinguishes between active underwriting activities and membership
of Lloyds.

Michael Howard had resigned from all his underwriting obligations
immediately upon being appointed as a junior minister on 2 September
1985. On this point there was no dispute. The point raised by Bryan
Gould was that, even having resigned from the syndicates of which he
was a member, Michael Howard remained liable for his obligations
and likely to receive profits. Parliamentary draughtsmen had attempted
to draw up a specific clause exempting Lloyds from the Bill and the
Opposition parties would attempt by all the means at their disposal to
keep Lloyds within the proposed legislation. The Minister, argued
Bryan Gould, would be seen to argue for the exclusion of an institution
from the provisions of legislation, in which he still retained an active,
pecuniary interest. Michael Howard argued that he no longer had any
direct financial interest in Lloyds and that in any event, he would be
unable to divest himself of his primary obligations to Lloyds. Bryan
Gould countered by saying that if Lloyds was kept within the ambit of
the Bill, and subsequently required to conform with the provisions
relating to compensation for losses incurred, then any future profits the
Minister might expect to receive or any losses he might be expected to
make good would be affected by the amount which Lloyds would have
to pay out to disgruntled losers. Bryan Gould used the specific
argument of the PCW syndicates, which had caused so much public
disquiet. Michael Howard argued that the Bill before them did not
have a retrospective effect and that, even if Lloyds were included in the
Bill, this would not effect the PCW losses. Bryan Gould pointed out
that it was impossible to say at that stage whether or not any further
losses would be identified in the future.

The argument wound on for some time and eventually the chairman
of the committee was asked to adjudicate on the matter. He found that
Michael Howard did not have a pecuniary interest in the proceedings
and that his vote should stand. It is of later interest to note that Michael
Howard subsequently disqualified himself from dealing with the
clauses relating to the inclusion of Lloyds within the Bill.

Bryan Gould had neatly identified a major conflict of interest right at
the start of the proceedings in this question of the Minister's interests.

He said this, when describing the appointment as a 'typical piece of Government arrogance':

'The problem is ironic and acute because we are dealing with a Bill whose *raison d'être* is to minimise and deal with conflicts of interest. I do not hold the Minister personally responsible for the problem that we face, but nevertheless the hon. and learned gentlemen appears, from his declaration of interest, to be involved in a conflict of interest of precisely the sort that the Bill seeks to outlaw.'

It seemed to me that this point was very important when analysing the Government's approach to the problem of conflicts of interest. After all, if they refused to accept that the principle extended to the choice of minister to pilot the Bill through committee, then one might be entitled to examine their other views to ascertain whether a similar attitude had been expressed. Some weeks after the ending of the committee proceedings, I put the question to Bryan Gould again and asked him whether he still held to the view that Michael Howard should have disqualified himself from the proceedings. He said:

'Yes, I do believe that very strongly. I've got nothing against Michael Howard and I'm sure that there was no actual conflict of interest, but the fact that there was a potential conflict of interest was all that we should have been concerned with and I think that it's a measure of the decline in the standards of public life that he was able to stay in that committee.'

The next aspect is a pertinent example of the inherent impracticality of civil servants in their attitudes towards practical problems. Throughout this book I have given illustrations of aspects of criminal behaviour which became difficult to combat because of the intransigent attitude of certain Government departments towards adopting practical solutions. I have recorded the views of a number of agencies of the perceived inefficiency of the DTI in exercising the powers which they already have to combat fraud and one would have supposed that the Government intended to tighten up the provisions in order to make them more effective. This example is interesting also because it illustrates the nature of Michael Howard's attitudes towards the other members of the committee. It would not be unfair to say that many members of the committee felt that he exhibited a less than generous attitude in debate towards amendments being tabled by Opposition members. This factor was mentioned in committee on a number of occasions. During one part of the debate on 4 February 1986 the following exchange took place. The speaker was Mr Dale Campbell-

Savours, the MP for Workington, and he made a good point against Michael Howard:

'The Government may feel that our amendments do not meet the objectives of the legislation or are defective, but they may accept the principle. We have set out to argue a principle. We accept that our amendment may not be the way in which to resolve the difficulty. The Minister should accept that a difficulty may arise, but there must be a solution, so will he try to find it? When we discuss future amendments, I hope that he will not set about their clinical destruction as a sadistic ritual.'

Returning to the second point of investigative speed and efficiency, the Opposition attempted to provide a power of entry to premises to search for evidence of the commission of the offence of carrying on an unauthorised investment business. The original Bill made it an offence to carry on such a business but did not provide a power to search premises to obtain the necessary evidence. It is failures like these to provide proper powers in specific cases which have caused so many investigative difficulties in the past, difficulties which were identified by the members of the Roskill Committee. The Bill proposed that any proceedings should only be commenced after consultation with the Director of Public Prosecutions or the Secretary of State, which would effectively leave the practical investigatory role in the hands of the DTI, whose role has received so much criticism in the past.

It is an unfortunate fact of life that those who indulge in the criminal misappropriation of other people's money do not exhibit a willing tendency to co-operate with investigations into their affairs. Readers may find it strange, but it has not been unknown for criminals to use false names and give false addresses in their business affairs, to use nominee 'front men' to run the offices to which their victims have access and to attempt, as much as possible, to confuse the issue when they become the subject of investigation. Another factor which has traditionally identified the activities of these people is their marked absence, together with the books and records of the business, from the scene of the crime, if they find out that an investigation is taking place or even pending.

All joking apart, these facts were well known to the civil servants who assisted in the drafting of this Bill, yet they did not include the one power which would provide for a swift and efficient seizure of incriminating evidence and Michael Howard attempted to justify this exclusion in debate. In so doing, he exhibited a woeful lack of understanding of the needs of criminal investigators to be provided with adequate facilities to enforce the law. Perhaps he should not be blamed too much, as the provision was drafted by civil servants who had close contact with the DTI and it was almost inevitable that they should seek to retain the primary responsibility for enforcing the new law. Michael Howard said:

'The Government take the general view that it is desirable to keep to a minimum the statutory provisions to give the police or other authorities the right to enter and search private premises . . . Clause 92 already enables the Secretary of State to require the production of documents from any person so that he may investigate someone who appears to be carrying on an investment business. Although there is no right of entry to premises, anyone who fails to comply with such a request without a reasonable excuse would be guilty of an offence . . . Because we believe that the power in clause 92 is sufficient for those purposes, we do not regard the power of entry as being necessary.'

It seems incredible that such an argument could have been seriously put forward, and Bryan Gould expressed his dismay at the failure to provide a power of search and pressed the Minister to restate his objections. Michael Howard reiterated that clause 92 provided a power to require the production of documents, a failure to comply being an offence. The clause did not differ very greatly from the power of the DTI to require production of the books and records of a company under section 447 of the Companies Act 1985 and that procedure has not been universally effective, yet the Minister was obdurate. When discussing the granting of search powers to investigators he said:

'Having regard to the introduction of that power and to whether in those circumstances it is necessary to give police or other authorities the right to enter and search private premises, and also in the light of the general principle that such provisions should be restricted to a minimum, the view is taken that it is not necessary to confer such a right in all the circumstances that we are considering . . . That is a self-evident view, capable of being disputed but not of benefiting from prolonged dissertation upon it.'

Bryan Gould accused the Minister of exhibiting a touching faith in human nature and identified the professional criminal who would use the request to provide documents for inspection as an excuse to get away. Other members of the committee urged the Minister to reconsider his position. Dale Campbell-Savours argued that it was 'extraordinary that the Government were prepared to tamper with the jury system but would not ensure that the police have reasonable means at their disposal to obtain evidence'.

Mr Campbell-Savours reinforced earlier complaints when he later said:

'Why does the Minister not show any flexibility? Instead of ruling the amendment out, could he not consult a few of the people we have talked to recently?'

Michael Howard, faced with concerted opposition and provided with no support from his own side, restated his belief in clause 92, but he agreed to reconsider the amendment, a concession which drew a somewhat ironic comment from Bryan Gould when he said:

'I welcome that first glimmer of light and sign of flexibility from the Minister, and hope that we shall be able to encourage him to follow a similar path on later occasions.'

Much later, the Minister introduced a number of amendments to the Bill, and one such amendment introduced a power of entry with a warrant. It appears that the amendment only confers the power of entry upon the Secretary of State, or his delegated representative, which means, in effect, officers of the DTI. If that is the case, then we have indeed been provided with another power similar to section 447 of the Companies Act 1985, useful in theory but impracticable in application if left solely within the authority of the DTI. It will not be a power which they will be willing to share with the police, and they themselves will be unwilling to upset the sensibilities of their senior masters who believe that the power of entry to premises should be restricted as much as possible. We shall be left with the status quo identified by the Minister, of investigators asking for relevant documents to be produced, probably, as before, by appointment.

The next point which represents an aspect of 'efficiency' is the right of SROs to a degree of immunity from civil action at the suit of their members. The point at issue is simple. An SRO will be required to provide regulatory control of its members. As such, it will be required to undertake a regular examination of its members' activities. The SRO represents a level of insulation between its members and their public clients and owes a duty to itself to ensure that it regulates its members properly, for fear of having its regulatory recognition removed by SIB, and owes a duty to the clients of its members to ensure that they are protected.

The Opposition members of the committee attempted to introduce an amendment which would provide SROs with a degree of immunity from civil action at the hand of their membership while maintaining the right of investors to bring action against SROs for negligence. The aim was to strengthen the hand of the SROs to enable them to carry out their duties more efficiently because they would not be faced with the likelihood of civil action being used as a gagging device, should they seek to take swift action against a member, if the evidence warranted such a course. The immunity had already been granted to SIB and it was proposed to extend it to the SROs.

The committee argument quickly became bogged down in the effectiveness of individual SROs' negotiating with their members regarding the limitation to be placed upon the members' right to bring an action against the SRO, a suggestion which had all the inherent likelihood of success. Paddy Ashdown, the Liberal MP, described it as 'turkeys voting for Christmas'. Bryan Gould extended the degree of concern by saying:

'To issue a writ for libel is a well-known practice simply to stop or to make it impossible to pursue a course of action. Given that, at the extreme, we are dealing with hardened people who will try every legal recourse open to them, I am sure that that is what they will do . . . The mere threat of issuing a writ involving the SRO in litigation will be enough to deter many people running SROs from effectively regulating those for whom they are responsible.'

Subsequently, in proposing certain amendments, Michael Howard did introduce a proposal granting immunity to SROs from action by members and by investors. It may be felt that this was an unfortunate move on the part of the Government as the long-term likelihood is that any subsequent actions that might be brought will be against the SROs at the suit of unhappy losers. Certainly, Bryan Gould, in the debate which followed the proposed amendments, made a number of telling points. He described the granting of blanket immunity to SROs as 'self-regulation on the bad old model', designed by powerful and private cliques to defend their members' investment business rather than the public. Paddy Ashdown said that the Government had granted this degree of immunity to the SROs because it had been placed in 'an armlock and half-nelson by its friends and paymasters in the City'.

Lastly, I want to look at the clause which attempted to exclude Lloyds from the provisions of the Bill. There are many important elements which were included in the Bill and I do not want to give the impression that the Government had not given due weight to their consideration. It has not been easy to decide which aspects to choose for discussion and which to exclude, so I have chosen those which I believe give the best illustration of those aspects which I wish to emphasise, notably the perceived influence upon the Government by those interests within the City who wish to see a degree of 'interpretive flexibility' remaining within whatever legislation the Government finally introduces. That such interests exist cannot be doubted and Lloyds must be seen as being one of the biggest and most scandalously obvious examples.

I have deliberately excluded Lloyds from this book, in the belief that the topic requires a book all to itself and, at the moment, we are insufficiently equipped with the full facts to be able to draw proper conclusions from what has happened within the institution. However, no book which seeks to deal with investment fraud could ignore the topic completely, and I shall concentrate therefore on a specific aspect of Lloyds, in order to identify its investment role.

The fundamental purpose behind the Financial Services Bill was to provide an efficient framework of investor protection, thus introducing a means of combating City fraud at all its levels and in all its guises. The aim was to reinforce public confidence in the City of London and its institutions in order to enable London to take its rightful place in international investment markets, providing services which attract the greatest number of users and thereby earning profits for the City, the country and its people. If that is accepted as a general statement of philosophy, then it is right to ask, 'How on earth can Lloyds be excluded from the Bill?' Bryan Gould asked the same question in committee when he said:

'Much of the concern about City fraud and how institutions operate has its genesis within Lloyds, so it is perverse to proceed to legislate on City institutions after lengthy preparation to provide investor protection, eliminate fraud or provide remedies for fraud while deliberately excluding Lloyds. That is the point the Government must answer.'

When the Financial Services Bill came to be drafted, the Government deliberately included clause 40 which stated quite simply:

'The Society of Lloyds and persons permitted by the Council of Lloyds to act as underwriting agents at Lloyds are exempted persons as respects investment business carried on in connection with or for the purpose of insurance business at Lloyds.'

Why did the Government provide this exemption clause? There can be no doubt that certain activities carried on within Lloyds represent investment business. These activities were identified by the Government in a statement by the Parliamentary Under-Secretary who said they included:

'The management on a collective basis by managing agents of the affairs of Lloyds syndicates; the process of giving advice and assistance to members and potential members of Lloyds by members' agents; and the investment management of members' insurance funds, usually carried out by underwriting agents.'

Bryan Gould accepted that it was not the insurance business carried out by Lloyds which posed problems and made it clear that it was not the insurance activities which the Opposition wished to bring within the ambit of the Bill, but the investment business. Lloyds had only recently provided an unfortunate example of self-regulation, which was used by the Opposition as a support for their argument. Bryan Gould:

'Lloyds is, and has been for some time, a matter of fundamental concern to all those who watch the City and who are concerned about its future health and good reputation. The problem that both the Government and Lloyds face is that Lloyds is, par excellence, the instance of self-regulation. It is a living example which has operated over many years of how self-regulation performs and what results it produces without any element of outside supervision . . . We have seen at Lloyds on so many occasions that practices that become the vehicle for fraud are embraced also by those who are supposed to be regulating those operations.'

This dichotomy was expressed elsewhere by Dennis Skinner, in more forthright terms. He said:

'The Government and its supporters in the City quite fancy the idea of self-regulation. They like to have ballots for trade unions, they like to have trade unions brought into the law, they've introduced three or four Acts of Parliament recently, in order to enforce trade unions to have to do things that previously they did in a self-regulatory fashion. But in the City, they're anxious to keep the self-regulation process so that if there are any scandals, it's kept within the family. So that this wonderful casino, this great posh betting shop, should be allowed to carry on without the law interfering. When you consider that there are fifty Members of Parliament who are members of Lloyds, including one on the Labour side, the rest on the Tory side, you can imagine just how much power there is . . . and there are many, many more who are 'names' who are Members of Parliament, it's a giant lobby. Now compare that to eleven who are sponsored members of the National

Union of Mineworkers, and you can see the powerful lobby that there is within the House of Commons, so I think it's a question of protecting their own interests.'

The most that could be said, apparently, on behalf of the Government case was that Lloyds should be excluded from the Bill because it had its own legislative identity, which had embarked upon a major restructuring of the Lloyds regulatory system. Some commentators relied upon the existence of the Neill Committee, which had been set up by the Government to hear evidence on the effectiveness of self-regulation at Lloyds in January 1986, and which was expected to report to the Government after the debate of the Financial Services Bill was over.

Some made the point that if the Neill Committee found it necessary further legislation would be introduced to strengthen the protections at Lloyds. In resisting the Opposition case to include Lloyds, Tim Yeo, MP, said:

'We should wait for the outcome of Sir Patrick Neill's inquiry, if the Minister will assure the committee that the Government will give priority to introducing regulatory legislation, if the inquiry finds or if other evidence emerges, that Lloyds fails to match up to the standards that we are setting for other investment markets and businesses.'

Why therefore, was the Neill Committee so important? I asked a number of commentators this question, and no one could really find a good thing to say for it. The general consensus of opinion among those interested who had an opinion, was that the Neill Committee was conceived as a time-wasting exercise, intended to exclude Lloyds from the provisions of the Bill. Bryan Gould identified it in the committee debate as 'one of the most transparent of delaying tactics, designed to trap the unwary'. Brian Sedgemore described it as 'bogus', although his opponents would not be surprised at his comment. When I put the question to Professor Gower, he told me that he did not believe that Lloyds would be brought within the ambit of the Bill, although he was not totally pessimistic. He said:

'No, I think that the probability is that it will not, but I think that there is a chance that something not dissimilar may be applied. I was afraid that the setting up of the Neill Committee was just intended to brush the whole thing under the carpet but I suspect that they are taking it rather more seriously, possibly, than the Government wished them to. What I mean is that they appointed this committee in the hope that they would get a report from them which would say, "Well, everything is now all right at Lloyds and nothing needs to be done." I suspect that the Government may not get a report quite like that.'

Lloyds has represented one of the worst examples of conflicts of interests and the scandals that have emerged in the publication of the PCW affair, to name but one example, represent merely the tip of the iceberg. I put the point to Bryan Gould when I interviewed him and he said:

'I think what has happened was that disquiet about Lloyds mounted very rapidly, for obvious reasons, it extended quite a long way into the Tory back benches; the Government then got pretty alarmed because they knew that the committee was going to be making a big thing about getting Lloyds into the Bill, and I think that they feared, unless they did something, they could well lose on that, and I think they would have done. So, they cooked up the Neill Committee as a sort of wheeze, a very transparent diversionary tactic in my view, and it has worked, to that degree. I think it's now virtually impossible for us to get Lloyds in the Bill, although I think on general principles that there's absolutely no doubt that it should be.'

The final word on Lloyds must be left to Brian Sedgemore, who in the committee debate reported a conversation which he claimed to have had with a financial journalist regarding Lloyds. He reported the conversation as follows:

'In hardly any other sphere of public life is there a body of people whose heads are so buried in the sand, so devoid of reality and so devoid of the fiscal and fiduciary morality which most of us would expect to be commonplace in any organisation . . . They know that in time the Lloyds Act will become distant, you will disappear from the scene, Sedgemore, and they will hope to return to their cosy incestuous world and get on with the job of making money. In the past they have allowed theft, fraud and tax evasion to become custom and practice and they will think of new methods of arranging those in the future.'

Such a statement, which I do not doubt was made as reported, exemplifies why Lloyds should have been included in the Financial Services Bill. That it wasn't gives considerable support to the argument expressed by those who, like me, believe that certain City practices will never be outlawed, regardless of how well-meaning the Government is or how determined the legislature.

CHAPTER TWELVE
An Unprecedented Body

Publicity is justly commended as a remedy for social and industrial diseases. Sunlight is said to be the best of disinfectants; electric light the most efficient policeman . . . the potent force of publicity must be utilized in many ways as a continuous remedial measure.

Justice Louis D. Brandeis, US Supreme Court Judge.

In the last chapter, I quoted Sir Kenneth Berrill, the Chairman of the Securities and Investments Board as saying: 'We are much nearer an SEC than people think.' Much has been written in the newspapers over the last eighteen months of the workings of the Securities and Investments Board and on many occasions reference has been made to the SEC. I found myself wondering how many people really know what the SEC is, or what it does. There exists a powerful lobby within the financial sector in the UK who do not want to see any kind of financial regulation at all if it can be avoided, and the minimum degree possible if it can't. I do not apologise for this unequivocal statement as I have seen all too often the evidence of the activities of these people in all kinds of financial dealings. These people represent a small percentage of City practitioners yet they continue to wield an influence which is grossly out of all proportion to their numbers. These men have been partly responsible for a policy of the concerted dissemination of the grossest disinformation concerning the activities of the SEC and this has created, in the mind of the public at large, the idea that the SEC is some form of administrative ogre, designed to stifle entrepreneurial flair. Various uncomplimentary articles on the SEC have appeared in certain sectors of the financial press, and selected public figures have been encouraged to include disparaging remarks on the efficiency of the SEC in keynote speeches.

The theory that is promulgated is that too much regulation stifles business activity and discourages investors and that, if we are perceived to be operating an SEC type of regulatory organisation, we shall discourage investors in our markets. This is such an old lie, which has been told for so long that I am amazed that it is still being put forward. In reality, the converse is true, as was expressed during the committee stage of the Financial Services Bill by William Cash, the MP for Strafford. He quoted an article which examined the American Commodity Futures Industry. He said:

'When the US Commodity Futures Trading Commission (CFTC) was established by the Government to regulate the industry some ten years ago, there was jubilation in London. It was widely forecast that the increased rules and regulations imposed by the CFTC would deter many users of the markets and drive business across the Atlantic. Instead, exactly, the opposite happened. It was found that properly regulated markets were an attraction, especially to newcomers to futures like the financial institutions, which were accustomed to dealing in regulated stock exchanges.'

His words were echoed by Bryan Gould, later in the debate when he said: 'People like to deal in properly regulated markets. That is a lesson that we should all remember and apply throughout our proceedings.'

More than enough newsprint has been expended on articles dealing with the creation of the SIB and its satellites in the last few months and I do not intend to rehearse arguments which you will have read in the press regarding the operation or conduct of the way in which the SIB is intended to work. If you have read this far in this book, then you have already illustrated your willingness to find out about the SIB and what it will mean in principle, for yourself. This book is for those people who want to protect themselves in the future from the activities of the fraudster and the con-man and it is for this reason that I intend to concentrate on some of SIB's recommendations for the future regulation of the financial industry, so that readers may know what is expected of the SROs whose duty it will be to act as primary line regulators of the industry. In conducting this review, I intend, as far as possible, to compare SIB's recommendations with the regulations imposed by the SEC in an attempt to provide a reasonable comparison of the ways in which a long-established Securities Commission has operated and to ascertain if there are any lessons which we can learn from their experience. Before we launch into such a review, it is appropriate briefly to examine the history of the SEC, in order to place it in its historical perspective.

The aftermath of the First World War signalled the beginning of the end of the pre-eminence in financial affairs of the great European imperial powers and identified the real emergence of the United States of America as one of the world's rapidly expanding financial leaders. Pre 1929, Wall Street experienced a boom in securities dealing the like of which had never been seen before. An atmosphere of *laissez faire* prevailed, permeating every dealing room and corridor and attempts to require financial disclosure or to prevent the fraudulent sale of stock were not seriously pursued. The man on the Brooklyn omnibus hurried to get into a market which offered unlimited opportunities for profit, giving little thought to the dangers inherent in unbridled market expansion. Writing in 1932, in the post-crash era, the economist Bernard Baruch said:

'I have always thought that if, even in the very presence of dizzily rising prices, we had all continuously repeated "two and two make four", much of the evil might have been averted.' Tragically, this simple economic formula was ignored and gamblers, driven by a mania for financial speculation and the offer of easy credit, set out to make a killing on the stock market. During the 1920s approximately twenty million people involved themselves in some form of speculative enterprise. One report suggests that of the $50 billion worth of new securities offered for public subscription during this episode, half proved to be worthless. This atmosphere of 'get-rich-quick' was fuelled by a new form of buying 'on margin' whereby potential investors would purchase securities by putting up merely a down payment, and paying interest on the balance of the outstanding price. Allowing the value of the securities thus purchased to rise, on paper, realised more collateral to purchase yet more stocks, without the need to provide any more hard cash, a practice known as 'pyramiding'. This procedure continued to work as long as a bull market prevailed, but when the market entered a downturn phase and prices started to decline, the brokers who were holding considerable quantities of paper began making 'margin calls' upon clients, in order to balance the market values of portfolios with their paper values. To provide sufficient funds to satisfy these margin calls, speculators began to sell securities, which depressed the price of stocks still further. The inherent worthlessness of a vast quantity of the paper securities on offer meant that confidence in the market was quickly extinguished,

thousands were ruined and the history books were left to record what
we have come to call the 'Wall Street Crash' of 1929.

The philosophy that lay behind the methods of restoring that
confidence led to the creation of the Securities and Exchange Commission and coined one of the most apt descriptions of the requirements of a securities commission. It was voiced by one of its former
chairmen who described its success as, 'The uniform thread that keeps
the Commission an integral part of America's economic destiny is the
fusion of good people, important problems and workable laws.'

The Americans have always understood that in a capitalist economy
it is simply not sufficient to offer the investor a market in which to invest
his money, without giving him the best possible opportunity to realise a
return on his investment. This is not to say that they seek to minimise or
alter the risks inherent in the market, exemplified by 'market forces',
but they try to minimise the outside risks to the investor so that he
knows that at least he is getting a fair run for his money. Putting it
another way, the British have traditionally assumed that everyone
involved in financial dealing is a gentleman, and they appear to be
shocked when they discover that it is not so; the Americans, on the
other hand, assume that everyone within the market is a potential
crook, and legislate for the possibility.

In simple terms, the SEC is a politically balanced Commission
funded by central Government, whose Commissioners serve for a
limited period and who can be removed for cause. It has complete
authority over the administration, organisation and regulation of the
securities industry and concentrates its efforts on overall policy and
surveillance, as well as specialising in specific areas of concern such as
market manipulation and insider dealing. It is responsible for the
general administration of the activities of the broker/dealers and the
markets, but leaves the day-to-day organisation of those bodies to their
respective self-regulatory organisations who are required to answer to
the SEC in the event of administrative failure.

The various securities exchanges operate their own surveillance and
compliance departments which are charged with the responsibility for
ensuring the smooth running of the exchanges; the broker/dealers are
supervised by an organisation called the National Association of
Securities Dealers. Whichever aspect of the securities industry a practitioner chooses, registration with the SEC and membership of an exchange or the NASD is mandatory. Membership of either requires a considerable degree of documentary examination, compliance with a struc-

tured set of financial requirements, together with a constant overview, to ensure that certain regulatory controls do not become too relaxed.

One of the criticisms laid against the SEC is its size, employing over 2000 people. While this is true, its staffing is relative to the functions the organisation is required to perform, including elements of administration which in Britain are shared among the Stock Exchange, Companies House, the Take-Over Panel, the DTI and the Fraud Squad. The most publicly known division is that which is responsible for enforcement. This department carries out regular investigations into allegations of market manipulation and insider dealing, while maintaining an active international intelligence gathering office which collates information on all aspects of criminal influence within securities markets. This office liaises with the Interpol network to supply information to interested police forces all over the world. The existence of the SEC does not mean that fraud no longer exists, far from it, but the investigators employed by the Commission are well provided with very sophisticated monitoring facilities and backed up by some highly motivated lawyers who are prepared to take on Wall Street's biggest players in an attempt to combat what they perceive to be the major causes of financial concern.

The main function of the SEC is to provide leadership and guidance to the supplementary compliance and supervision departments employed by the individual exchanges and the NASD. Complaints will be forwarded to the SEC from these organisations for investigation. The SEC will also maintain its own monitoring facilities and bring action if the exchanges fail to spot activities which need correction. By and large, the relationship between the supervisor and the supervised works well because there is a large degree of facility for agreement to be reached without the need for legal proceedings. In many cases, the first line of approach by the Commission is to issue nothing more than a mild rebuke, if the circumstances warrant it. On the other hand, if the Commissioner considers it necessary, it will bring the full weight of its powers to bear on a transgressor and issue proceedings, backed up by criminal prosecutions carried out by the Justice Department, whose penalties include long prison sentences and triple-penalty damages.

The staff of the Commission, for administrative ease, enjoy civil service status, all except the lawyers, who while being paid Government grade salaries, which, let it be said, are considerably higher than their counterparts might earn in the United Kingdom, do not enjoy a similar protection of employment rights and can be dismissed from their posts for lack of professional competence or other perceived inability. (I doubt whether such a proviso would enjoy much popularity among certain civil servants in this country.)

The one immediately obvious difference between a young lawyer working for the SEC and his British counterpart, employed by a Government department, is the considerable degree of kudos enjoyed by the American lawyer. There is no stigma attached to a young man or woman who follows this route and in many respects it is encouraged. The same cannot be said for a young graduate in the United Kingdom, unfortunately, as the salary scales alone prohibit any ambitious lawyer from seeking any form of employment with a Government agency. One has only to read the recruitment columns of *The Times* to realise the truth of that assertion.

Bearing this factor in mind, I put to Professor Gower the question of whether or not he still held to his original preference for a statutory commission in the UK. He said, in his usual forthright way:

'I don't think it matters a damn whether it's statutory or not. The fact of the matter is that SIB is going to be exercising statutory powers. Fundamentally, it makes no difference whether it is a body incorporated by statute directly, or a body incorporated as a company, limited by guarantee. It would obviously make our position more intelligible to the outside world and equal to overseas regulatory bodies if we were named in the statute and set up directly by the statute but there are great disadvantages. Once we become a quango, we're going, almost certainly, to be subject to some of the public accountability restraints; and if we are to do our job properly here, we've got to pay City salaries, not civil service salaries. That is a great reason why we on the whole prefer to remain as we are. From the point of view of our powers, it seems to me to make no difference whatever. In other words, those people in the City who still think that they haven't got an SEC have got a Securities Commission. The fact that it's a Securities Commission which happens to be incorporated as a company limited by guarantee seems to me really on the whole to be neither here nor there. It does have this enormous advantage, because at the moment, if we could only pay the sort of salaries that the civil service pays, we shouldn't be able to get the legal team we need, we shouldn't be able to get the accountants and we shouldn't be able to get experts in other branches of the City.'

It has never ceased to be a matter of some mild amusement to me that the Americans who operate some, if not all, of the most highly efficient and profitable financial markets in the world, should be perceived as having the most draconian of securities controls. Britain is now required to get in step with the rest of the world, in financial terms, not the other way round, and any failure on our part to provide an efficient form of securities regulation is going to be perceived in the US and elsewhere as proof positive of the continued existence of the British disease of fraud and malpractice, which will drive out American investment in our markets. This fact was brought home to me when I was in America studying at the SEC. One of their senior regulators had previously studied the proposals put forward in the White Paper and he had said to me:

'You guys can talk about regulation for as long as you like but, until you come to terms with the reality of what financial regulation really means and stop pretending that it can be carried out by gentlemen in their spare time between deals, then you will continue to suffer from the sort of scandals that make you a joke. When you take regulation seriously and make the money available to finance those intentions, then we'll take you seriously. Until then, don't waste our time.'

With these sentiments in mind, consider the proposals set out by SIB for the future regulation of our home markets; see if we have really confronted the problem and compare them with the methods used by our American counterparts. I intend to concentrate on those provisions which are designed to protect the individual investors and leave the provisions relating to the recognition of SROs or Investment Exchanges. It should be borne in mind that any SRO which claims to exercise control over the activities of its members will be required to prove that its regulations are at least equivalent to those proposed by SIB.

It will be a criminal offence under the new Act for any person to carry on an investment business in the United Kingdom without being authorised or exempt from authorisation and any contracts entered into with an unauthorised person will be unenforceable by him. The following constitute carrying on investment business, as a business:

1. Dealing in investments: dealing is defined as buying, selling, subscribing for or underwriting investments or offering or agreeing to do so either as a principal or as an agent;

2. Arranging deals in investments: this is defined as making or offering or agreeing to make arrangements with a view to another person buying, selling, subscribing for or underwriting a particular investment;

3.   Managing investments: managing is defined as managing or offering or agreeing to manage, assets belonging to another person if those assets consist of or include investments or may do so at the discretion of the person managing, offering or agreeing to manage them;

4.   Advising on investments: advising is defined as giving or offering or agreeing to give, advice as to the purchase, sale, subscription for or underwriting of investments or as to the exercise of rights conferred by investments;

5.   Establishing collective investment schemes: establishing, operating or winding up a collective investment scheme, including acting as a trustee of a unit trust scheme.

These five definitions are provided in the *Regulation of Investment Business*, a publication issued by SIB. As you can see straight away, the definition covers virtually all persons who are involved with the investment market. Investments include securities, rights to securities, certain money market instruments, certain options, futures, contracts for differences, units in collective investment schemes and certain long-term insurance contracts, and powers exist to extend the definition of investments where appropriate. The definitions of investment business are very similar to the regulations defined by the SEC.

To become authorised, an investment business must be able to show that it complies with a 'Fit and Proper' test, which is that it has sufficient capital requirements, that it complies with the 'Conduct of Business' rules, that it complies with the stringent client money provisions and that it has the power to monitor and enforce these rules within its own company or business.

The concept of 'fit and proper' is difficult to define in an objective sense and each individual investment business which applies to be recognised by SIB will have to satisfy the board that it passes the test. The SROs will be required to ensure that each applicant for recognition by them reaches the same standard. To reach that standard, the individual company must be able to provide a business profile identifying the sort of business which it intends to carry on.

Financial requirements will be strictly monitored in relation to the type of business contemplated. The important requirement will be the maintenance of a sufficient degree of liquidity to ensure against the failure of a firm simply because it is under-capitalised, thus placing client funds at risk. This will also minimise the necessity to use the facilities of the compensation fund.

The American capitalisation requirements are very stringent and require regular monitoring and reporting to the relevant SRO, whether it be an exchange or the NASD in the case of securities dealers, or the CFTC in the case of commodities or futures dealers. The American regulations provide that the supervisory body can suspend a member's authorisation if his capitalisation requirements fall below a certain minimum level and he will have to satisfy the supervisors that his capital has been increased before they will permit him to continue to trade. The SIB rules anticipate requiring a minimum capital requirement for each type of business, and those businesses which offer investments containing a greater degree of risk, such as futures and options, will be required to provide greater capital reserves, to compensate for the greater degree of uncertainty of market fluctuation involved. The rules for calculating these provisions are voluminous and each business will be expected to be able to calculate its position to comply with the rules. SROs will be required to maintain supervision of all members' capital provisions in order to ensure that they do not slip below the minimum requirements.

This provision is fundamental to the smooth running of any investment business, particularly if those activities which I described as the 'slippery-slope' frauds are to be overcome. This requirement will help to eradicate those fly-by-night commodity futures operations which are capitalised on a shoe-string and which exist solely for the purpose of ripping off their unsuspecting clients as quickly as possible in order to provide themselves with the necessary operating capital.

The next requirement which will be strictly enforced is the Board's reliance on 'Conduct of Business' rules. It is a measure of the almost institutionalised failure of investment businesses to conduct their business fairly and honestly that the SIB felt it necessary to spell out these rules in detail and to define clearly the requirements of the law of agency, a law which for so long was treated with such a cynical degree of disregard. SIB have said:

'In general, a client is a person for whom the firm is providing a service, or otherwise acting as agent . . . a broker who accepts instructions to "buy for me" or "sell for me" is clearly under a duty to act as the investor's agent in the proposed transaction . . . In practice, the Board will expect firms to treat all customers as clients unless there is a clear understanding on both sides that a different relationship subsists. A fiduciary relationship cannot be waived at the firm's discretion, no matter what disclosure is made to the customer at the time. The Board believes that Professor Gower's dictum, "once an agent, always a fiduciary" should underlie its rules.'

It is incredible that these simple rules needed to be spelt out in such defined terms, but there it is. Again, these requirements, if strictly enforced, will assist in undermining the activities of those shady stock peddlers, one of whom was described to me recently as having been sacked from X Securities Ltd for being too crooked, a concept not dissimilar to being kicked out of the Gestapo for being too cruel, or those shabby futures dealers who wander the City like the proverbial financial albatross, propping up the corner of a desk here, introducing a few punch-drunk clients there, in return for a series of rebated commissions and a 'no questions asked' policy on the part of those who employ them.

The 'Conduct of Business' rules will include a number of requirements, the more important of which include the following provisions.

All investment businesses must make quite clear when discussing investment proposals with a potential client the degree of independence they possess. They must not imply a greater degree of independence than they possess in reality. This rule is to prevent advice being given which appears to carry a degree of independent judgement when in fact the advisor is simply carrying out his contractual obligation to an employer. If a firm recommends another company in the course of such business, they must declare any interest they may have or connection which may exist between them. This will bring some degree of control to the activities of insurance salesmen who appear to be giving independent advice when they are simply selling the product of their employers and which may not be suitable for the individual client's needs. The aim is to give the client an opportunity to examine a series of investment proposals to ascertain which is best for his needs and to obtain truthful advice from salesmen. If a salesman is contractually tied to a certain company, he will be required to explain this fact and that he can only recommend their products.

The next requirement prohibits the practice of overriders or benefits in kind. This practice has many names which are common within the industry and I have found a degree of difficulty in deciding which description most nearly fits the bill. In the end, I settled for a simple word which, I believe, most people will understand. The word is 'bribery'. This rule forbids the practice of the provision of special payments to investment firms in return for the introduction of large volumes of business, or any other kind of payment which might be construed as an inducement to bring in business. The Board takes the view that such arrangements cannot be the subject of such disclosure provisions as will adequately describe their scope and that, therefore, they should be outlawed. The rule will not forbid low-value Christmas presents, such as are commonly given between normal business participants, nor does it prevent a modicum of reasonable business entertainment. It does however prevent the sort of low-level, barrel-bottom scraping inducement such as an all-expenses-paid 'golf' trip to Bangkok, masquerading under the heading of 'investment research', which will be jolly bad luck for all the non-golfers who have tradition-ally undertaken these trips to the soft underbelly of the Orient. It also prohibits the practice of a futures broker introducing his clients exclusively to one clearing broker in return for benefits in kind, unless the clearing broker identifies the introducing broker as his exempt representative. It is to be hoped that the prohibition of such practices will be reflected in a better service to clients, although I am not convinced that such old-established activities will be stopped simply because SIB says so. I have a grave suspicion that it will take a series of test-cases to satisfy the system that such practices are finished.

Advertising a company's services has always proved a matter of concern for those who would wish to see the City subjected to a greater regard for the concept of truthfulness. In future all advertisements will have to contain specific risk warnings, printed in the same size of type as the body of the advertisement. These warnings are intended to draw the attention of a reader to three risk considerations. Firstly, the volatility of the investment; secondly, the liquidity of the investment; and thirdly, the probability of the investment requiring further future liabilities. The advertising will have to be fair, accurate and complete, and those advertisements which invite money 'off-the-page' will be subjected to considerable scrutiny to ensure that any representations made regarding past performance or projected performance in the future are scrupulously accurate.

This requirement should I believe encourage a far greater degree of accuracy on the part of advertising copywriters in the future. Do you remember the risks I exposed you to in the first chapter when I invited you to open an investment magazine? These new provisions should mean that those risks are reduced. Look at it this way. Are you likely to part with your hard-earned money to an advertisement which offers you an opportunity to invest in commodity futures or certain OTC stocks, when at the same time the advertisement tells you that the value of these products can fall just as quickly as it can rise, that there is no organised market for these particular shares and that you may experience difficulty in selling them? Or that you may be required to make more payments of margin capital simply to keep your particular futures contract open? At the same time, the advertisement will need to state by which SRO the company placing the advertisement is regulated, so that if any complaint is felt to be justified, the right SRO can be contacted without difficulty.

Any recommendations which are published by a company in future, whether by circulars or tip sheets, will have to be soundly researched and capable of substantiation. The firm publishing the document will be required to maintain accurate records of documents prepared and details of circulation.

All contracts between company and client will, in future, be required to contain a far greater degree of information than hitherto. The basis of the business arrangement beween either party will need to be defined more accurately and the computation of all fee charges, commission rates and capacities in which the firm may act must be expressed clearly. This requirement should prevent the practice which some firms have used of describing the calculation of commission in such vague terms that the client is unaware of the true nature of the amount he will be expected to pay, and most of his original investment becomes swallowed up in commission charges. The most important exemption will be that these provisions will not extend to what are called 'execution only' clients. These are persons who know sufficient about the business in which they deal that they simply intend to use the services of a broker to execute their instructions. A great temptation will exist in future for brokers seeking new clients to suggest to them that they will provide a service in outlining various strategies, but they will claim that the client was making the investment decisions and that therefore they were 'execution only' clients and not covered by the provision.

The next requirement is going to be the subject of considerable amusement to investigators and compliance officers in the future when they come to examine how Piers St John Chinless-Wonder, ex-public schoolboy and short service commission Guards officer, turned commodity futures account executive, managed to lose £50,000 for Aunt Agatha in the space of two weeks, trading in stock index futures. The board will require all firms to operate a 'know your customer' rule. Companies offering investment services will have to show that they took reasonable steps to ascertain the truth of a client's financial position and to be able to prove that the investment recommendations they made to the client were of a type and kind suitable for that person's financial position and understanding. Firms will be required to introduce methods of conducting such enquiries with non-professional investors and a greater degree of care will be required in those areas which pose a higher degree of volatility. In addition, firms will be required to show that the client understood the risks involved in the transaction. This throws the burden of responsibility onto the firm to prove that they took all reasonable steps. Some commentators have wondered if this is not a particularly harsh requirement as it places considerable responsibility on the shoulders of the industry. So it should. The Americans have absolutely no difficulty with a similar and even harsher requirement and it doesn't seem to have caused any slackening in the numbers of people who wish to make investment decisions in that country. The rule was introduced to put a stop to a degree of unbridled 'advice' being proferred by unqualified operators to persons whose investment needs were not best served by being placed in various high-risk areas, but who knew no better and were grossly misled by the 'investment advisor'.

The next provision must be considered to be one of the primary requirements of an honest industry. It is described by the board as the 'best execution' rule. This means that, where a firm deals for a client, it must charge to or pay to the client the same amount of money as the firm paid or received for the investment concerned, subject only to any pre-agreed commission, fee or mark up, which is disclosed to the client. Dealing as a principal will only be allowed in future after a specific written agreement has been entered into between broker and client and, if such an agreement exists, the broker will then be required to show that the client received the 'best execution', ie that the transaction was carried out on the best possible terms to the client. This rule restates the duty owed by an agent to this client, what lawyers call a fiduciary duty. Again, I find it incredible that a market which claims to be so honestly managed by its practitioners should need this simple legal obligation spelt out in such basic terms. It will require very careful monitoring however as old habits die hard and practices such as 'clipping', which involves the broker knocking off a couple of pounds from each client's sale transaction or 'marking up', which means adding a couple of quid to the client's purchase price, have been widespread in the market for so long that they have become almost institutionalised.

In an attempt to bring some form of regulation to the OTC market, the Board will require all off-exchange securities in the future to be marketed on the basis that the client knows that the security which he is contemplating purchasing is not traded on a recognised exchange and that there is no recognised market for the security concerned, which may, in turn, make the security difficult to sell. This requirement has been introduced to try and minimise the number of people who are induced to enter into purchases of certain highly speculative OTC stocks in the belief that they are obtaining the same degree of efficiency that they would obtain on the floor of the Stock Exchange. If the firm marketing the security makes the only market in that share, the firm must declare that fact and must not use phrases such as 'market price' or any other form of words which implies that the security is traded on a recognised market. Companies that wish to operate as market makers must notify this fact to the Board, together with details of the securities which they wish to market. The Board will require these securities to be marketed in firm, two-way prices, in realistic numbers, to any customer. The market makers may withdraw the security from the market upon notification, but withdrawal will mean that the security cannot be re-instated for a specific period subsequently. A daily list of closing prices must be supplied to the Board or to a public information network, designated by the Board.

This requirement should minimise the risk to the private client of another unfortunate practice which occurred when the market-maker suddenly decided that he would deal in the shares on what was called a 'matched-bargain basis' only. This meant that the market maker would try and match a person who wanted to buy a defined number of shares and a person who wanted to sell the same number at the same price. In a market where the bottom has just fallen out of the price of one of these more esoteric offerings finding someone who suddenly decides he wants to buy, in order to match him with someone desperate to get rid of his now worthless holding, represents, I suggest, nothing more than a triumph of hope over experience.

In America, most OTC stocks must be sold by at least two market makers and there must be at least 100,000 shares in public hands. Total assets must exceed $2 million and there must be a minimum of 300 shareholders. These requirements are to provide a degree of trading volume to OTC shares which are supervised by the NASD.

The Board will require all transactions in future to be time-stamped.

This is such a simple regulatory measure and so easy to arrange that it seems hard to understand how it has not been required before. It has been mandatory in America. When a firm receives an order from a client, it will be required to time-stamp the receipt of the order and then time-stamp its execution. This will provide a record, which must be kept by the firm and which will be available for subsequent examination in the event of dispute over the execution of an order. Time-stamping will help eradicate the problem of late execution because a client will now be able to see when his order was executed. It will then be possible to make a comparison with the contract price and the market price to see if they tally. Together with this requirement will be an ending of the practice of maintaining 'suspense accounts'. This practice has provided a degree of facility to unscrupulous brokers to enable them to hold on to bargains to establish whether they are going to be profitable or unprofitable, so that they can subsequently decide where to allot them. Take the activities of a fund manager who, using the services of his stock broker friend, purchases a large quantity of shares at the start of the account period, and the stock broker holds their purchase in his 'suspense account'. While still in the account period, the value of the shares increases dramatically and the fund manager instructs his broker to sell the shares and they split the profits realised. If, however, the value of the shares declines within the account period, the fund manager instructs his broker to allot the shares to the fund which he manages, and the pension fund or unit trust swallows the loss. Neat eh! Now, I know that this sort of thing doesn't go on and that it only exists in the minds of suspicious cynics. In fact, it doesn't go on so much that the SIB has had to state a rule forbidding the practice. The abolition of the practice of using suspense accounts and the requirement that all bargains must be appropriated upon execution will assist in driving out this practice that doesn't happen, once and for all.

Certain other practices will be banned, including the vexed question of 'churning'. At the moment a broker can charge commission on any transaction, whether it causes profit or loss to the client. In some companies, the degree of commission charged is so high that it really doesn't matter a damn whether the client wins or loses as the broker is the only one who makes any money. The SIB does not say how churning is to be defined; it admits that the 'practice is difficult to prove and safeguards are not easy to devise'. The Board is considering introducing a rule whereby a firm will have to report their earnings at a client's expense to the client on a regular basis, particularly where a client is traded as a discretionary account.

The Board will require all firms to maintain means of ensuring that the new rules are adhered to. In other words, all firms which market investments will be required to show that they have adequate in-house compliance procedures and that their staff members are properly trained and adequately supervised. This aspect alone is going to cause considerable soul-searching for the more peripheral companies who currently conduct business in the City. Efficient regulation costs money and some of the costs for this process will have to be met by the industry. It would be iniquitous if the City attempted to pass on all those costs to the clients in higher dealing costs or commission rates, although the investor should expect to have to bear a proportion of the new costs. In America under SEC/CFTC rules, all investment companies are required to maintain elaborate in-house training and staff monitoring procedures, and to employ a specified compliance manager, who is responsible for ensuring that the relevant rules are enforced, to ensure that proper supervision is maintained. In addition, all American entrants to the industry have to fulfil certain educational requirements in order to prove that they possess certain minimum standards of knowledge of the workings of their market. I would imagine that a similar requirement in this country would strike terror into the hearts of some of the City's more flamboyant 'investment advisors'.

A complaints procedure will be required, and firms will be expected to investigate complaints impartially. Clients will have recourse to the SRO if they are unsatisfied and, if all else fails, to the Board.

Two other elements are worth consideration, both of which have caused considerable difficulties in the past. The first is the Board's intention to ban the practice of 'cold-calling' in all but a few, specific instances. Cold-calling is the practice of making unsolicited telephone calls to members of the public, using a very well-researched script, in an attempt to sell 'investment' facilities. Apart from anything else, such a practice is an unjustified intrusion into the private life of the recipient of the call.

Such a practice will be permitted in certain aspects of life assurance products and certain types of unit trust, because these can have cancellation rights written into the contract document, by which a client can change his mind within a specified period. The sort of areas in which it is sought to ban the practice are in the sale of speculative investment products such as OTC securities, and commodity futures and options. There is an exemption to this ban, apart from the right to call existing clients, which is that a call will be permitted after written permission is granted by the potential client. You should exercise great caution in future if you don't want to be bothered by these sharks, and read very carefully the kind of junk mail that comes through your letter box offering investment products. Unsolicited mailing has not been banned and a considerable upsurge in mail-shotting will be experienced. If you bought shares in British Telecom, TSB or British Gas, it is almost inevitable that your name will be on a mailing list. You will continue to receive a considerable quantity of unsolicited mail, much of which will offer you all sorts of services, for which you only have to return the small reply-paid card, indicating your wish to know more about commodity futures, or how you can discover the prize which you have already won. You didn't even know that you had entered a competition, but never mind. All you have to do is to fill in your name and address and a day-time telephone number to assist their mailing department to ensure that they've got your correct details and, hey presto, you have suddenly given them written permission to ring you, so read them all carefully. Better still, put them straight away where they belong, in the rubbish bin!

If you should find yourself in receipt of a series of cold calls which you don't want, there are a number of methods which can be used to discourage the caller. You can always complain to the relevant SRO if you can find out his or her name, or you could complain to SIB. They will, in fairness, have so many more urgent matters to deal with that you may feel that a bit of self-help is more appropriate. For the more robust, a few, carefully chosen, short, Anglo-Saxon words describing certain physiological impossibilities usually does the trick. For those of a more genteel nature, a police whistle, kept by the phone, and blown very hard into the mouthpiece has a most satisfying way of bringing an unwelcome phone call to an end. It was a method we used to advocate to women who received certain other kinds of unwanted telephone calls and I am told that it is highly effective.

On a more serious note, the other requirement which the Board will enforce will be compliance with regulations requiring the safeguarding of a client's money, held by an authorised business. The Board's regulations will take precedence over any requirements which may be defined by individual SROs. This rule is of paramount importance and reflects the seriousness with which it is viewed in America. Indeed, it would be true to say that of all the American regulatory requirements supervised by the relevant SROs in that country, the requirements dealing with company capitalisation and client-fund segregation are given the utmost priority.

In future, all clients' funds must be held in a separate bank account from that of the firm and the accounts must be identified by the use of the words 'client' and 'trust' in their titles. The primary aim is to be able to identify clients' monies and to protect them from unauthorised use by the investment business and, in addition, from any other creditors, if for some reason the company has to be wound up. It is likely that all clients' funds will be permitted to be maintained in an omnibus account, which will place upon the investment business a considerable degree of responsibility to ensure that the accounting procedures for the identification of client accounts are efficient and well administered. All monies held for the client whether in his own right as a customer, or on his behalf as proceeds of settlement, must be paid in directly to the client account. They cannot be held in the firm's account. There will be a strict prohibition of the practice of 'borrowing' from the client's account on behalf of the firm or another client. One client's profits cannot be used to satisfy another's debts. If these regulations are strictly enforced, this will have a considerable impact on the activities of a large number of under-capitalised futures brokers, many of whom will find themselves facing financial difficulties if they have to meet substantial margin requirements at the end of a day's trading, particularly as their open contracts may reflect a number of client positions. As happened in America in the aftermath of their financial revolution a few years ago, a large number of these smaller, less efficient, firms will go to the wall. There will be a shakeout of the less well-structured participants and a degree of amalgamation among the larger firms, which can only prove to be of long-term benefit for the consumer.

It may be thought that I have been rather harsh in my comments regarding certain parts of the investment industry. I do not apologise for these statements as I believe them to be fair comment. For too long I have watched elements of the British financial sector operating to the detriment of their clients, protected by the unwritten rules of 'gentlemanly conduct' which have traditionally governed certain types of City activity. It became hard to maintain much faith in an institution which publicly preached the virtues of 'utmost good faith' and 'financial probity', while turning a blind eye here and tipping the wink there to practitioners who were using the system to rip off their unsuspecting clients. Some of these men enjoyed a degree of esteem which my colleagues and I found hard to fathom. It didn't take long before I realised that most of these operators had been dealing in these ways for such a long time that they simply took it for granted because this was the way it had always been done. Those practitioners have had it their own way for too long and the City has been offered opportunity after opportunity to put its house in order and has consistently failed to prove equal to the challenge. Now, the regulations will have to be imposed from outside, by an independent body, and the City will be a better place for it.

Even now, those who would resist the changes which are coming are still making their voices heard. When the Financial Services Bill was debated in the House of Lords, a carefully orchestrated publicity campaign received a degree of coverage from the press, drawing their attention to the views expressed by certain practitioners in the international investment business sector. It seems that a survey was carried out by a firm of accountants of the views of some of these gentlemen and they expressed their reservations regarding the contents of the Bill. One of their complaints apparently was that the 'fundamental flaw in the legislation was that it was designed for the Aunt Agathas and not the professional investors'.

One can only take a step back and marvel at the crass insensitivity of some of these operators. Why do they think the Gower Report was commissioned? What do they think prompted a Conservative Government to grasp the nettle of financial regulation in the face of concerted opposition? Does their complacency regarding the losses sustained by hundreds, if not thousands of small investors mean that they are content to sit back and watch the situation get worse and worse, for fear of introducing changes which are common currency in other, more financially efficient countries? Thankfully, their views were not adopted by Roy Croft, the chief executive of SIB. Speaking at a seminar held by the London Chamber of Commerce, regarding the lobbies which existed to resist moves towards a greater degree of investor protection because of the operational changes which would be needed, he made the following observations:

'The United States has had detailed investor protection and related regulations in force for some considerable time, and New York is hardly a financial wilderness. Indeed, the experience is that properly regulated markets tend to be expanding markets . . . Yes, one of the main reasons for introducing the whole new system is indeed the

protection of the legions of members of the public who have their
money invested, whether in shares, life assurance policies or occupational pension schemes. And it is quite true that the Bill is not primarily
intended to protect professional investors. But that is as it should be.
Professionals should, by definition, know what they are about in
financial dealings whereas Aunt Agatha is likely to be in very foreign
territory. We are not insensitive to the problems of the professionals.
Our aim is to distinguish clearly between rules affecting professionals
and amateurs in such a way that the proper protection of Aunt Agatha is
achieved without discouraging the professional participants in the
markets.'

The dinosaur became extinct because it was unable to adapt to a
rapidly changing environment. It is to be hoped in the face of change in
our financial markets that, if the remaining entrepreneurial dinosaurs
cannot adapt, then they will become similarly noticeable by their
absence. The air will be a lot sweeter without them.

CHAPTER THIRTEEN
Looking After Number One

In about twenty-five years' time there will be quite a lot of people who will be inheriting something, because for the first time we will have a whole generation of people who own their own homes and will be leaving them, so that they topple like a cascade down the line of the family, leaving to others not only their homes but some of their shares, some of their building society investments, some of their national savings certificates, only on a bigger sale than ever before. The overwhelming majority of people, who could never look forward to that before, will be able to say: 'Look, they have got something to inherit. They have got a basis to start on!' That is tremendous. That is popular capitalism.

Margaret Thatcher, 1986

Throughout this book, I have attempted to discover whether the proposals for the future, when compared with the failures of the past, will provide the necessary degree of protection for the new investors envisaged by the Prime Minister. I have used as many direct quotations as I could, in order to see if those who seek to promote or benefit from the new investment environment match their expressed intentions with realistic action. I have also thought it right to provide as wide a degree of critical opinion as possible, in an attempt to view the topic from both sides of the political spectrum.

I have tried to place the practical aspects of a political philosophy in its wider historical perspective by examining the effects of promoting a wider share-owning democracy at a time when the markets in which those shares must be traded in the future are becoming ever more de-regulated and accessible to a far wider number of non-professional participants.

The changes in financial services are not restricted to Britain and they were not brought about in a vacuum. The Government did not introduce the proposed legislation for greater investor protection simply because it seemed like a good idea at the time. The changes in the City have been a long time coming and, as with so many other evolutionary developments, have possessed such a degree of historical inevitability that it was only a question of time before all those countries involved got into line.

The financial revolution has been precipitated by a number of disparate elements. The rapid development of communications technology has meant that I can talk to a colleague on the other side of the world as easily as I can talk to my neighbour. Add to this the international air of de-regulation which has swept through securities markets, lowering traditional barriers to outside influence and introducing new sources of capital, and an irresistible impetus for change is generated. The greater trend towards investment banking, which can provide a whole range of new services for the securities industry, coupled with a general increase in the volume of disposable income available for investment purposes in the more affluent West, has meant that competing services must become more efficient if they are going to attract sufficient capital to maintain their market position. In order to maintain efficiency, these services must offer the widest range of facilities to an increasingly sophisticated clientele using the latest technology, with informed knowledge of the most effective financial instruments available to service their requirements.

At the same time, however, we cannot lose sight of the need to maintain a strict degree of regulatory control within the market. This is the dichotomy which faces market regulators everywhere. Too much control and you stifle initiative, making the market less efficient and less profitable. Too little control, and those whose behaviour the market wishes to prohibit will literally 'steal the world'. This aspect has long been understood by the SEC, who watch with growing concern the increasing number of American stocks which are being traded off US exchanges, and which are thus outside US regulatory control. Their concerns are being forcibly expressed to our Government and attempts are being made to forge closer regulatory links in order to facilitate a free-flow of information between departments.

Capital markets need money to survive. In order to attract that money they must be enticing to speculators. If the speculators perceive that they can obtain more efficient and safer facilities elsewhere in the world, they will put their cash there, to the detriment of our markets. Behind the expressed philosophy of the Conservative Government to open up the market to a wider share-owning public lies the realisation that if they fail to attract more people willing to part with their money in transactions of a speculative nature, then the markets will become increasingly the preserve of the international institutions, which would not necessarily be in the best long-term interests of our country. Foreign investors may not always have the interests of the British economy closest to their heart, but home-grown private speculators provide independent liquidity.

The stimulation of the growth in ownership of private property has always been a Conservative philosophy and their policies have always been aimed at increasing the degree of private ownership, whether it be by way of house purchase, national savings, building society accounts, or, latterly, share dealings. Have their attempts to stimulate investor confidence been matched by the nature of the protections they have introduced in the proposed investor protection legislation?

The biggest disincentive to investor confidence is the perception that the market is fraudulently operated. A proliferation of the fraudulent practices described in this book will result in a steady decline in the numbers of private investors who are prepared to part with their money in enterprises of a speculative nature. To protect these potential investors, the Government has introduced a number of changes and reforms, both in legislation and in regulatory method. Will they be sufficient?

In an attempt to bring a greater degree of efficiency to the investigation and prosecution of fraud, we have seen the introduction of the Fraud Investigation Groups. Successful results, by which the FIGs' effectiveness can be judged have so far proved to be elusive. Two FIGs have been at work investigating the allegations into the missing millions from insurance brokers Alexander Howden and from the PCW syndicates. Currently they have reported little success. Much has been made of the hopes for the future effectiveness of the FIGs, but even as early as December 1985, when the concept had been in operation for only twelve months, there were reports that FIGs' resources were already overstretched.

What of the police? Despite very positive recommendations in the Roskill Committee's report for the introduction of a full-time career plan for those detectives who wished to specialise in the investigation of complex fraud, at the time of writing no official proposals have been put forward for the implementation of such a policy.

This failure to treat fraud seriously as an independent crime problem flies in the face of reason. The most recently available figures for criminal statistics released by the Home Office in 1986 have shown that the combined cost of theft, burglary and robbery in England and Wales for the previous year totalled £1014 million. The figure for fraud recorded by the Metropolitan and City Police Company Fraud Department alone for 1985 was £867 million. The fraud figure in London was three times the total cost of all other property crimes in the metropolis put together. This figure is reflected in the increased charges imposed by the institutions for the costs for their services.

The Commissioner for the Metropolitan Police, Sir Kenneth Newman, in his annual report for 1985 recorded that the value at risk under investigation at the end of the year showed a 28% increase over the previous year, while the number of people arrested or summoned for the same period showed a 31% decrease. The Commissioner reported that the reduction 'reflects the fact that investigations have tended to be more complex and involve larger sums of money'. Later in his report the Commissioner admitted that demands on the branch consistently exceed the level of available resources.

Dr Michael Levi, in his report on *The Incidence, Reporting and Prevention of Commercial Fraud*, found that, of the company executives surveyed, there was an almost unanimous degree of accord for the proposition that fraud detectives should receive specialised training. Currently, no further training facilities or specialisation procedures are apparently contemplated, indeed the Commissioner's annual report records the fact that the two Fraud training courses previously held have been amalgamated into one course. The justification for this action is defined as 'rationalisation, making more effective use of scarce teaching resources'. Despite the fact that a suggestion was put forward by police to the Roskill Committee that some degree of semi-permanency would be introduced within the Fraud Squad, allowing 30% of staff to remain for an extended period of posting, at the moment no official policy decision can be identified to corroborate this proposal. All that can be ascertained is that there exists an ad hoc arrangement whereby certain officers stay put for longer periods, without any formal agreement. No proposals exist for the creation of a unified career structure within the department.

The Roskill Committee's report has been public property for nearly a year. So far, there appears to be an acceptance that certain kinds of evidence may be admitted in court by use of television and video, which would enable interviews, conducted abroad, to be played in court. This procedure would enable witnesses abroad to be examined and cross-examined without requiring their attendance before an English court. In addition, the proposal to remove the right of trial by jury for complex frauds appears to have been shelved. But what else has been adopted? The most far-reaching recommendation made by Roskill was for a completely independent commission to be responsible for the investigation and prosecution of allegations of fraud, in an attempt to bring together the disparate elements of investigatory authority currently possessed by the police, the DTI, the Customs and Excise and other departments. The Government has proposed the setting up of a 'serious fraud office'. What progress has been made on that front?

Well, the proposals have been under consideration, this much we do know, and certain senior appointments have been proposed, but there appears to have been a considerable degree of institutionalised reluctance among senior members of the respective authorities involved to come to any kind of reasonable compromise. The major stumbling block would appear to centre on the vexed question of a command chain, and, perhaps, more importantly, who would hold the reins of control. The DPP has always resisted the invitation to take control of the day-to-day management of police investigations, on the grounds that the administrative questions on the deployment of manpower and the degree of priority to be attached to necessary enquiries should be the primary responsibility of the Chief Officer of Police, and partly because he does not relish too public a belief in his perceived control of police enquiries, for fear that such a perception could have unhappy political consequences, particularly in a society where the executive arm aspires to police by consent.

The DTI have never really relished working too closely with the police, partly because, not possessing the same executive powers, they do not share the same robust attitude towards the most practical way to deal with professional villains (the action ethos), and partly due to their jealously guarded right to conduct investigations under Section 447 of the Companies Act 1985. If these powers were also bestowed on the police, as recommended by Roskill, then their Companies Investigation Branch would quickly become an anachronism. The police, ever conscious of their budgetary restrictions, would like to be able to conduct investigations under the instruction of the DPP, because that assists to remove the inter-departmental financial constraints and facilitates official permission to travel abroad, while wishing to retain

their independence to conduct investigations free of outside interference from academics, theorists and lawyers.

The DTI have effectively handed over a large chunk of their
previous responsibilities for everyday supervision of the markets and
their participants to the Securities and Investments Board. This
decision was described in the White Paper as 'unprecedented'. They
will still retain the power to conduct overall supervision, but in practice,
the immediate power will rest in the hands of SIB. The DTI have been
in the process of completing arrangements with the Securities and
Exchange Commission regarding the degree of co-operation the SEC
can expect in future transatlantic investigations. There was a considerable number of self-congratulatory press reports regarding the
existence of a new accord reached between the two departments. What
does this accord mean in principle?

The SEC and the CFTC demanded the right to subpoena foreign
witnesses in foreign countries when conducting investigations. They
also demanded a right to lift foreign bank secrecy rules. These
proposals, which go to the very heart of the necessary investigatory
requirements needed to prove allegations in the United States, have
been strenuously opposed by the British civil servants and negotiators.
The Americans have been left with an undertaking that, when the
Financial Services Act becomes law, the Securities and Investments
Board could isolate an institution which failed to co-operate with an
American investigation by threatening to withdraw the authorisation of
any UK business that conducted dealings with it. Now, I am no expert
in commercial law but it occurs to me that if a company found itself
being threatened with de-authorisation for conducting business with
another lawfully authorised business within the jurisdiction of the
English courts, simply because that company had failed to co-operate
with an investigation conducted by a foreign jurisdiction, they would
have a right to challenge that decision before the High Court.

In addition, the UK/US pact does not appear to extend to investigations in the Channel Islands or the Isle of Man. The agreement
between the two countries appears at this time to be largely in spirit
rather than in practical reality.

The proposals contained within the Financial Services Act do
represent a real step forward in investor protection. If they are correctly
applied, future investors should be able to satisfy themselves that the
business affairs of the company with which they are placing their
money are properly managed, that their staffs are properly supervised

and that their funds are segregated from those of the company. In addition, there will be provision for an independent compensation fund. The Act has restated the importance that will be applied to the recognition of the fiduciary relationship that exists between broker and client and it lends weight to the requirement that the client should receive fair treatment from his broker.

In practice, however, the provisions of the Act do little more than provide for a state of affairs which, in an ideal world admittedly, should have been capable of enforcement under the law of agency, without the need for specialist legislation. That is not to say that the legislation is not welcome. If that is what it takes to bring the cheats in the industry to heel, so be it. In the main, the legislation tends to look backwards, dealing with wrong-doing which was widespread before, while failing to look sufficiently to the future. It is to be hoped that we shall come to see less and less of the sort of activities which have marred the reputation of certain financial services for so long, perpetrated by companies who were under-capitalised, inefficient or just plain incompetent. Generally speaking, these operations will rapidly become a thing of the past. Whether or not the legislation provides sufficiently for the future, we shall have to wait and see!

So, what of the future? What problems will become manifest within our markets and what pitfalls will await the unwary investor? What can you do to protect yourself if you become the subject of an approach from an 'investment advisor'?

As far as the markets are concerned, we shall continue to see a proliferation of allegations of insider dealing, coupled more and more with the associated activities of risk arbitrage. This is a phenomenon which at the present time is too profitable for those engaged in its practice to forgo. As markets became more internationalised, the profits to be earned from dealing on inside information will increase, and the organised groups that even now actively engage in the use of specialist information will proliferate and become even more sophisticated. The SEC devote considerable degrees of resource towards the investigation and prosecution of insider dealing. In order to bring a degree of clout to what is after all essentially a covert activity, they have developed techniques which are very unpopular, but which have proved to be necessary.

In their investigation into the affairs of Dennis Levine, the Wall Street investment banker suspected of earning in excess of $12 million from the use of inside information, the SEC investigators discovered the existence of a secret Swiss bank account, maintained by Levine at a subsidiary of the bank in the Bahamas. Under normal conditions, this would have been the end of the road for the investigators, as the bank would have relied on the bank secrecy laws maintained in the Bahamas to protect the identity of their client. The SEC decided that they were fed up with being stonewalled by off-shore bank secrecy rules which did nothing, in their view, but protect criminals from prosecution, a view which I must confess to sharing. The bank concerned, the prestigious Bank Leu, had branches in New York. The bank officials were presented with the possibility of having injunctions placed upon their assets in New York, if they were backward in coming forward with the information regarding the beneficial ownership of the account in the Bahamas.

They gave the matter a little consideration and then, having first negotiated immunity from prosecution for their part in the affair, and having negotiated immunity from Bahamanian bank secrecy laws, passed over the information requested. In a masterpiece of understatement, the bank's chief legal officer was quoted as saying:

'We decided it was in the best interests of the bank to co-operate.'
I'll bet!

The Americans by this action signalled clearly to the rest of the world their intention to pursue insider-dealing allegations to the limit. The use by them of the power to freeze the assets of institutions who are unwilling to co-operate in such investigations creates a fascinating scenario for the future. The development of business 'marriages' between leading international banks, stock brokers and securities dealers has meant that many financial services will now possess outlets which are subject to American jurisdiction in some form or another. One example is the Union Bank of Switzerland, which owns a seat on the New York Stock Exchange, is currently awaiting the outcome of an application for a securities-trading licence in Japan and recently bought Phillips and Drew, a leading London broking concern. Imagine a situation where the SEC, during the course of an investigation, discovered that illegal trading had been allegedly conducted through an off-shore facility of one of our leading banks, who possessed assets within the jurisdiction of the American courts. Would this bank suddenly discover that it was in its best interests to co-operate, as well?

If the UK is to bring any realistic action against institutionalised insider dealing, then the investigation unit of the Stock Exchange must be staffed with investigators who can match the expertise of those engaged in this most damaging practice. At the same time, it will be imperative for the DTI to negotiate workable mutual assistance treaties with other jurisdictions, which will allow investigators to pursue their enquiries behind the doors of the secret bank accounts, the nominee companies and the spurious trust funds.

The laundering of criminally obtained funds will proliferate and the scope for hiding such assets will widen. The Government has proposed legislation to permit the confiscation of the assets of drug dealers and narcotics traffickers, and suggestions have been put forward to extend this provision to the proceeds of crime generally. Anyone who has any experience of our criminal process will instantly recognise a series of considerable difficulties contained within such a legislative proposal. Trying to prove such an allegation would be fraught with difficulty, a fact which is partially acknowledged by the proposers who have, in the case of drug traffickers, shifted the burden of proof to the criminal, who must prove his assets were acquired legitimately if they are not to be assessed as proceeds of trafficking. If this legislation were to be extended to accommodate other criminal offences, the burden of proof would have to be placed back upon the shoulders of the prosecution, at least in part, to prove that a specific sum of money came from an identifiable offence. While the proposals for dealing with the proceeds of drug offences may have gone some of the way to providing a realistic means for confiscating illicit profits, they are emergency measures. I cannot imagine a similar provision being applied to all offences, as this would inevitably be seen as an unwarranted intrusion into the requisite degree of proof needed for our criminal process to be satisfied that guilt has been established.

As with so many other politically inspired but legally impracticable legislative proposals, this recommendation has the smack of 'firm Government' about it and comes at a time when the need to reassure the voting public that the Government intends to deal efficiently with criminal wrong-doing is paramount. Faced with crime statistics which tend to indicate that Government policies are not as successful as might be hoped, the Cabinet is aware of the need for a greater public perception that they are doing something practical about crime. What would be better than a proposal to remove the criminal assets of wrong-doers, to placate the party faithful?

What we are not told is where the increased resources to conduct such enquiries will come from to finance the highly time-consuming and complex enquiries which will be necessary to uncover the provenance of the proceeds of organised criminal activity. Any professional criminal with experience of financial affairs is unlikely to maintain any large accounts within the jurisdiction of the English courts. His illegal activities will be financed abroad, in sums of money paid into foreign bank accounts, using off-shore company nominee names. Any funds he needs within the country will show up as company assets, laundered through a series of securities or commodity futures trading transactions, and forming part of the legitimate trading of the company. His house will be rented, paid for by regular cheques from an off-shore company, drawn on an off-shore bank, his car will be hired and paid for in a similar fashion. His everyday needs will be met by using an internationally accepted credit or charge card, paid on an account held off-shore. His immediately realisable assets will be negligible. His wife, if she's got any sense, will be the director of a company in her own right, from which she will draw a salary, feed, clothe and educate her children, without any obvious recourse to the assets of her husband. To identify other assets abroad, sufficient for their confiscation to be contemplated, will prove to be a task of Herculean proportions and will require considerable resources for the task. In addition, each jurisdiction through which the suspect money passes must be willing to accommodate these enquiries and to co-operate with the British officers. We already possess legislation to require criminals to pay compensation to their victims, to confiscate assets used in the commission of criminal offences and to make professional criminals bankrupt. This legislation, introduced no doubt in a welter of frothy publicity, together with statements of firm resolve, has rarely been used to its most practical effect. There seems to be little point in introducing yet more legislation unless the relevant funds to make it effective are made available at the same time.

Turning away from the use of the markets themselves, what about the private client, the individual investor? What will the future mean for him?

A number of existing problems will become more complex and some new investment proposals will creep in to the fraudsman's armoury. Among the more obvious are the proposed changes for unit and investment trusts. Hitherto, unit trusts have been very stringently controlled within a tough regulatory framework. Partly due to this severe restriction on those areas of the market in which the trusts were permitted to operate, unit trusts have been very successful and relatively free from scandal. Unit trusts have represented an attractive means of investment for the less sophisticated investor prepared to

undertake a slightly higher degree of risk. Recent proposals have
indicated that unit trusts will now be permitted to expand their
operation to include investment in hitherto prohibited areas of investment, including unquoted securities and those on the Unlisted Securities Market. In addition, investment managers will be permitted to
invest in money market funds both in the UK and overseas, using both
cash and currency funds. Further investment proposals are made for
investment in property, commodities, financial futures, options and in
mixed funds.

It is to be hoped that the relevant risk warnings attached to the
marketing of such instruments will point out the increased degree of
risk.

Proposals have been put forward to create a Recognised Investment
Exchange for the marketing of OTC stocks. The Stock Exchange has
already published proposals to create a recognised third-tier market,
but their plans have not enjoyed universal approval among the current
OTC market makers, partly because the Stock Exchange have insisted
that practitioners in the third-tier market must be members of the
Stock Exchange. The Stock Exchange has laid great emphasis on the
responsibilities of the market maker who intends to introduce a new
stock in being able to check the *bona fide* nature of the stock concerned.
Certain OTC opponents of the Stock Exchange's plans have indicated
their beliefs that it is not in the interests of the industry for the OTC
market to be controlled by the Stock Exchange. The more cynical
among us might agree that it would not be in the interests of the
practitioners perhaps, but it would certainly be in the interests of
investors, particularly in the light of the figures showing the high failure
rate of companies which qualified for Business Expansion Scheme
status and were traded on the OTC market.

Marketing of investment proposals in the future will be subject to
new restrictions. Certain types of investment will still not be advertised
openly, although they will be permitted to be advertised to existing
clients. Open-ended investment schemes, investing pooled clients'
funds in commodity futures, are one such example. In future, it is
proposed that authorised commodity futures dealers, while not being
permitted openly to advertise such a scheme to the public at large, will
be able to advise their existing clients of the scheme which they market.
In addition, they will be permitted to offer their scheme to be marketed
by other authorised investment firms.

Marketing investment schemes and opportunities will become a growth industry, and you should be aware of the new variety of practices which will develop to encourage you to be considered as an existing client. Do you remember how I described the methods used to encourage you to return enquiry cards to investment businesses? While writing this chapter I have come across such an example, which was sent to a friend of mine, who, in turn, passed it on to me. It was from LHW Futures Ltd, a company which has attracted a considerable amount of publicity in the financial press over the structure of its commission charges and its sales techniques. Incidentally, LHW Futures Ltd applied for membership of the London International Financial Futures Exchange, and it was refused membership. It appealed against this refusal and its appeal was subsequently dismissed. Apparently, LIFFE refused LHW on the basis that it did not enjoy the 'financial and business standing suitable for a member of the Exchange'. LHW claimed to be the UK's largest retail futures broker with more than 6500 clients, and to have earned £30 million in 1985 in gross commissions. Incidentally, if that figure is correct, it means that, on average, each client paid £4615 in commissions alone.

The mailing received by my friend offered him admission to a competition, the winner of which would receive an account containing $2000, for which the first trade would subsequently be conducted on a commission-free basis. All he needed to do was to answer three simple questions. In addition, the recipient would, if he returned the enclosed card, receive a free three-month subscription to an in-house publication. The point of the mailing however was to obtain his telephone number. The card requested details of his home and business telephone number, using the spurious excuse that 'Should you win the competition, we will need to contact you urgently.' Having successfully managed to send a letter to his home address in the first place, one wonders how urgent the need would be to inform him that he had won the prize, which another letter could not accomplish just as easily.

Marketing techniques such as these, enjoying, as they do, a remarkable similarity to playing bingo in one of the daily tabloids, place such offers in their proper perspective, which is nothing more than another example of the casino mentality. But, be warned. The amount of junk mail which will continue to land on your doormat will grow rapidly. One company which specialises in marketing lists of potential customers bought the entire list of shareholders in British Telecom. Lists such as these contain not simply names and addresses. Computer data bases can now be referred to which will identify the other shares owned by an investor, the value of such investments, the volume of trading conducted by each individual, his socio-economic grouping and, in some cases, his home telephone number.

Certain types of investment-related activity are outside the scope of the investor protection legislation and we shall undoubtedly see a proliferation of such schemes. One of these aspects relates to the sale of physical property which the customer can see and of which he can take possession. Be extremely wary of the 'investment' potential in furs, wines, precious stones, foreign coins, stamps or limited edition etchings, pictures, prints or, a recent addition to the list, commemorative plates. These and other similar items are not covered by the Financial Services Act. They are being pushed more and more as investments and should be treated with care. If you like the look of them, then buy such things by all means, but don't be deluded into believing that they have any intrinsic future investment value, per se.

The other growth area which is already starting to cause considerable concern is in the rapid growth of the purchase of property abroad, most notably time-sharing apartments. Time shares are beset with a welter of foreign legal problems and drawbacks which in the main are often not well explained to or understood by the holidaymaker, suddenly confronted by the possibility of owning the right to use a villa or an apartment for a specific period for years to come. The holiday areas of Spain and Portugal are being flooded by con-men, British, German and Dutch for the most part, who are actively marketing time-share concepts to holidaymakers who have found themselves being parted from cheques or inveigled into contracts to pay large sums of money by highly sophisticated salesmen. If you are considering buying land abroad, look upon it first and foremost as a holiday for the future, not as an investment. Take proper, legal advice from a lawyer in this country who specialises in foreign property transactions before parting with any money or signing any document. Certain steps have been taken by some of the leading building companies who specialise in building time-share apartments to form a trade association to create a set of guidelines for members of their group. This is fine as far as it goes but the standards they have created are of a minimal nature, and provide no protection for the person who looks upon such an enterprise as an investment. The rules do not apply to non-members of the group and there are no powers to enforce the standards quoted. Always consider the necessity to protect yourself first.

So what can you, the investor, do to protect yourself? There are a number of simple precautions which can be taken to ensure that you avoid the clutches of the cheat, the thief or the con-man.

Before you do anything else, decide what sort of investment you wish to undertake and how much disposable cash you have to spend. Ask yourself quite clearly what it is you want to achieve from your investments, and above all, discuss your aims with your respective partner. I lost count of the number of times I found that one partner had kept all the relevant details from the other. Do you want capital growth, do you want income? Are you saving to pay for grandchildren's school fees, or to provide yourself with a pension? Work out exactly what you want to achieve, before you start asking any so-called experts, so at least you are sure in your own mind what your objectives are, and then stick to them!

Next, please forget about the taxman. The last thing you should be worrying about is the Inland Revenue. I saw too many examples of people who lost their investments because some con artist told them he had discovered a new tax-efficient investment vehicle. In my experience the taxman only wants what he can legitimately charge, he doesn't want a penny more. Yet more people than you can shake a stick at will turn themselves inside out to put their entire fortunes into the hands of some cheapskate who claims to have found a way to avoid paying a few quid in tax. Believe me, if these people were so efficient, they wouldn't have to be offering you these dubious services. Avoid like the plague the investment advisor who offers tax efficiency before sensible profit. They will spend more than enough time juggling your finances between one scheme and the next, just to save a few measly pounds and, on the way, you could lose everything. You would be far better off going to a local, qualified accountant, after you have made your profit, paying him his fee and taking his advice. You will notice that I used the word 'sensible' in connection with proposed profit. Commonsense will tell you that the promoter of a scheme offering a rate of return which is out of all proportion to the rest of the market is either a financial genius, in which case why does he need your money, or someone to be avoided.

Now, having decided what sort of investment you want to make, spend a little time in choosing the right advisor. First of all, make sure that he is a member of a self-regulatory organisation, or is authorised by the Securities and Investments Board. You can do this by writing to the relevant SRO or to SIB, and asking for a list of authorised members. If you don't know the addresses or the names of the SROs, your bank manager will have a list of addresses and telephone numbers. If he doesn't, change your bank. Having found a list of investment advisors, write to at least a dozen and tell them exactly what it is you want to achieve. Wait and see what sort of replies you get. Do not send any money at this stage, but keep all the replies you receive. Examine the replies, most, if not all, of which should offer you some sort of interview at your home. Decide which ones you prefer, and then ask your solicitor to conduct a company search on each of the companies you are considering. Obviously if it is one of the major names then you may feel this is unnecessary. However, a company which may offer an interesting service but of which you have never heard may be just what you are looking for, but you would be advised to check their company records. A solicitor can perform this service for you for a relatively small fee. After all, if you are thinking of investing thousands of pounds, doesn't it make sense to spend a few pounds to check the company out? If the company hasn't lodged any accounts for the last few years, then give it a miss. If the company hasn't made any profits in the last few years, look somewhere else. If its company records are hopelessly out of date, avoid it. If its directors claim to have aristocratic titles, whether British or foreign, check that they exist.

By now, you should have a short-list of half-a-dozen companies, all of which are offering the sort of investment services you require. Arrange for a representative to call on you but make sure you know exactly what it is you want to talk about before he comes. If he suspects that you do not know what you want then he can make all sorts of proposals which may not be suitable for your needs. Take a good look at his business card, and keep a copy. If it has got a lot of funny letters after his name, ask him what they mean and get him to explain them. Make sure that the representative explains everything to your entire satisfaction. If you are not sure you understand what he means, tell him and make him explain again. It's your money he's after, make him work for it. If he appears unwilling to explain matters to your complete understanding, or appears to be trying to rush you into a decision, then simply cross him off your list. Under the new provisions relating to certain unit trust and life assurance contracts, the salesman will be required to tell you if he is bound to offer one company's products or whether he is empowered to offer a range of services. If he doesn't tell you right at the start, then ask him. If he doesn't give you a straight answer, ask him to leave.

Do not be pressurised into signing any agreement then and there. You will lose nothing by telling him that you are considering a number of proposals. Tell him that you will consider his offer, but that you would like him to put his proposals in writing. If you do not receive a written proposal, containing all the terms of the proposed agreement plus the charges or commissions he intends to charge, within a reasonable space of time, then he is not worth worrying about.

When you have received all the proposals, then the decision is up to you. At least you have done what you can to ensure that your advisor is a *bona fide* member of a well-capitalised, authorised investment company. Make sure that your client contract agreement contains all the relevant information you require. Your advisor will be subject to specific rules laid down by his SRO as to the nature and content of his client agreement form. He should arrange an interview with you to ensure that he knows what your investment needs are and how much you can afford to invest.

Make sure you know exactly how your commission rates will be charged. If necessary, demand that your advisor provides you with a monthly statement of how much commission he is earning at your expense, particularly if you are giving him discretion to act on your behalf. Compare this with your investment figures. If his earnings exceed yours, change your advisor, as he is 'churning' you.

Never, never give money to a faceless voice on the end of a telephone. If you receive an unsolicited phone call, tell the caller where to get off, in whatever terms seem appropriate to you. Alternatively, use the whistle method. If you receive junk mail advertising investment services, put it in the waste bin. Always remember, anyone advertising investment services will always put his own interests before yours. Performance fees are usually front-end loaded, which means that he will take his earnings before your money is invested. You would be surprised how often investment advisors' advice will mirror their own speciality. Stock brokers will recommend equities, insurance brokers, term assurance, investment companies, unit trusts, etc.

Remember, off-shore companies are outside the jurisdiction of the English courts. It doesn't matter how tax-efficient they claim to be, any investment which is based in any of the off-shore jurisdictions cannot be subjected to any realistic investigation if the wheel falls off. Only crooks, tax evaders and people with something to hide need to shelter behind off-shore secrecy. If an investment proposal is a good one, offering an honest service with *bona fide* aims, then why do the promoters need to protect themselves behind a shield of nominee directors and impenetrable legal barriers? In my experience, off-shore investment companies operating out of some of the more exotic locations, providing services for mainland UK clients, have a tendency to fail with monotonous regularity.

Never, ever put your family's future at risk. If the salesman insists on emphasising that the investment he proposes is a risky one, in which you stand the chance of losing your entire investment, then believe him and don't risk it. People who emphasise the considerable degree of risk of total loss of your funds are in fact telling you that you will lose all your money. If you are looking for genuine investment opportunities, do try and avoid any kind of speculative futures contracts, if you can. The facts are simple. 80% of all people who part with their money in futures speculation lose everything. If you are a gambler by nature, or you are just looking for a punt, go ahead. Better still, go to the betting shop. At least you can watch your money losing. If the scheme you are in is a highly speculative one, then do not risk any more than you can genuinely afford to lose. Do not throw good money after bad by trying to recoup your losses. That is what the futures dealers hope you will do. Once you have lost it, as you will inevitably do, give up and go home.

Last, but not least, please remember the three cardinal rules for survival in the casino economy. Two and two make four; nobody gives you anything for nothing in this life; and if a scheme sounds too good to be true, it probably is. You've worked hard for your money, so don't throw it away.